Margaret Heffernan is an [...]
She produced prize-winni[ng ...]
moving to the US to run multimedia technology companies.
Her third book, *Wilful Blindness*, was a finalist for the *Financial Times* Business Book of the Year Award, and her fourth, *A Bigger Prize*, was awarded the Transmission Prize. She advises senior executives around the world, is a professor at the University of Bath, and writes for the *Financial Times* and *HuffPost*. Her TED talks have been seen by over 13 million people.

www.mheffernan.com

Praise for *Uncharted*

'In a year when rigid planning and unfeasibly precise predictions have been exposed as worse than useless, Heffernan's prescient book shows how to be prepared, adaptable and resilient in the face of inevitable crises and uncertainty around the corner.' *Financial Times*, **Business Books of the year**

'I have never read anything quite like *Uncharted*. I was captured on page one and captivated to the very end. My whole idea of what the future might hold, the impotence of most forecasting, sagas of amazing acts of preparedness. She shook core beliefs and made me look at the world – and myself – differently. It doesn't get any better than that.' **Tom Peters, author of *In Search of Excellence***

UNCHARTED

How Uncertainty Can Power Change

MARGARET HEFFERNAN

**SIMON &
SCHUSTER**

London · New York · Sydney · Toronto · New Delhi

First published in Great Britain by Simon & Schuster UK Ltd, 2020
This paperback edition published by Simon & Schuster UK Ltd, 2021

1 3 5 7 9 10 8 6 4 2

Simon & Schuster UK Ltd
1st Floor
222 Gray's Inn Road
London WC1X 8HB

www.simonandschuster.co.uk
www.simonandschuster.com.au
www.simonandschuster.co.in

Simon & Schuster Australia, Sydney
Simon & Schuster India, New Delhi

A CIP catalogue record for this book is available from the British Library

Paperback ISBN: 978-1-4711-7982-2
eBook ISBN: 978-1-4711-7980-8

Typeset in Perpetua by M Rules
Printed in the UK by CPI Group (UK) Ltd, Croydon, CR0 4YY

For
Jonathan
Raj
Robert
and
Roger

CONTENTS

INTRODUCTION

We think about the future all day, every day. What time do I need to leave the house? What's for breakfast? Can we picnic at the weekend? Should I change jobs? Move house? Online and offline, the news is mostly speculation: what will happen in Congress, in Parliament, in traffic, in the markets. However much we might aim to live in the present, we can't cross the road without thinking ahead: will that car reach me before I'm safely across? Our brains have evolved to anticipate whether we'll like this food, this person, that book. Entire industries – property, travel, banks, insurance, pensions, technology – analyse, construct and sell permutations of the future. So we cannot *not* think about it: neither our brains nor our lives will allow it.

Prospection bestows tremendous evolutionary advantage, alerting me to danger or reassuring me that the noise I hear isn't a burglar but a cat. For the most part, it works so well that we scarcely notice when we get home on time, pack the right clothes, select satisfying homes and holidays. Apps train us to assume accuracy in plotting routes, choosing hotels, restaurants and lovers with levels of confidence and precision our ancestors never imagined. We have come to expect the future to be minutely and perfectly predictable.

And then it rains after all, the train's late, traffic is held up by a crash, the neighbourhood is noisy, the job hateful and the election doesn't go our way. Trump. Brexit. The end of history. The fall of idols. Booms and busts and out of the blue, #MeToo. The predictability of life, on which we've come to depend, seems to fall away and we're left angry, intolerant, fearful.

Our expectations are wrong. The future isn't perfectly knowable and never has been. Our brains may be the single most complex object in the known universe, but they still make mistakes. Today's technology may be the most advanced the world has ever seen, but it too is imperfect: incomplete, biased and full of error. Google isn't always right. Maps steer us to the wrong place and unpredictable accidents make us late. Artificial intelligence trusts correlations that turn out to be irrelevant, selective or ill-informed. DNA knows nothing about broken legs or toxic pollution.

Ineradicable uncertainty remains inherent to human life; Hannah Arendt called it the defining characteristic of the future. That this leaves us uncomfortable and anxious is why humans have always searched for ways to see what's coming: oracles, shamans, soothsayers, augurs, horoscopes, religions. Longing to reduce uncertainty and doubt has driven much of our progress. The more we noticed, remembered, wrote down and shared, the more knowledgeable we became and the better able we were to pass on our learning for future generations to increase. This has made us better and better estimators, able to plan, to manage, to anticipate. The entire construct of management – forecast, plan, execute – hinges on our capacity to make well informed estimates. The more we practised it, the more accurate we became.

It makes sense to imagine that that progress is infinitely sustainable, but it isn't. Along the way, fundamental change has occurred. We have moved from a complicated world to a complex one. The two aren't the same – and complexity isn't just complicated on steroids. Complicated environments are linear, follow rules and are predictable; like an assembly line, they can be planned, managed, repeated and controlled. They're maximised by routine and efficiency. But the advent of globalisation, coupled with pervasive communications, has made much of life complex: non-linear and fluid, where very small effects may produce disproportionate impacts. General Stanley McChrystal distinguishes the contrast between the First Gulf War (1990–91), which he says was complicated – an intensely planned application of overwhelming force, executed by the book – and the Iraq War (begun in 2003), which was complex: a fluid, volatile environment of shifting opacity where a lone individual with a cell phone could tip the balance. On a more mundane level, the manufacturers of plastic straws thought theirs a predictable business until 2019, when public opinion declared the product unacceptable, while the maker of electronic keyboards discovered that a single negative review on Amazon could reduce sales by 50 per cent.

What this shift means is that, while we can still be generally certain about many things, much remains specifically ambiguous. We know climate change is real, but that doesn't mean we can predict when or where wildfires will break out or when extreme weather events will destroy which harvests.

The Bank of England acknowledges that there will be future banking busts, but cannot say when or why. Their executives aren't stupid; they're just candid about navigating daily tsunamis of data and interactions, of which some are meaningful, much is obscure and quite a lot is pointless. The Bank recognises that much of the system – Trump's tweets, corruption trials in Korea, the outbreak of a new virus – lies beyond its influence. Complex global systems incorporate a multitude of factors, each influencing others but controlled by no one person or nation. We used to ignore these systems but their problems have become ours now, when a bank halfway across the world crashes or a government falls.

Apple's iPhone may have been 'designed in California', but making it depends on raw materials and suppliers from Ireland, the Philippines, China, Taiwan, Japan, Austria, Korea, Singapore, Thailand, Germany, the UK, the Netherlands, Indonesia, Puerto Rico, Brazil, Malaysia, Israel, the Czech Republic, Mexico, Vietnam, Morocco, Malta, Belgium and most of the United States. This complex supply chain is designed to reduce costs, take advantage of labour specialisms, employment conditions, currency fluctuations and tax breaks. But they expose Apple (and similar phone manufacturers) to natural disasters, labour disputes, economic volatility, social turmoil, religious strife, trade wars and political discontent: all factors over which the company has no control, little influence and poor foresight. We're so dazzled by the ornate complexity of such manufacturing systems that we forget, or prefer to deny, that contingencies have multiplied, fragility has proliferated, accurate prediction has become harder.

To be able to do and know so much and yet to be unable to predict what we crave to know is painful and frustrating. So we perpetuate the age-old search for sources of certainty. That leaves us susceptible to pundits and prophets: experts and forecasters who claim superior knowledge. But academic Philip Tetlock, after studying their track records over twenty years, concluded that the more famous they are, the more likely they are to be wrong.[1] Other models prove unsatisfactory too. DNA tells only part of our story; the rest is driven by more factors than we see or know. Psychological profiling is flawed by subjective models, attribution errors and inadequate data. History doesn't repeat itself but often misleads us with aesthetically pleasing analogies that underweight critical differences. Proponents of each model oversell their promise and each one falls down, defeated by the ineradicable uncertainty of life.

Technology offers a newer, shinier model, purporting to provide certainty, while in fact merely masking ambiguities. Big data, analytics, machine learning and artificial intelligence may help us to see more, to glean patterns previously impenetrable to the human brain alone. But their capacity to assess mountains of data at speed obscures their flaws. A large dataset might describe a group or neighbourhood of voters well, but still be unable to predict with certainty how an individual will vote next time. Algorithms are, as the mathematician Cathy O'Neil once said, opinions encoded in numbers. They impose subjective assumptions on data that's skewed and incomplete. Unique or rare external events may render what was formerly predictable suddenly unforeseeable, making historical data irrelevant or useless. (This is frequently true of epidemics.)

And finally there is the problem of life itself: the tendency of organisms, atoms and subatomic particles to behave in non-random but fundamentally unpredictable ways.

The utopian fantasy of the tech industry – that all the data in the world will yield perfect predictions – appropriately provokes privacy champions. That isn't its only challenge. These predictive systems are frequently wrong, as when they recommend to me a book I've written or one I already own. Those flaws are trivial, because the recommendation is so cheap to produce and easy to ignore. But when determining who should have access to social services or healthcare, or who might commit crimes, such errors carry more weight and warning. Meanwhile, managers of AI technologies tell me that every now and then – unpredictably – their systems need to be reset. They don't know why.

Moreover, depending on technology incurs a high cost. Every time we use it, we outsource to machines what we could and can do ourselves. The more we use GPS, for example, the more the parts of our brain responsible for navigation and memory shrink.[2] And the less we know our neighbourhood. This is known as the automation paradox: the skills you automate, you lose. So the more we depend on machines to think for us, the less good we become at thinking for ourselves. The fewer decisions we make, the less good we become at making them. We risk falling into a trap: more need for certainty, more dependency on technology; less skill, more need. We become addicted to the very source of our anxiety.

Moreover, as Shoshana Zuboff has so eloquently diagnosed, the technological opportunity to nudge, tempt and even mandate behaviour is a wickedly clever way to enforce predictability. Enough carrots and sticks and there's no need to anticipate behaviour that can be compelled. Knowing your car will be immobilised if you fail to pay its insurance extravagantly reduces uncertainty in decision-making. Technology aims to solve the so-called problem of human complexity by force-fitting a predetermined model onto the surprising variety of human existence. But absolute certainty about all aspects of life would be tyranny. At a time in our history where we have huge decisions to make – about the climate, about technology, capitalism, democracy – we need our freedom more than ever. It is in the interstices of uncertainty that we encounter the need and find the freedom to forge our identity and our future.

The first part of this book looks at how all of our models for knowing the future let us down. It isn't an argument for apathy or resignation. But it is only in rejecting pundits and propagandists of determinism that we free ourselves to explore the contours and landscape of possibility. Our choice is not between false certainty or ignorance; it is between surrender or participation. So we need to be bolder in our search, more penetrating in our enquiry, more energetic in our quest for discovery.

Experiments are what you do when you don't know what you can do; they're ideal for complex environments because they yield clues about the systems we inhabit. Transformative scenarios reveal and develop unseen possibilities, changing both people and problems through radical diversity and confrontation. Cathedral projects – conceived and built over centuries – show how individuals and institutions have explored without maps to achieve what looked impossible.

Artists spend their lives in exploration, seeking change before they have to and embracing ambiguity for its richness and nuance. The survivors of existential crises have huge wisdom, won at high cost, about what we need in order to endure when the unexpected arrives. Just because we don't know the future doesn't mean we're left helpless; there's genius and creativity in preparation. Start wherever you are; in a complex, non-linear world, there can be no step-by-step rule book, only an infinite mandate to explore. Approach the future with fervent curiosity, not with an ideology or itinerary but with a methodology that progresses with questions: what do we need to do now? What do we need to *be* now? What must we preserve at all cost? Rich futures are mapped by those with the energy to convene, the passion to learn from the widest variety of human imagination, paying attention, changing course, discovering and inventing what the world demands of us all.

This is an optimistic book. Not because it promises that all is for the best in the best of all possible worlds. Optimists aren't idiots. They do better in life − live longer, healthier, more successful lives − for the simple reason that they don't ignore problems or give up easily. Psychologists distinguish between two kinds of optimists. Explainers accept that bad news is neither permanent (things can improve) nor universal (good news is happening somewhere else). Expectant optimists, by contrast, see problems but anticipate improvement; they have a fighting spirit. Both kinds of optimism alert individuals to fresh opportunities and to the resources needed to pursue goals. Where pessimists may avoid problems, optimists cope and solve. They are specially productive because optimists are more likely to reach out for help, to collaborate and trust others. That gives them more capacity and resilience than they could ever possess alone.

At a time when we are deluged with propaganda undermining human talents in favour of the perfection of machines, the sheer creativity of human interaction has never been more critical. We have huge capacity for invention – if we use it. We have limitless talent for questions and exploration – if we use it. We can imagine what we've never seen before – if we practise. Lose these gifts and we are adrift. Hone and develop them and together we can make any future we choose.

Anyone who tries to tell us they know the future is simply trying to own it: a spurious claim to manifest destiny. The harder, more subtle truth is that the future is uncharted because we aren't there yet. So this book can't provide a map, a recipe, an app or any perfect certainty about destination or time of arrival. What it will do is provide the questions to lead you in the direction you choose. Many of the most inspiring people start in a place of uncertainty, are filled with doubt, yet arrive triumphant at places in life they could not see when they set out. Their successes are deeply human, derived from curiosity, imagination and not a little bravery. These individuals were prepared to navigate the unknown in pursuit of the ill-defined because they realised that the only way to know the future is to make it.

PART ONE

PREDICTION ADDICTION

1

FALSE PROFITS

The only function of economic forecasting is to make astrology look respectable.

— JOHN KENNETH GALBRAITH

Who knew what was in the air? Even a breath can be a catalyst.

Enjoying the waters just beyond Narragansett Pier, Rhode Island, the economist Irving Fisher kept swimming. A happy marriage, two daughters. The full professorship at Yale was a lifetime appointment and the future seemed as dazzling as the summer ocean. But looking back to the shore, he was surprised how far the current had carried him. It took all his energy to regain the beach. He arrived at last exhausted, unnerved by the speed with which his glorious future had turned precarious.

For the rest of his life, Fisher would wonder whether that episode in the summer of 1898 had been an early warning sign. Was the swim so tough because he was already infected – or did his exhaustion trigger the crisis? Whichever way it happened, by the autumn Fisher scarcely recognised himself. Everything tired him and every afternoon he ran a fever. His doctor was stumped. Not a man to appreciate uncertainty, Fisher demanded a saliva test. When it came back positive, the physician felt too abashed to face his patient. Instead, he quit, never submitting his bill.

It was left to Fisher's wife, Margaret, to deliver the diagnosis: tuberculosis. At the time, TB was the single greatest cause of death in the western world. Autopsies showed almost every city dweller to be infected. But even without the data, Fisher knew the danger he faced: as a teenager, his father had died from the disease. Now aged thirty-one, what kind of future did he face?

Millions asked themselves the same question. By 1898, educated people knew that tuberculosis was an airborne bacillus, but there was no vaccine and no certain cure. Nor was there any reliable prognosis: the disease could lie latent for years, even a lifetime, or you could be dead in a matter of weeks. So diagnosis was almost worse than useless. Had Fisher received a life sentence, or just experienced some mild discomfort that would never return? As painful as the disease was the doubt.

As with all epidemics, moralists were quick to construct punitive theories to explain its cause. The disease was divine retribution for alcohol or tobacco consumption, sexual 'self-abuse', even dancing was suspected. Or perhaps society was to blame: commentators noted that TB thrived in places where urban crowding, pollution, mixed races proliferated. One surgeon, Ambrose Ranney, insisted that whether the disease killed you could be discerned through analysis of the lines of the brow, the hue and texture of the skin.[1] From causes to cures, everyone searched for predictive patterns.

Fisher turned to diet. He eschewed meat, forswore alcohol, and became an energetic advocate for prolonged mastication. At Yale, he urged athletes to correlate the length of time that they chewed their food with their athletic performance. He endorsed the new breakfast cereal Grape-Nuts, certain its extreme chewiness would make its consumers stronger. Diet became a life-or-death mission for Fisher – but not only for Fisher. Convinced that the health of a nation determined the wealth of the nation, he estimated the annual economic cost to the US of tuberculosis at $550 million – around $254 billion today.[2]

Although the TB bacillus had been isolated by Robert Koch in 1882, no cure was known until 1944 when Schatz and Waksman discovered streptomycin. Until then, patients remained suspended in crisis: fearful of the future and desperate for any remedies or signs that might foretell their future. For Irving Fisher, uncertainty was not an abstract idea but a visceral reality.

He was not alone in his uncertainty. Just a casual scan of events at the start of the twentieth century reveals a concatenation of wars, terrorism, political assassinations, earthquakes, royal suicides, epidemics and famine. What did these events portend? Did they spell progress or doom? Market crashes, revolutionary movements, new political parties, scientific breakthroughs, radical technological change and a chaotic cultural scene just barely contained order, anxiety and mayhem. The old-fashioned and the avant-garde – Peter Rabbit, Picasso, Singer Sargent, Munch, Gilbert and Sullivan, Stravinsky, Chekhov and Ibsen – jostled for attention as consumers marvelled at the first plastics, motorbikes, rubber gloves, zippers, telephones, radio programmes, x-rays, colour photographs, cinemas and the *Daily Mail*. Whole new countries took shape while scientists struggled to understand the impact of four-dimensional geometry, new moons and gases, the new science of relativity and quantum theory.

Whether through fear of the unknown, or hope to capitalise on new trends, a large, eager and susceptible market arose, desperate to know what the future might hold. And for the first time in history, technology provided tools that promised to make forecasting scientific. The telegraph and telephone enabled the collection of large amounts of up-to-date information. The emergence of statistics as a rigorous mathematical discipline, together with the growing sophistication of economics, facilitated serious data analysis. An ever-expanding railway network could disseminate newsletters, newspapers and magazines to an anxious, eager market of punters and pundits.

Astrology became a big commercial business at this time too, but it was in financial markets that forecasting first became a big, important industry. Panics in the US in 1893, 1896, 1901 and 1907 had exposed how little reliable information consumers, investors and managers had about the health of companies, industries or the economy at large. Into that vacuum rushed three men: Irving Fisher, Roger Babson and Warren Persons. All three were eager to sell reassurance, inspiration and advice. Each believed that, through data, they could discern future trends in the markets and hoped to build important businesses doing so. And all three, carrying the diagnosis of TB, viscerally understood the pain of uncertainty and sought to alleviate it.

Almanacs had been around for centuries – supplying farmers with information on sunrises and sunsets, tides and weather – and the new forecasting ventures aspired to something similar for investors: business barometers with which to analyse the present and forecast the future. But the metaphor posed more questions than it answered. With more economic and business data than ever before, how could they tell what was meaningful or trustworthy? It is easy to take the temperature with a thermometer, but in the early days of modern economics, no one quite knew which data was its equivalent. Farmers knew from experience what weather their crops required, but nobody really understood what kinds of economic conditions were needed to temper an overheated market, grow a slow one or stabilise volatility. Did different industries always thrive in the same market conditions? The density of unknowns meant it was left up to the forecasters to choose what mattered to whom, why and when. And they had a field day.

Each of the forecasters built commercial businesses selling their special take on the future. Fisher, whom Milton Friedman considered the greatest economist the United States has ever produced, was one of the first to try to analyse national economies, seen through the lens of the money supply. His working assumption was that too much money in circulation would produce an inflationary boom; too little a recessionary bust. At the time, government didn't measure money supply, which left Fisher trying to do so. He needed indicators of activity – but none existed. He started tracking prices, only to discover that they didn't always move in lock step: some went up as others sank. So he created indexes, aggregates of data he hoped would reveal overall patterns in economic activity. It was impossible to collect everything so he needed to be selective. But how could he identify representative data when he didn't know what the whole contained?

Whatever he chose, Fisher's theory required mountains of data. He packed his home with employees collecting it on index cards. What his homemade indices revealed was volatility – in prices and in markets. So Fisher became obsessed by a search for stability – where did it come from, what influenced it and what sustained it? How could stable currencies be realised? The more data he collected, the more questions emerged, all needing answers before Fisher could hope to anticipate where the economy was going.

Giddy with new insights, Fisher became one of the world's first economic pundits. His Index Number Institute, syndicating indexes and forecasts through newspapers and newsletters, made Fisher famous for financial commentary, analytical nous and his immense capacity for data analysis. Competitive, commercial and publicly spirited, he was easily drawn into commenting on a whole range of topics from prohibition to simplified spelling and calendar reform. But his fortune was made when he sold his card index system to the Rand Kardex Company for $660,000 (approximately $8 million today). Spread thin and often mocked for his humourlessness, Fisher nonetheless commanded attention and credibility for his mathematical rigour that promised to bring economic forecasting one step closer to a science.

Economics has long suffered from 'physics envy', and nowhere was that more explicit than in the early days of forecasting. One of Fisher's rivals, Roger Babson, believed that almost everything in life could be reduced to Newton's laws of cause and effect. Like Fisher, Babson had contracted TB as a young man and devised his own eccentric, ascetic health routine involving freezing air and a strict diet. Pictures of him in the Massachusetts winter, dressed in a long woollen gown as he works in front of a wide open window, show a man bent on proving that knowledge and determination could beat any odds. In particular, Babson was on a mission to redress a power imbalance. As a young bond salesman, he had discovered that banks held a monopoly on business information; investors knew only what institutions told them.[3] He had seen first-hand the human cost of that exclusivity too: visiting the stock exchange during the panic of 1907, he actually saw men turn grey.[4] So Babson brought to his new business an evangelical determination to empower individuals with data as sound and thorough as any bank's.

Babson wanted people to understand how intricately companies were connected to the economy as a whole, and he became famous for his Babsoncharts – spectacularly baroque graphic designs on which he tried to display the full complexity of an economy: stock and commodity prices, manufacturing data, railroad traffic, agricultural production, building construction, business failures and other indicators of economic output. Onto this data, he placed what he called the 'normal line', indicating periods of expansion and recession. Ever the fervent Newtonian, he put his trust in the Third Law of Motion: for every action, there is an equal and opposite reaction. He believed that a period of depression was always matched by a period of prosperity and that the steeper the decline, the faster the market would recover.[5]

Like many then and now, Babson imbued economics with morality; cause and effect resonated with crime and punishment. So booms were the product of wasteful exuberance that needed to be purged by sensible self-discipline. These views made him a contrarian: when markets went up, he foresaw extravagance and urged healthy restraint. Profiled as 'the man who refused to die', his success and fame conflated his apparent victory over tuberculosis with the moral lessons implicit in his market predictions – excess spelled danger and health demanded moderation. Each piece of data contained some meaning, he thought, and Babson maintained a boosterish faith that everything – health, behaviour, food, parenting, handwriting – was predictive of something and that he was the man to decode them all.

By 1910, he too had become a national pundit, called on to pronounce on everything from markets to medicine, education, diet and religion. No matter the topic, whenever Babson made predictions, he always looked for excess that needed reining in, or restraint that demanded a bigger push. Both Fisher and Babson became irrepressible entrepreneurs, financing their forecasting businesses with their own money and running them from home. They both worked through a process of deduction, applying their theories to mountains of data in the belief that their efforts would elucidate patterns that predicted the future.

By stark contrast, Warren Persons built his forecasting business, the Harvard Economic Service, right inside the university that funded it, hoping that, far from Wall Street, it could remain aloof from punditry and secure a solid reputation for scholarship and objectivity. A masterful statistician, he took an inductive approach, sceptical that any theories fully captured the complexity of economic markets. The best you could do was watch and measure what was in front of you and ask if you had seen such correlations and patterns before. In essence, he forecasted by analogy, believing that history repeated itself, albeit imperfectly.

The Harvard Economic Service was the world's first economic advisory business to serve a worldwide market of the elite, and in the 1920s it began to collaborate with Keynes' and Beveridge's London and Cambridge Economic Service. But for all its academic credentials, a problem lay at the heart of Persons's approach. Even if he believed himself immune to theory, didn't his attention to some trends over others imply a theory? In denying his assumptions, did he risk being blind to them?

All three men were personally invested in their competing theories and methods – their businesses and professional reputations depended on them, as, to a large degree, did the future of the forecasting industry as a whole. There were fortunes to be made in prophecy and their large, aggressive sales teams competed in a torrid market, each disparaging the others. Persons compared Babson's ideas to astrology and said that Fisher's data was unreliable. Where both men's methods were opaque and easily castigated as pseudo-science, Persons published hundreds of pages explaining how he worked – which just left him open to intense, methodological criticism from rivals and colleagues alike. Across the industry, rivals sniped at each other, trying to prove that they, and they alone, held the key to the future.

The test came in October 1929. At the beginning of the month, Fisher had been buoyant, claiming that stocks had 'reached a permanently high plateau'. Stability at last! When the market collapsed on 24 October, while conceding there might be a slight price retreat, he saw nothing 'in the nature of a crash'. For months afterwards, he insisted that a rapid recovery was imminent. His faith cost him dear, his son later commenting that 'his eagerness to promote his cause sometimes had a bad influence on his scientific attitude. It distorted his judgement.'[6] It also meant that he lost his fortune holding on to his shares in Rand Kardex.

Persons's Harvard Economic Service was equally blindsided and afterwards maintained that, with no historic precedent for the crash, a normal and swift recovery must follow. Month after month, the service kept predicting a recovery that failed to arrive. Cleaving to his big idea – that the economy always moved in cycles like the tides – proved too rigid in the new environment. The service closed in 1931. That so prestigious a group had failed so dismally soon gave rise to more disturbing questions: did such a commercial venture belong in an academic setting? Had the elite nature of the service and its clients influenced their predictions? Was the Harvard Economic Service unwilling to deliver bad news and, even worse, had its optimism contributed to the crash?

Only Babson, the least scientific of the three men, came out with his reputation enhanced. The reason was simple. Ever the contrarian, he had been predicting a crash every year for the past three years. 'I shall repeat what I said at this time last year and the year before; namely that sooner or later a crash is coming . . . Fair weather cannot always continue.' He basked in his triumph, snapping up some of his failing competitors and blaming his rivals for encouraging speculation. But in May 1931, he announced that the market had bottomed out and that it was time to get back into the stock market. He was wrong: the US economy wouldn't recover for a decade.

Persons moved on to consulting, where his statistical punctiliousness was said to dismay clients. Fisher, his reputation in ruins, went bankrupt – his investments had all gone bust. Though Babson was the forecaster who left behind a fortune and the college that still bears his name, his ideas – about markets and medicine – are now discredited. His 'normal line' wasn't brilliant, but random. Not one of these three men had accurately foreseen their own legacy. While they had seen themselves as wildly differentiated rivals, in fact these three pioneers had much in common. Beset by personal uncertainty, they believed that deciphering patterns in their data would give them control over their lives. They had more faith than skill, imbuing their theories and data with the certainty and consolation they and their readers craved. They imagined themselves objective scientists uncovering laws about markets as absolute and reliable as the laws of physics and believed that financial numbers unambiguously revealed immutable scientific truths. In all of these beliefs they were wrong.

What they left behind was the commercialisation of a fantasy: the belief that the future is knowable, that all life is susceptible to certain laws if we could only figure out what they were, and that there are some special people or processes that can reveal what the future holds. They ratified our addiction to prediction and proved that fame and fortune could be made from it. But these early pioneers also discovered three profound problems endemic to forecasts that dog them still today: they are incomplete, ideological and self-interested.

The first problem is models. Fisher and Babson relied on simplified versions of the markets they sought to understand. They didn't have the resources or the means to capture all the data on the economy – and even if they had, they lacked the tools to handle it. So they had to make choices about what to leave in and what to leave out. All economists do this kind of editing in an effort to see more clearly what is really going on. Today's technology accommodates vastly far more data but the intrinsic difficulty of models remains: the more data is compressed, the more its predictive power is compromised. Paul Krugman, who won the Nobel Prize for economics at least in part due to the beauty of his models, once quipped that he thought the data left out of his models might be more important than the data that went in.[7] It's an explosive and challenging remark that reveals the intrinsic difficulty of models: they will always be subjective and incomplete representations of complex reality.

The second problem lay in agendas. However much the early forecasters believed themselves to be men of pure, scientific enquiry, they all held cherished, implicit beliefs about how the world worked, about what mattered and what did not. Alan Greenspan later called these beliefs ideologies. Testifying before Congress following his failure to foresee the banking crisis of 2008, he said, 'Ideology is a conceptual framework with the way people deal with reality, everyone has one. You have to.'[8] Between 1994 and 2008, his own belief – that deregulated markets are safe – had caused him to ignore a whole series of failures in the unregulated derivatives market, right up to the crash in 2008. He hasn't changed his mind about regulation, but what he has done, as many others have not, is acknowledge that his mental model is an ideology and that forecasts always contain an agenda.

Moreover, all of these early forecasting businesses were commercial enterprises. They depended on customers who themselves had preferences and priorities. How far were forecasters driven to please their payers? The first person to raise this question had been Keynes, whose early interest in business barometers had led him to work with Persons. But writing to colleagues at the Harvard Economic Service in 1925, he raised the possibility that there was a conflict of interest in the very nature of the business. Didn't these men, and their companies, *depend* on boom and bust? The drama of market cycles, the chance of riches and the tantalising promise that, with special information, you could win – didn't this lure create an implicitly corrupt relationship with clients? With elegant tact, Keynes wondered at the position in which the Harvard Service (and by implication all forecasters) put themselves. 'I feel it would be a great pity if the Service were to get into the state of mind of having, so to speak, a vested interest in the due recurrence of the boom and slump.'[9] In this one casual remark, Keynes opened up a question that resonates to this day. If boom and bust was good for the forecasting business, how easily might the industry itself, instead of reporting data, start to try to influence events instead?

According to Robert Skidelsky, Keynes's biographer, the economist was always alert to vested interests; they were a big and frequent idea for him. He appreciated that economics was a complex system but also recognised that it was a human one, inhabited and influenced by those who studied it.

Economists could never be impartial observers. Their models are profoundly susceptible to the beliefs of the human beings who design and run them; they aren't and cannot be morally neutral. Because economics requires moral choices, Keynes believed, it could never be a science.[10]

Rejecting the hope that economics might one day be like physics and as forecastable as the tides, Keynes was far more comfortable seeing uncertainty and discontinuity as sources of hope. These meant that policymakers were not passive bystanders but could intervene and influence what happened next. But perhaps his shrewdest insight was that the prediction business had a commercial interest in giving forecasting more precision that it legitimately possessed.

'The problem with precision,' Skidelsky explained, 'is that where there's more precision, there's more drama. And if there's more drama, there's more money.'[11]

What Babson, Fisher and Persons had discovered, and Keynes had identified, was that forecasters gained bigger reputations and could make more money by being bold; they had a vested interest in exploiting our hopes and our fears. What none imagined was that the drama of the markets would evolve so spectacularly from drama to showbiz to hype to propaganda and the manipulation of consumer behaviour. Human discomfort with uncertainty, together with a craving for reassurance, has fuelled an industry that enriches itself by terrorising us with uncertainty and taunting us with certainty. Master of the genre, a kind of bastard grandchild of Babson, Fisher and Persons, is Jim Cramer, host of the US investment show *Mad Money*, in which he boomerangs around his TV studio to the dramatic cacophony of bullhorns, cash registers and bowling pins as he celebrates or mourns flourishing or decaying businesses. Predictions are the candy of his sweetshop and viewers eagerly swallow his advice, with prices on his picks visibly rising as the show airs.

What happens next is off air: investors in Cramer's picks don't make money. Academic analysis of his advice has showed that, over time, his believers either made no profit or incurred losses. If you slavishly followed his tips you would lose a third of your money in under two months. The analysts conclude: 'Because there is scant evidence that Cramer has skill in selecting under-priced stocks, it is puzzling why viewers act on the recommendations at all.'[12] The chief beneficiary of Cramer's drama is Cramer.

In reality, without inside information, it is impossible to beat the market consistently.[13] This is one reason why the market is increasingly dominated by passive investment funds that promise only to match market indexes, not beat them. But when we fall for exuberant forecasters, we collude in their fiction. Our desire for certainty leaves us susceptible to other people's agendas and business imperatives. This is never truer than in competitive and turbulent times, when the difference between winning and losing is so marked.

On the face of it, the fame of pundits ought to subject them to more scrutiny, not less, making them more accountable for what they predict. But according to the academic Philip Tetlock, that isn't the way it works. Decades of studying forecasters has shown him a perverse trend: the more famous the pundit, the *less* reliable they appeared to be. They survive because almost nobody follows up to see what happened afterwards. If prediction were a science, you'd demand proof; even the Greeks trusted most those oracles with a solid track record of success. But, for the most part, we don't check.

But Tetlock did, crunching twenty years of data. And he concluded that big names were held hostage by their 'big ideas', driven to see consistency where it didn't exist. Tom Friedman, Paul Krugman and Niall Ferguson may once have started as objective truth seekers but, over time, just like Alan Greenspan, they have developed their own ideologies: mental models of how the world works. They cleave to what they know and are loyal to the grandeur and power of their big ideas – sticking to them often in the face of overwhelming evidence. In a crowded, noisy, competitive market, their followers and personal brands lock them into conceptual boxes where they remain captive to consistency.

Tetlock relishes taking pot shots at illustrious commentators captive to big ideas, none more so than the CNBC pundit (and Jim Cramer's frequent co-presenter) Larry Kudlow. An economist in the Reagan administration, he has no economics qualification, but his big idea was supply-side economics: a theory that economic growth is best created by reducing taxes and regulation. When President George W. Bush instigated tax cuts, Kudlow predicted a boom. With each year that passed, Kudlow continued to insist the economy was booming – even if nobody else could see it. In 1993, he predicted that Clinton's tax rises would squash economic growth – and when the late 1990s boom ensued, attributed it to Reagan's tax cuts back in the early 1980s. Ten years later, he was rewarded for his intellectual intransigence when President Trump made him director of the National Economic Council.[14]

Incomplete, ideological and self-interested: the harder economists try to identify sure-fire methods of predicting markets, the more such insight eludes them. The rise of big data and artificial intelligence enables firms to analyse quantities of information far beyond the dreams of earlier forecasters: not just prices, money supply and national economies but satellite images tracking the number of oil tankers on the seas or cars at shopping malls. Yet uncertainty remains endemic, and the growth of passive investors testifies to the gradual acceptance that there are no magic formulae that accurately anticipate financial markets. Very few organisations or investment managers are willing to have their results analysed to determine whether they have a smart approach – or have just been lucky.[15] In the competitive market for analysis and advice, when winning models do emerge they are so quickly copied that any advantage evaporates. The only true source of advantage is new knowledge, but that is, by definition, unpredictable – because if it were predictable, it wouldn't be new.

But the power of prophecy to make reputations has not abated. When two researchers at the Oxford Martin School announced, in 2013, that 47 per cent of US jobs would disappear to automation by 2035, they hit the bullseye. The research offered ample drama – a big number of disappearing jobs – while the sheer precision of it – *exactly* 47 per cent – sounded like certainty. When I read it, I was instantly puzzled. Twenty-three years hence, *exactly* 47 per cent of jobs could be *known* to have disappeared? But it was the very grittiness and size of the numbers made them sound like fact and seized the world's attention. Soon the numbers were embedded in PowerPoint presentations, newspaper and magazine articles.

Bill Gates talked about them. Davos discussed them. *The Economist* wrote about them. Striking workers quoted them. Radio and television programmes gasped at them. It was possible the report was correct, but it was impossible – and still is – to know. But everyone from government officials to philosophical pundits projected inevitability onto what was no more than a hypothesis.

The authors of the original paper disclosed from the outset their 'novel methodology', but that didn't seem to prompt any scepticism about an untested, unproven approach. Nobody I talked to about it had read the paper itself (co-sponsored by Citibank), so they couldn't explain how the number had been derived. Subsequent studies, from the inter-governmental Organisation for Economic Co-operation and Development (OECD), concluded that just 9 per cent of jobs were auto-matable.[16] A PWC report in 2017 plumped for 30 per cent of jobs at risk in the UK, 38 per cent in the US and just 21 per cent in Japan. McKinsey estimated that 60 per cent of occu-pations were at risk. A subsequent report from the World Economic Forum predicted that, while 75 million jobs globally would be destroyed, 133 million would be created.[17] Among the cacophony of guesses, the only idea established without doubt was that these forecasts were guaranteed media attention.

But the gritty Oxford Martin numbers performed mightily for their authors. Such exposure *is* currency in universities today. Academics need people to talk and write about their work – that is how they rack up citations that help determine career prospects. Their institutions need the attention too, as those citations also help push them up in the rankings of UK universities. There are big personal and institutional incentives to produce headline numbers like these. As Babson and his contemporaries proved, in the forecasting market, everyone competes for attention.

An inescapable quality of forecasting lies within that word: it can be about *casting forwards*, seeking to shape, to cast a mould, for what lies ahead. The forecast in Shakespeare's *Macbeth* is a classic example. When they predict that he will be king, are the witches telling Macbeth what they know will happen, or are they priming him, dropping into his mind an idea he cannot shake off? In the prediction business, it's but a small step from selling forecasts as a business to using prophecy as a sales technique to shape or accelerate a future you seek to dominate. That's the subtext to the by-now perennial headline declaiming this is the year for virtual reality. It isn't true; the makers just hope, by getting you to believe it, that they can make it true. Nowhere has this subtle shift from prediction to propaganda been more prominent than in the marketing of autonomous vehicles. The driverless car, we have been told for years now, is inevitable. There's no point even learning to drive any more, so immediately will the liberating technology be upon us.

The piratical image of Google's Sergey Brin sporting Google Glass as he struggled to explain how autonomous vehicles will both free the blind and reclaim green space from car parks shimmers with visual irony. Just as bizarre, as he signs a Bill facilitating the new technology, is Governor Jerry Brown's celebratory reference to California as the home of the gold rush – an epic of exploiting hopes and dreams if there ever was one.

The real drama is the one nobody wrote about: the absence of questions. It is hard to see how the blind would use driverless cars if, as most believe, safety requires that the driver remain capable of last-minute intervention. It remains unclear why, if drivers already on the road are joined by those who currently can't drive, the streets would be clearer. More cars in use sits oddly with the notion of needing fewer parking spaces, while promises of 100 per cent safety left thoughtful consumers wondering if there had ever, in history, been a 100 per cent safe product. Since any obstacle automatically stops these cars, couldn't any pedestrian merely step in front of them? Or would that risk require that pedestrians be caged in, so as not to impede traffic? Where would all the cars go at night and what would happen in snow or fog when sensors don't work? That all the cars would be connected and might therefore be able to drive in convoy more efficiently was cool, and clearly the manufacturers would have a field day collecting drivers' data, but this is also a hacker's dream.

In short, the forecasts were so dazzling, the rhetoric of inevitability so dramatic and so confident, everyone stopped thinking about implications and was instead seduced into submission by the beautiful, frictionless fantasy. We call it salesmanship because there are products and money attached – automobiles are the largest manufacturing business in the world – but if the technology were correctly seen as a campaign we'd recognise it as propaganda: we are being recruited into an army of believers.

Quashing pragmatic questions is not the only consequence of such grandstanding. It also discourages policy questions about the impact of AVs on the labour market, on civil liberties and on public transportation.[18] In a perfect world, where everyone has easy access to a driverless car, there's apparently no need to invest in infrastructure or to address the geographic segregation that plagues so many cities. The more we believe, the less we question, the more probable the forecast becomes. A simplistic commercial view of the future is being forced onto a world as though there are no alternative possibilities, when in fact there are many.

The same sleight of hand is intrinsic to almost all discussions of artificial intelligence. Wild promises are made about the capacity of AI to predict disease, crime, recidivism, career trajectories, lifespan. Inevitablism discourages practical questions. Data scientists know that, with a large enough dataset, projecting trends with gross accuracy is easy, but it's near impossible to reduce from that to pinpoint accuracy for an individual. Philosophical questions abound – and not only about who owns the data and for what purposes. The rhetoric flowing from Silicon Valley casually assumes that a person *is* simply an aggregation of data. Accepting this begs questions of what aspects of existence can't be standardised and measured, and therefore the value and importance of what gets left out. Does anyone seriously propose a standardised measurement of how much I love my partner or my child? But omit that and an individual profile full of data still is not me. Which means that when artificial intelligence assumes that I am the sum of the data available about me, it will make mistakes. Just as, we already know, it makes mistakes on the simpler issue of facial recognition.

Ethical questions, too, are casually overlooked. Where does the data come from, who gave their consent and who's making money out of whom, for what?[19] AI systems already in operation make mistakes, but it remains unclear whether responsibility lies with the companies deploying the software, the businesses that design it or the legal system that permits it. These early implementations of AI resemble nothing so much as drug trials on an unsuspecting public in a market with no oversight. Such questions cry out for public debate and the difficult, slow task of crafting consensus and rules. But businesses are advised to avoid that. When consumers balk at technologies that track where they go or how they drive, the advisory firm Deloitte recommends that they be worn down with the argument that 'enhanced surveillance and/or geo-location capabilities are part of the world we live in now, for better or for worse . . . The genie is out of the bottle.'[20] If it's inevitable everywhere, why bother having the argument?

Promising improbable benefits, the propagandists exploit one enormous advantage: ignorance. The future hasn't happened yet, so we can't be completely certain that they are wrong. But that's no reason to swallow whatever we're told, sold or dazzled by. It's a good reason to ask better questions. That is what some research firms hope their forecasts can generate: not numbing certainty, but deeper, more exploratory thinking and debate. A prediction is really just a hypothesis.

As chief of research at Gartner, a technology advisory firm, Daryl Plummer produces forecasts that he hopes will provide an antidote to the fetid hype of tech inevitablism. His customers are companies that depend on distinguishing hype from reality. Gartner's strategic planning assumptions start when analysts present propositions which, if interesting enough, they are sent off to verify, quantify and make actionable. Then, Plummer says, 'Their peers tear them apart and then they have us review the final version.' Only when the evidence base is seen to be solid and logical is it published.

When it comes to prediction, Gartner's analysts follow a similar process: a lot of debate, a bit of a slugging match and a lot of challenge. Ninety-five per cent of predictions are changed along the way. That doesn't mean Gartner always gets it right, but, in striking contrast to popular pundits, it is a routine part of Plummer's work to scrutinise their final predictions and compare them with what happened. His prediction accuracy report gives Gartner analysts feedback on their thinking that impossibly long-term speculations aim to avoid. At conferences, the company proudly broadcasts the many areas in which the company has been right – but it also shares the topics on which it's been proved wrong.

'We predicted that Windows 8 would be the last release of an operating system by Microsoft,' Plummer recalled. 'It was wrong because of how we defined what an OS was – and Microsoft redefined it. But if you're not wrong, you're not trying hard enough. Sixty per cent accuracy is optimal; if you are right more than that, you're diluting what you're predicting. Nobody here is hired because they're psychic; they're hired to generate insights that are useful – even if they turn out to be wrong. It's useful if it gets you thinking.'

Plummer is making a provocative and important point: that what matters most isn't the predictions themselves but how we respond to them, and whether we respond to them at all. The forecast that stupefies isn't helpful, but the one that provokes fresh thinking can be. The point of predictions should not be to surrender to them but to use them to broaden and map your conceptual, imaginative horizons. Don't fall for them – challenge them.

'Inevitability', Plummer laughed, 'is just a statement seeking a reaction. You're putting a stake in the ground: this is the faith I have and you should believe what I believe – because if we *all* believe, well then angels get their wings!'

Over a century of modern forecasting has revealed and exacerbated intrinsic problems that remain unsolved. Even the newest technology leaves models incomplete, their designers unable to see what's missing until it presents problems. All interpretations of the present are rife with assumptions – ideologies and big ideas that organise, but also influence, prediction. The self-interest of forecasters, be they pundits, academics, technologists or companies, cannot but motivate what is seen and sold. But those problems won't, and can't, stop human beings from thinking about the future. So if we can't be perfect, could we at least do better? Is there any chance that self-interest and ideology could be removed, or at least reduced?

Those questions lay at the heart of Tetlock's Good Judgment Project, a tournament initiated by IARPA, the US Intelligence Advanced Research Projects Activity. For them, forecasting is neither a commercial venture nor entertainment. With billions of dollars invested in intelligence that informs decisions about security, terrorism, energy, environmental, social and political policy, there is a clear and urgent need for objective, accurate insight. IARPA challenged five teams of researchers to identify people and methods that could produce proven, measurable standards of reliability. Each team tackled nearly 500 questions about world affairs in a prediction tournament designed to compare results: which, if any, could sustainably achieve significant levels of accuracy?

Tetlock recruited volunteers for the Good Judgment Project who weren't in it for the money, to build personal reputations or on ideological crusades. At the end of each season's work, they received a $250 gift certificate; that's all. The collective intelligence of the teams mitigated individual biases and ideological differences. Each participant drew on a very broad range of information sources and constantly revised their assessments. Their forecasts – individually and in aggregate – were logged and subsequently compared to what happened. In the first year of the tournament, Tetlock's team proved 60 per cent more accurate than the control group – superior to university teams at MIT and the University of Michigan. The following year, they did 78 per cent better, out-performing professional intelligence analysts who had access to classified information. Confronted by that margin of success, IARPA saw no point in continuing the contest and stopped it. Tetlock's process had won.

The Good Judgers didn't make binary forecasts; they almost never gave an absolute yes or no to any question. Instead, they assessed probabilities: how likely was it that an event would occur or not? Probabilities changed the way that they thought about the future, allowing them to accept uncertainty and to reject the dramatic absolutism so beloved of popular audiences. It made them more thoughtful and more accurate. Measuring the results of their work showed Tetlock that, yes, some individuals – he calls them super-forecasters – are better than others. But depending on any single voice or loud opinion is folly.

There is much that is hopeful in this outcome. The project showed that ordinary people who were open-minded, educated, prepared to change their minds, humble and attentive could gain real insight and awareness into what might happen in the next year or so. These were people who were prepared to see multiple, not single, causes of events and who were comfortable updating or changing their initial expectations. They weren't beguiled by consistency but, like the analysts at Gartner, learned from their mistakes and got better over time. They appreciated that all forecasts are probabilities, not absolutes. And working in teams, they did even better.

Tetlock believes in doubt but isn't paralysed by it. Few things, he says, are absolutely certain or completely impossible. While he lacks the evangelical salesmanship of a Babson or a Fisher, he has put the Good Judgment Fundamentals curriculum online to share what he has learned. Taking its tests, which calibrate confidence against accuracy, I found that, in areas where I had expertise, I was overconfident and estimated probabilities too narrowly. In areas where I knew I knew little, I was under-confident, assessing probabilities so broadly as to be meaningless – a 50 per cent probability, after all, tells you nothing. Implicitly, the training moves you away from purely wishful thinking because predicting what you want to happen just produces poor results. Instead, it starts to make you ask better questions – of yourself and others – and to be more comfortable with the suggestion that you could be wrong.

But the time horizon for accurate forecasts is dauntingly small: the Good Judgment Project found that, while many forecasters were accurate within only about 150 days, its own super-forecasters weren't confident beyond 400 days.[21]

That number should give anyone pause when confronted by loud pontification about life and events far into the future. Organisations that invest time and effort into intricate five-year plans or thirty-year plans can't believe that they represent any kind of absolute truth. They shouldn't mistake the gritty realism of numbers for anything more than informed guess-work, rife with assumptions, ideology and bias.

When you assess a forecast can make a decisive difference to seeing it as true or false. The future doesn't unfold evenly but often reveals new information long after it looks like the story's over. When, in the days and weeks following the Brexit referendum, the British economy appeared to defy the predictions of imminent decline, it was easy to conclude that dire warnings from those campaigning to remain in Europe had been bad, stupid and wrong. After all, in the days and weeks after the 2016 referendum, the UK had remained the fastest growing economy in the G7. But then, in the first three months of 2017 and on into the first six months of 2018, it became one of the slowest, missing out on a boom enjoyed by the rest. Neither forecast – of utter resilience or total disaster – had proved right, but either could be validated in different timeframes.

Sooner or later, everyone, even the best of the best, gets it wrong. The Good Judgment Project itself is no exception: it called the Scottish referendum correctly in 2016 but got Brexit and Trump wrong. There is no one person, process or prophet who gets it right every time. But that message is hard to hear against a noisy backdrop of daily prophecy. Listen carefully to the news: today, just over half of the items I heard weren't reports of events but speculation about the future. It's tempting to dismiss most of it as guesswork, posturing, propaganda, lobbying, marketing or hot air, but that doesn't mean it is without impact. I'm haunted by the headline about 47 per cent of jobs vanishing by 2035, not just because nobody can make reliable forecasts that far out. Not just because it feels more like PR than anything else. But because it was so quickly absorbed as fact. Instead of appearing unknown, debatable and uncertain, suddenly the future looked foreclosed. In that guise, it becomes propaganda. When we trade the effort of doubt and debate for the ease of blind faith, we become gullible and exposed, passive and irresponsible observers of our own lives. Worse still, we leave ourselves wide open to those who profit by influencing our behaviour, our thinking and our choices. At that moment, our agency in our own lives is in jeopardy.

When he was asked at Davos how forecasters had got both Brexit and the Trump election so wrong, Tetlock was laconic and relaxed. He has, he told me, an existential comfort with uncertainty. Public hunger for certainty had misinterpreted probabilities; expectations of forecasters, he said, were simply misplaced. 'The very best forecasters are wrong a lot. We live in a world where there is a lot of irreducible uncertainty. And in the very best forecasting systems, even systems that are very well calibrated, there are going to be conspicuous cases where they look wrong. It is in the nature of the political world that there is uncertainty . . .'[22]

***

Because the future is unknowable, the best we can hope for are probabilities – which themselves may be incorrect. Even ssional statisticians and mathematicians find probabilities rintuitive and difficult, at odds with gut instinct.[23] For those of us who are not super-forecasters, this leaves us with a dilemma. Which forecasters should we trust? If by 'trust' we mean an absolute belief that we'd stake our lives on, the answer is: nobody. Not our neighbours. Not our boss. Not our financial advisor. Not corporate propagandists. And not ourselves. We could and should treat predictions as hypotheses and ask better questions of ourselves: if there is vested interest, where does it lie? What's at stake? What am I being sold? Is this propaganda, bad science, careerism or entertainment? Does the hypothesis emanate from individuals working alone or from a team? What's their track record? How far out are they looking? What are the counterarguments? How wide is the range of opinion? What's the agenda? Only when we kick our addiction to prediction do we stop being spectators and become creative participants in our own future.

The future is uncharted and life remains uncertain. But doubt is so uncomfortable that people will invest a great deal to eliminate it, as the founding fathers of forecasting discovered. They tried and failed to map the unknown, and uncertainty persists throughout their story even to this day. While Fisher lived until he was eighty, Babson to ninety and Persons to fifty-nine, neither they nor we will ever know whether their cold air or chewing regimens extended their lives. We don't even know whether they had TB at all, because no reliable test for the disease was commercially available at the time each received the terrifying diagnosis. We know that there's a high probability that they were infected, and we know that they thought they were. That belief is a powerful motivator is what gives prediction its power.

2

DOES HISTORY REPEAT ITSELF?

To remember this world is to create it.

— TONI MORRISON

Eleanor Maguire gets lost a lot. Her sense of direction is so poor, she says, that she doesn't even bother trying to drive. As professor of cognitive neuroscience at University College London, she understands better than many that if navigation absorbs most of her attention, she'll have little capacity left to think about traffic. Far safer to walk.

Geneticists might see her lack of spatial awareness as a flaw, but Maguire has transformed it into a formidable strength. The difficulty she has finding her way around London made her curious about people for whom this ability has become second nature: London taxi drivers.

'Even GPS doesn't help me, so I was really trying to cure myself!' she laughed. 'I could see that there were huge differences in human navigation and I was trying to understand why some people can learn this stuff well and others, well, they just can't do it.'

To qualify as a licensed London cab driver, candidates must take The Knowledge: a series of tests that requires learning to navigate 25,000 streets within a 6-mile radius of Charing Cross station. Typically, candidates spend three or four years riding around on a scooter with a map, wandering and memorising the spatial relationship between streets, landmarks and popular destinations. Maguire scanned the brains of seventy-nine male taxi drivers at the beginning of their training and could identify nothing that might indicate who might succeed or fail: she found no general intellectual, mnemonic or structural differences between the candidates' brains. The candidates started their training, therefore, on equal terms.

During the course of their training, many drivers dropped out – hours criss-crossing London on a scooter in traffic with rain and snow takes commitment. Thirty-nine drivers qualified in the end. Unsurprisingly, Maguire noted that the successful drivers had put in far more hours than those that failed. She gave all candidates memory tests about the spatial relationships between landmarks and found, again predictably, that the successful cab drivers were better at this. But they weren't better at other kinds of memory tests. But when Maguire did MRI brain scans, she saw that the successful cab drivers now showed a visible increase in grey matter in the hippocampus, while no such physical change was visible in those who failed to qualify.[1]

Hailed as a dazzling demonstration of neuroplasticity and neurogenesis, the results stimulated in Maguire an abiding curiosity about the nature of memory: how it works, how it changes, what parts of the brain it recruits and what they are used for. Her next finding excited the press less but was just as profound. In 2007, Maguire and her colleagues reported that five people with amnesia caused by damage to the hippocampus were less able to imagine future events. Memory, they found, serves many functions – and one of them is to allow us to simulate the future. The idea that without a sense of past we can't have a sense of the future isn't metaphorical. It is the physical reality of how our brains operate. We draw from the past in order to imagine what lies ahead.[2]

'The whole point of the brain', Maguire told me, 'is future planning. You need to survive and think about what happened when I was last here – is there a scary monster that will come out and eat me? We create models of the future by recruiting our memories of the past.'

Mentally, we are all time travellers. We might exhort one another to live in the moment, but the truth is that we can't, we don't – and we wouldn't want to. What gives life meaning is the rich and constant interplay between past, present and future. Maguire saw in the brains of taxi drivers that a new address generated the live construction of a map drawn from memories of landmarks and past routes and updated with current knowledge of driving conditions. Old materials, combined with the present, were required for a vision of the future route. But her work with amnesiacs added a twist: people who didn't have or couldn't find memories lacked material with which to map the future.

But to make memories requires us to be alert and attentive, aware of where we are and what we're doing. Distraction and overload, Maguire says, impede this, reducing our ability to create memories for future use. So too do some forms of technology. Just like a taxi driver, whenever we travel to a destination our mind is drawing and storing a mental map of the environment, logging landmarks and making memories.

But using GPS displaces this activity. We pay less attention to our surroundings and more attention to our phones or satnav. Less awareness, fewer memories – and as a result, the brain area responsible for navigation is used less and tends to shrink.[3] The less we engage with the here and now, the more impoverished our scenarios of the future become.

If we pay attention, reading a book or listening to a piece of music provides ingredients just as rich and pliable as physical or visual experience. Memory also contains feelings: I remember that place was cold; this kind of food was revolting; that person cheered me up. How I use these memories of the past depends on my situation in the present. If I have painful memories of the dentist and today I feel fine, the prospect of going to the dentist this afternoon feels grim. On the other hand, if today I have a terrible toothache, then my present may create a future scenario of relief.[4]

We create a multiplicity of these kinds of scenarios because context keeps changing and because our memories are unreliable, subject to bias and editing. We tend to pay more attention to the way that events finish than to how they start or unfold. A gruesomely painful event (like childbirth) may be remembered as more joyful than it really was because the outcome was happy (a healthy child). Big events are more readily recalled than trivial ones, many of which are lost. Maguire, who by now is a huge fan of memory, was at pains to point out that the fluidity of our memory isn't always negative. It allows us to be more flexible, adaptable and creative in our thinking.

Like many neuroscientists, Maguire is wary of analogies. The brain isn't like a computer and memory isn't like a videoplayer. We don't retrieve a memory, we don't replay the event; we reconstruct it on the fly, assembling a new picture, a fresh sensation each time. It's unhelpful to think of these as flaws or bugs, because the very fact that memory comes to us freshly assembled is why we can use it to come up with new ideas. These additions, subtractions and rearrangements may play havoc within our legal system, but they also propel us into new and unexpected creations and experiences and prevent us from becoming trapped or static. Our capacity to generate a vast range of scenarios is what gives us the capacity for change.

What Maguire and her colleagues are discovering pushes far beyond mechanical descriptions of our brain as simple sources of crude cause and effect. The emerging view of our brain (and, by extension, of our mental, emotional and physical lives) shows that we routinely create, assemble and discover a vast array of possibilities not only at big, dramatic cross-roads but throughout our lives. Like London cab drivers, we can map thousands of possibilities with a lively, free-flowing combination of routine and creativity, knowledge and improv-isation. How rich or poor the results are depends on how much attention we bring to our surroundings and to ourselves. But there is nothing predictable or predetermined about what we will produce with the ingredients of our minds. We neither forsake our past, nor are we mired in it.

Such a view is pretty much the opposite of the narrative approach to life that argues, in essence, that each of us con-structs a narrative and sticks to its plot and characterisation. In the same way that forecasters persuade by constructing a compelling story, strong narratives can become a trap too, constraining and limiting how we see ourselves and other people. Instead of illuminating freedoms, choices and imagination, narrative proposes that we are slaves to plots we can't know and didn't write. The fallacy of narrative lies in the fact that human beings don't experience themselves in just one way, but in a wide variety of ways over time. Our history is not static but fluid. Yesterday's cab route won't necessarily be today's, because of road works, a colleague's tip, the overnight appearance of a crime scene or just a moment's lapse in attention. A career choice early in life need not be deemed an error in the light of a change of profession decades later. People change, events change them and their own choices move them to places where they see more of life, differently. These contingencies, accidents, flukes aren't errors or bugs; however uncertain, they are an infinite source of life's richness, opportunity and freedom. That the past is a very poor predictor of the future is not true only of financial markets. It is a source of hope and redemption for anyone with a poor start in life.

'Whenever I failed at something, I gave up. I blamed other people. That's just what I did, it's what everyone around me did.' Jacob Dunne is a solid student, flourishing in his last year at university. But nothing in his history predicted that this would be his life. He'd grown up in a single-parent family and done alright in primary school. But secondary school and adolescence proved typically challenging for a young man on a tough Nottingham estate. Kicked out of two schools and routinely told he was stupid, he saw nothing in life to give him hope or ambition. He became, he said, a ticking time bomb. Doing drugs and alcohol, he depended on gang life to give him a sense of belonging. The test of loyalty was violence. 'It started to become normal to go out and fight for an adrenalin rush,' Dunne recalled. 'And we used to do it to show each other that we were there for each other.'

One night, Dunne got separated from his friends but received a call from them asking for help. When he joined them, he threw a punch and felled James Hodgkinson, a paramedic visiting Nottingham for a cricket match. Dunne ran away and thought no more of it until, nine days later, he learned that Hodgkinson had died. He turned himself into the police and, pleading guilty, received a reduced sentence of thirty months for manslaughter.

At this point, there is nothing notable in his history but crime and failure. He is wracked with guilt – for what he's done to his mother, for what he hasn't done for himself. He's crying, frustrated that nobody has helped him. He has an overwhelming sense that he deserves more from life but that now the only identity available is that of a victim. He feels unlucky, alone and doomed.

On release, Dunne is homeless and can't access benefits. He doesn't think he stands any chance of getting a job. He feels bound to retrace the same steps, over and over again. But then something unexpected happens. A fluke. One of his probation officers asks if he will see two women who work in restorative justice. Jacob doesn't know what that is. They've been in contact with James Hodgkinson's parents who have questions about what happened that night. But there's no pressure; it's Dunne's choice to make. 'My initial response was to say no. Then I felt obliged to do it. I felt so bad about myself, maybe this offered some kind of decency. I didn't know what to expect, I just thought at least I can answer some of their questions and they can move forward in a more positive way. I heard horrible things about them sitting by their son's life-support machine, arranging the funeral, what kind of person James was. He became real. How can I ever appreciate the harm caused without hearing it from those closest to him?'

Nothing about the exchange makes Dunne think he can change. The probation officers keep bringing questions and take Dunne's replies back to Hodgkinson's parents. A correspondence begins. Hodgkinson's parents ask what he will do with his life, but Dunne has no idea. He wants to tell them something so he mentions going back to school. In the past, he'd found education meaningless, but now he feels a strong urge to develop himself as a human being.

At the age of twenty-two, sitting in a classroom of sixteen- and seventeen-year-olds, he feels embarrassed, knowing some of the kids he'd gone to school with would have degrees by now. He is also driven by shame and a deep desire to repair the harm he'd done. But on their own, those feelings would never be enough to keep him going.

Studying English, maths and psychology, Dunne learns about memories and how we constantly reconstruct them. The learning prompts questions: how had he been interpreting what had happened to him? How far had he constructed a story that trapped him into an identity that felt doomed and led nowhere? What different story could help him grow?

One day, he is approached by a man he remembered seeing at church with his mother. Another fluke. At first he fears the man might try to convert him to Christianity, but the request is more modest: would Dunne come and talk to some of the volunteers on the young offenders' team the next day? At first he's petrified, but unable to come up with a good reason to refuse. To his own surprise, he turns out to be good at describing what happened to him: direct, no bullshit, straight from the heart. He speaks again, at a conference about restorative justice. He is starting to feel like a citizen.

As Dunne tells me his story, the narrative wanders. He is looking around for different ways to think about himself, different ways of seeing the world. His mother has died, and she becomes a memory of someone he could have helped and loved more. This is a new thought for him. He now remembers that she never washed her hands of him, had always believed in him. Her death gives him a fresh excuse to feel sorry for himself again – but this time he doesn't take it. His own bereavement helps him appreciate what James Hodgkinson's parents had endured. 'Hurt people hurt people. That's what they do. That's what I didn't want to do. What helped me were David and Joan Hodgkinson. If ever I gave up, or failed my exams, what could I say to them? It was only when I got my place at university that they felt comfortable meeting me because they realised I meant it when I said I was going to change. What was extraordinary is that after that, they said: "You don't have to go to university just for us!" But by then it wasn't just for them; it was for me. They set me free.'

Dunne's story doesn't have a tidy end. He's currently finishing university – a degree in criminology – and isn't quite sure what he will do next. His story is neither predetermined nor is it ahistorical. What he senses is that he has possibilities.

Although Dunne's story is dramatic, and moving, it isn't unique. Most of us can find times in our lives when we might have turned one way but went another. These are times when we feel we have freedom, but we need skill to notice it and valour to use it. The act of imagination required to see choices and imagine better ones is how we craft the lives that are our own. When George Santayana wrote: 'Those who cannot remember the past are condemned to repeat it,' he was writing specifically about the development of young people, from childhood to old age.[5] Progress, he argues, depends on retentiveness; if, every day, we had to learn from scratch, we would remain infantile. Instead, new learning creates new perspectives and memories which themselves prompt the creation or identification of new possibilities. With no knowledge of the brain science underlying this process, Santayana, in his famous epigram, understood the interplay between time zones that underpins the incessant construction of our futures.

The German philosopher Karl Popper described a parallel process in human history. He argued that the fundamental driver of all human progress is the growth of knowledge. We obviously can't predict what we don't know yet, and we can't know how, in what directions, or at what speed, human knowledge will develop. And therefore, Popper concludes, history can't repeat itself. Neither can history itself be a predictor because it can't take into account what is yet to be learned. There are, he argued, no laws, tantamount to the laws of physics, that determine what happens next. Popper was refuting Marx's famous edict that history repeats itself, seeing in Marx's determinism the heart and soul of author-itarianism. Eliminating the power of choice and action, Popper believed, is what autocrats seek to do. Identifying choices for ourselves is how we remain free.

Yet the idea that history does repeat itself is so often repeated that many have come to believe that it can be a meaningful predictor of the future. But if history really did repeat itself, then historians would by now be able to identify recurrent patterns and fundamental principles with unvarying actions and predictive power. But, since Herodotus, historians have discovered no such laws. What we have instead are numerous examples where not only did history fail to repeat itself but believing that it did led to blindness and blunder.

The poster child for this error is the Maginot Line: fifty-eight underground fortresses built in the 1930s along 1,500 kilometres of the French border with Italy, Switzerland, Germany and Luxembourg – the largest single fortification in the world after the Great Wall of China. These massive and elaborate installations, complete with underground trains, kitchens and operating theatres, were impregnable to tanks and aerial attack, but the line's path assumed that the Germans would repeat their strategy in the First World War and launch any new attack along exactly the same geographical axis.

But, at its vast scale, the Maginot Line was no secret; the Germans watched the line being built and changed their plans accordingly. Instead of repeating the 1914 battle plan, they attacked through Belgium and the Netherlands. Within five days, Germany had successfully invaded France. The Maginot had both reflected and created in the French Army a rigid, static mindset. Depending on the fortification cost the army all their mobility.[6] Its ruins stand today as a vivid reminder of the dangers of believing in the past as a predictor of the future.

To be fair, the French weren't alone in imaging the future war would be similar to the preceding one. Hitler resisted building up a submarine fleet because he believed that that was what had brought the United States into the first war. In Britain in 1936, General Archibald Montgomery-Massingberd decided that the army's estimated budget for forage for horses should be increased ten-fold – from £40,000 to £400,000 – but allocated a trifling £121,000 to motor fuel, even though the technology of warfare had undergone huge change.

In believing that the future would be like the past, the British and the French succumbed to the power of aesthetic similarity. When two things look similar, we assume that they are the same and therefore predict that they will behave in the same ways.[7] This feels logical but it's often wrong. The difficulty posed specifically by historical analogies is that they overweight parallels and leave us blind to crucial differences. History doesn't repeat itself, but thinking that it does makes forecasting flawed.[8]

The most routine historical analogy deployed by politicians is the Munich Agreement of 1938: the archetype of the failure to stand up to a brutal dictator. Macmillan used it, to disastrous effect, to guide his strategy during the Suez Crisis. Eisenhower relied on it during the Korean War and he and Johnson both used it at the beginning of the Vietnam war. In 1965, while Harold Wilson and the British urged negotiation, Eisenhower weighed in, telling Johnson: 'We, however, have learned that Munichs win nothing.' Later, urging negotiation again, Johnson insisted: 'To give in = another Munich. If not here – then Thailand.'

By all accounts, Johnson wanted to find a way to stop the bombing, but his fear of history repeating itself stopped him from trying a different path. Once he started equating the North Vietnamese with the Nazis, Johnson feared that the South Vietnamese President Ngo Dinh Diem might prove another Chamberlain: an appeaser whose failure would provoke another global war. Channelling Churchill's rhetoric, Johnson insisted that, to withstand the North, President Diem would 'have to meet them in the bushes, and you're going to have to meet them in the mountains, and you're to going to have to meet them in the forests . . .'[9] Meanwhile, William Bundy, assistant secretary of state for East Asia and the Pacific, insisted that 'aggression of any sort must be met early and head on or it will have to be met later and in tougher circumstances. We have relearned the lessons of the 1930s — Manchuria, Ethiopia, the Rhineland, Czechoslovakia.'[10]

The problem here is that the belief that history would repeat itself inhibited fresh thinking about how to deal with the threat they believed they faced. They saw the South Vietnamese as similar to themselves, thirsting for democracy. And they saw North Vietnam as a fascist aggressor, set on world domination. In his memoir *In Retrospect*, Secretary of State for Defence Robert McNamara discusses how the Cabinet arrived at what he called 'our misjudgements of friend and foe alike'. His book describes how busy everyone was, how rushed the deliberations, how little time there was available for detailed exploration or even understanding of societies so different from Europe in the 1930s. Had they abandoned that shortcut in favour of open-minded enquiry, or even pursued different comparisons, they might have seen that they were relying on the wrong history, trusting to the wrong analogy. Choosing familiar parallels made the American government overconfident that they were operating in familiar territory when, in fact, they were not. Since then, of course, Vietnam has become an analogy of its own.[11]

More recently, General Sir Nick Carter recalled that a similar error helped to explain the confusion in British operations in Iraq. The military had believed that their years of experience dealing with insurgency in Northern Ireland would give them an advantage in Iraq, where in fact it led them to underestimate the differences between the two war zones. As we sat surrounded by the portraits of his predecessors as chief of the general staff of the British Army, Carter explained: 'We thought we were very good at counterinsurgency because of Northern Ireland. But the lessons we drew weren't the right lessons. We didn't think so clearly about how you need to use indigenous forces or intelligence services in order to be able to understand a population that's not at all like you. So it took us a long time to recognise that we had to understand population dynamics.'

Analogies are dangerous, the historian Margaret MacMillan argues, because they fail to take into account both the differences between events and open exposure to accident and contingency. No two events are ever exactly the same, and not just because of changes over time. Countries are different, personalities are different and everyone operating in the present is different to those from the past, so make decisions with information that their predecessors did not possess.

But when the Arab Spring began in Tunisia in December 2010, analogies popped up like daisies. Just the term 'Arab Spring' evoked comparisons with the European revolutions of 1848 and the Prague Spring anti-Communist rising of 1968.

Even more common were references to the fall of the Berlin Wall, another event that had defied prediction. In August 2011, one NGO commentator wrote: 'The Arab Spring is truly historic. People are standing up in a region where customs have required deference to the wise and elder. This is nothing short of a socio-cultural quake. Today's mostly youth-led revolt is new for the Middle East but not for the world. In 1989 and 1990, young activists saw the culmination of their *Leipziger Montagsdemonstrationen* as they peacefully challenged the status quo and proved to be smarter than the Communist East German state.'[12]

The belief that history repeats itself often leads people to think that it is *their own* history that is being repeated – but not someone else's. The Russians saw Russian history in the Arab Spring, with Medvedev fearing that, like the fall of the Berlin Wall, these demonstrations would prove destabilising for Russia.[13] Meanwhile, President Obama likened it to the Boston Tea Party and the beginning of America's war for independence, drawing analogies too with the civil rights protest of Rosa Parks.[14]

Everyone saw themselves in these events. So they felt confident they knew where they would lead and how they would end. The reliance on analogies implied inevitability: just like the fall of the Berlin Wall or the Boston Tea Party, the demonstrations would usher in a new era of democratic freedoms. But history proved a poor forecaster and few today look back on the Arab Spring and see so simple or triumphalist a narrative.[15]

It's a very human error to assume that countries, peoples and histories we don't know very well must be similar to our own and to conflate their history with ours. But historical analogies can be just as forceful, and just as flawed, when applied to homegrown events. In peacetime, there is probably no historical event that strikes such fear as the flu pandemic of 1918. Globally it infected 500 million people, of which 50 to 100 million died. That the flu killed young adults within twenty-four hours, and that it particularly struck the lucky survivors of the First World War, made it poignant and horrifying. The stories of such swift and sudden deaths have left an indelible mark on the psyche of every health professional ever since.

So when, in January 1976, doctors diagnosed thirteen soldiers at Fort Dix, New Jersey, with flu, no one took their illness lightly. Tests revealed that most suffered from A Victoria or A Port Chalmers virus – not the strain responsible for 1918. But with about seven samples, some uncertainty remained. After retesting, just two contained swine flu type haemagglutinin, closely related to the cause of the 1918 pandemic. But meanwhile, one of the flu-ridden soldiers went on a five-mile march against doctor's orders and died. Following an emergency medical meeting at Fort Dix with the Center for Disease Control, labs were mobilised to produce a swine flu vaccine.

The United States had experienced flu outbreaks in the years since 1918. The 1968 flu outbreak, known as Hong Kong flu, killed 33,800 Americans and provoked a general sense that the national response had been too little too late. In 1976, therefore, two analogies ran together: the abject horror of 1918 and the administrative failures of 1968. That fear set the agenda for the mobilisation of the full force of all healthcare institutions and of the federal government to ensure that this time history did not repeat itself.

The head of the CDC, David Sencer, argued and gained support for the mass inoculations of the American population. At this scale, no insurance company would indemnify the makers of the vaccine, so Congress rushed to pass legislation providing federal cover. On 1 July, Bruce Dull, assistant director for programs at the CDC, attended a flu forum in New York where he said that he could see no parallels with the 1918 pandemic. But his reassurances went unheeded; a mood of sublimated panic prevailed. Any unexpected death caused alarm; an outbreak of illness in Philadelphia, thought to be swine flu, turned out to be Legionnaire's disease. On 1 October, with inoculation underway, two men died of heart attacks following their jabs. Those deaths turned out to be pure coincidence. Within ten weeks, over 40 million people had been immunised, without a single case of the disease having been identified since the first findings at Fort Dix.

The mistaken application of an analogy proved costly in more ways than one. In the years that followed, it transpired that those who had been inoculated were four times more likely to develop Guillain–Barré syndrome, a life-threatening condition that can lead to respiratory arrest and paralysis. At least twenty people died. The CDC was accused of using scare tactics to promote its own agenda and importance, leaving a legacy of cynicism and scepticism about vaccines and nationwide health programmes. Forced to leave the CDC, David Sencer, the evangelist for mass inoculations, moved to New York City where he became the city's health commissioner. And that's where he was working when a new disease arrived: AIDS. Sencer seemed now to think that history was repeating itself, but this time it was the 1976 analogy that guided his thinking and his response. Determined not to be alarmed, he didn't rush into action. Only this time what he saw *was* a pandemic and the gay community rounded on him for failing to appreciate the scale of an unfolding tragedy.

***

When we expect history to guide us, we overweight continuity and narrative, while underweighting change and contingency. Aesthetic similarities often turn out to be no more than skin deep, their appearances masking important variation that could spark better questions and more illuminating debate. History could provide a rich array of components with which to construct images of the future, but we lose that richness when we reach for analogies.

But just because parallels are misleading doesn't render history useless. It means we have to use it differently. The great British military historian, Michael Howard, considers the comforting stories and patterns that we cherish to be 'nursery history'. He suggests that a mark of maturity is to use history to challenge, not confirm, comfortable assumptions about ourselves and others.

The nursery histories we favour aren't only simplistic, they're also selective. Which history do we attend to: the history of institutions or of protest? Of the powerful or the powerless? Each tells a different story with its own agenda, every bit as much as the models preferred by financial forecasters. In 2016, when the World Economic Forum christened the rise of AI and automation the 'Fourth Industrial Revolution', the metaphor meant something – but it wasn't anything that historians of the period recognise.

'The (first) Industrial Revolution is a step change,' Emma Griffin says. As professor of modern British history at the University of East Anglia, she is alert to how different the first Industrial Revolution was from today. 'Before it, everything was made by hand and comes from the land. Normal experience is to die in a world very similar to the one you were born into. Most people live in small settlements of fewer than 5,000 people. All of that changed during the Industrial Revolution. But today, we are already used to a very rapid rate of change. We are used to a globalised world and to living in big cities. That won't change. We could re-distribute working populations but we won't. That doesn't mean automation and AI don't change anything – but it isn't the kind of change ushered in by the Industrial Revolution.'

Introducing this analogy both amps up the drama– stand back, absolutely everything is going to change – and implies, as historical analogies always do, that there is nothing we can do about it: the history train of inevitability has left the station. It conveniently overlooks vast differences between the two periods, of which the most prominent is the franchise. In contrast to the period immediately before the first Industrial Revolution, adults today can vote, are educated and can communicate with one another. Citizens have the right to active and decisive participation in events. But the narrative being sold at Davos comes from those who expect to be its leaders and victors; their dazzling story marginalises other forces while minimising the tensions, costs and conflict that may ensue. Most of all it implies that there is no opportunity for intervention, debate or change. In that, such narratives fulfil Popper's definition of autocracy – that which limits the scope of our ability to identify our choices.

But if the traditional study of history hasn't produced predictive patterns, might our increasing ability to interrogate vast datasets yield more insight than analogies? Could models help? The question is more than academic: predicting outbreaks of violence could save lives. But academic researchers working with massive datasets from history, together with machine learning and neural networks, to try to identify predictive patterns found that people, states and political causes have changed shape too frequently to be subject to any stable definition. The onset, location and timing of conflict remains too ambiguous and uncertain to generate a reliable model, and violence has too many predictors to know in what circumstance which one of them will become pertinent.[16] Try as they might, they could not identify a series of narratives that could do much more than point out obvious sources of trouble.

But when we challenge narrative fallacy, then we can start to unlock new possibilities, not just in the past but in our own future. In the 1980s, the Irish historian Roy Foster was one of a generation of historians who, like Margaret MacMillan, probed and challenged simple narratives. For centuries, the history of Ireland had been one of perpetual victimhood, a story that gave the Irish themselves only a small role in their own past. When Foster wrote his *History of Ireland*, and later in *Vivid Faces*, he examined the intimate lives and choices of individuals caught up in events. These weren't tidy or simple, and nothing about the narrative was inevitable. Manifest destiny, he reminded me gently, was propaganda. 'The great stately rolling narrative, people coming out of bondage feeling their way up to the light,' Foster argues, 'was the way that history had been written. But it wasn't the way that people lived. It isn't the way that people do live. I just got so tired of reading moralising history. There *was* no enormous flow of continuity.'

The fissile nature of Irish society – including convulsive events like the Famine – could not be described adequately, understood or honoured if portrayed as though they had been just episodes along an inevitable path. Foster became determined to show how much *dis*continuity there was in the story. He took on the immense challenge of writing history as though he *didn't* know what would happen next – because that's how the people living through these events had experienced them. They did not, could not, know what we know now. Drawing on published and unpublished sources, tracing minute details of individual lives, viewing events through a wide variety of people and places, Foster succeeded in portraying Ireland's history as a series of choices and contingencies which, with no grand plan, shoved one event to the next. The best history, Foster told me, is written when we understand the past in the light of a future that never happened. But it's much harder to write that way because the narrative is so complex and contingent.

What is difficult but thrilling about Foster's history is that it seems to be saying: at any moment, it could have been, could be, different. Outcomes aren't inevitable; history isn't about manifest destinies but unexpected and unforeseen futures.

What happened next took place because of choices people made, people without the information we have today and with information perhaps now lost. History wasn't the runaway train on which we all sat like helpless, terrified children. This different view of history quivered with possibilities – some good, some bad, some seized, others overlooked – but all alive and human.

Think about what happens when you apply that mindset to the future: at any moment, it could be different. Outcomes aren't inevitable. What happens next is a choice. Foster was both reflecting and influencing his generation as it reconsidered its relationship with the past *and* the future. When the Good Friday peace accord was signed in 1998, it wasn't history repeating itself, nor was it some miraculous *deus ex machina*. It was the result of human beings making decisions very different from those that had gone before.

Knowing that history doesn't repeat itself is what makes it useful. We may glean what appear to be themes – humiliation provokes tyranny, for example – that make us pay attention to new information we might otherwise ignore or marginalise. Like Roger Babson, we can use Newtonian physics to expect equal and opposite reactions – but simultaneously use history to question whether, this time, it's true. Like Warren Persons, we can search for patterns, but instead of focusing on similarities, identify salient differences.

Just as the super-forecasters have to keep their minds open to change, or as London cab drivers have to know enough to change routes in the face of sudden obstacles, just as Jacob Dunne responded to lucky contingencies and was willing to try different ways of being, history offers us a rich inventory of ideas and ingredients with which to interrogate, explore and craft not old but new narratives of our own making. History doesn't repeat itself because we keep changing and it keeps changing us. It can't offer recipes but it can provide raw material with which to construct fresh combinations, drawn from where we have been, where we are today and where we wish to be tomorrow. That it offers neither inevitability nor guarantees isn't its weakness but its greatest power.

3

WELL-ORDERED SHEEP

'When I was pregnant with Johanna, all I wanted was a normal, healthy baby,' Julia recalls. 'I had every genetic test I could, but that was it. I was against birth plans, because really you never know what's going to happen. I didn't want to know whether it was a boy or a girl. You're having your first baby, even your doctors don't really know what's going to happen.'

Remembering the birth of their daughter, Julia and Mario both chortle. It feels so long ago, they were so innocent. Both approached parenthood as an adventure. With no particular desire to know or predict the future of their family, they were content to make it up as they went along. Young as they were, they understood that life is complex, full of contingencies, the unexpected and the unwonted. They accepted that no plan or research could foresee who or what their children would become. Back then, their outlook bespoke humility. Today it's experience.

Julia got her wish. Johanna was healthy, and grew into a pretty girl – sociable, amiable, with a bubbly personality she inherited from her Welsh parents. She loved primary school, although detested being asked what she'd be when she grew up. When she was three, her brother Luca was born. Being told she was getting a brother is, Johanna says, her first memory. With neat bobbed hair and bright brown eyes, the two children looked almost identical. Warm and affectionate, their parents had no particular ambitions for their children; they just wanted them to be able to choose their own paths in life. For Mario, this goal was paramount. He didn't want his history to repeat itself with his children. As a boy, he had resisted pressure to work in the family chip shop. Thrown out of the house when he refused, he'd run away to Julia's house, returning home only because her mother couldn't cook Italian food. Freedom, happiness and health were all they wanted for their young family.

But when Jo moved to secondary school, her easy, wide-eyed charm began to evaporate. She rarely went to classes and when she did she was bullied. No teacher sparked her interest and neither did most of the kids in her year. After a while, she didn't bother going to school and didn't see why she should. Her parents tried everything – promises, threats, ignoring her, cajoling her, anger, patience. Nothing seemed to work. Then she started vomiting and having seizures. That meant being in hospital, more time at home, less at school. Years went by. Friends wondered: was the problem with the girl, with the family, the school? Was it physical or emotional?

'Sometimes it would last a few weeks and then she'd be okay,' Julia recalled. 'Then something would trigger it again – any kind of stress. Johanna just got completely out of the loop as far as school was concerned. She was missing out on a social life too; to be so ill, separated from her peer group, the psychological impact, depression: those were huge worries.'

One of Julia's colleagues suggested the problem might be CVS, cyclical vomiting syndrome. When the diagnosis was confirmed, being able to name the disease brought some relief, as did talking to other parents whose children struggled with the same condition. But CVS has no known cause or treatment and some sufferers died. Jo's parents felt mired in uncertainty, anxious that their daughter's lack of academic qualifications would shrink her life chances. Not knowing what to do, they remained calm, supportive and encouraging. Being at home so much, Jo took up art and eventually developed a strong enough portfolio to gain admission to an arts foundation course at the London College of Fashion. She did well, but then got ill again and had to withdraw.

'She has no exams! She's so ill!' Julia remembers. 'But I'd tell myself, she's reading, she's curious, she will come through it in the end. You have to have faith that good enough parenting, a good home, she'll figure it out . . .'

Tentatively, Jo started to explore jobs: working in a library, reviewing restaurants, then copywriting at an ad agency. She took to social media, teaching herself how it worked and quickly stood out as an expert, writing digital strategy for the firm. Three years later, she left to run digital media for De Beers, a diamond company. She had no academic qualifications, but it was her online expertise they wanted. For a while it was fun, but Jo found the company stultifying and left. Unexpectedly she was contacted by a company she didn't know but who were interested in her social media savvy. A few weeks later, she found herself working for the British government, tackling radicalism and extremism online. She found she enjoyed the urgency of the work and the camaraderie of leading a team.

Nothing about this trajectory yields a coherent narrative. Jo was finding her way through life, little by little, experimenting with what suited her, and attracted employers. Every step she took revealed more of who she was and what she wanted from life. There was no map; she just explored.

Her brother Luca's route was just as meandering. His father's history certainly provided no path. Mario had enjoyed a successful career as an animator and artist, well known for a dazzling, inventive style that merges drawing, live action, choreography and classic animation techniques. The aesthetic of his son's favourite toys – Power Rangers – made him wince, but the little boy would spend hours in his bedroom, fighting pretend air battles, shouting co-ordinates. He showed all the academic disinterest of many young boys, until mediocre exams results and the failure to get into the university of his choice brought him up short. To his parents' amazement, he graduated with a first-class degree in physics and went to Cambridge to start a PhD. But what his parents didn't realise for a long time was what he yearned for: to be a test pilot.

Nobody took Luca's ambition seriously. It looked like such a pipe dream, Luca said – a childhood fantasy doomed by the requirement for perfect and uncorrected eyesight, which he didn't have. But when the criteria changed to allow for corrected vision, Luca was on it: getting the laser-eye surgery that would, a year later, make him eligible to apply for pilot training within the Royal Navy. But as the possibility of Luca enlisting improved, family discussions became heated. Mario was a lifelong pacifist and both parents describe themselves as anti-authoritarian. What had their son become? They feared for him and were mystified by an ambition so alien to their family.

'You have to have faith,' Mario decided. 'But it isn't faith that they'll do the right thing. It's faith that they'll notice quickly if what they're doing doesn't work. So they'll be unafraid, not because they *know* what happens next but because they'll figure it out . . .'

By the time Luca left Cambridge to train as a test pilot, Julia had become equally sanguine. An educational psychologist, she had seen too many kids who had grown up believing their lives would best be determined by following the rules and getting great grades. She'd worked with parents who brought huge files of reports on their children to her, desperate for reassurance of their future success, eager to impose a conventional model of success. But life, she argued, doesn't follow rules; that's what makes it life. There were no sure-fire tests or profiles that could guarantee what they wanted. History couldn't predict their children's future and nor would she. She counselled the parents to spend more time with their kids and worry less.

But worrying is what parents do. The positive function of worry is that it encourages horizon scanning: where are the people, activities, opportunities that might appeal to my kids? How could I broaden their horizons? Worry also makes parents more attentive, tuning in to change and danger. But worry becomes destructive and limiting when it demands instant alleviation – which is what most parenting products purport to offer. The worldwide market for parental advice, reassurance and certainty is so vast that it is impossible to quantify. What's obvious is that selling certainty to anxious parents is tantamount to selling sweets to their children.

'It doesn't matter if a child is heading for the Nobel Prize or falling behind in fifth grade,' runs the promotional material for the MUSE parenting app. 'Our deep cognitive modelling and patented machine learning technology allows us to predict life outcomes and to show you what you can do today to maximise the lifelong potential of your child.'[1]

The app was developed by Socos Learning, founded by CEO Vivienne Ming, who seems fuzzy about how deterministic life really is. She says of herself that she was 'supposed to win a Nobel Prize', but gender dysmorphia, depression, insomnia and an eating disorder derailed her.[2] Which, if any of these, was predicted or predictable, she doesn't say, nor does she reveal what the appropriate response would be for a parent able to see these in their child's future.[3]

The promise made on behalf of the MUSE app could be every parent's dream – or every parent's nightmare. If you could be certain your child would win that Nobel Prize, then knowing the future might be fabulous; since she's bound for a Nobel Prize, no need to worry about her drug habit. But if the future holds drugs and a jail sentence, perhaps parents would decide there was no point investing in the education of a deadbeat. All the ethical issues intrinsic to predicting the future are alive and oversimplified here. How MUSE predicts your child's outcome is opaque since, thanks to 'patented machine learning', it's a trade secret and Socos has no scientific advisory board. So all the app will do is tell you where or when improvement is seen. It is, in effect, conditioning you to behave like a good parent. But whose idea of good parenting is being promoted? The definitions of progress and success are all Ming's own, and whether her ideas are compatible with yours, or even trustworthy, you will never know.

Ming makes great claims for her technology, saying of her infant clients: 'We want to change the person you're going to become. It's not the same you but a non-smoker — *it's a different person*. I don't mean this in any spiritual sense. It's the person you were meant to be.' It's not clear how she knows who or what your child is supposed to be (since you don't), but she insists that its assessment of social skills, emotional intelligence, strategic thinking and creativity can determine life outcomes.[4] She believes her analysis of historic leaders proves it. But this is a logical fudge. When you look at very successful people in the past, of course their positive qualities are what you notice first. But assessing leadership is rife with attribution errors, which suggest but can't prove that exceptional leaders succeeded purely because of those individual qualities, conveniently discounting good luck, the era they lived in, the people who helped them, the weaknesses and bad luck of adversaries. It's common also to overlook, marginalise and trivialise all the areas where they failed. Despite the overwhelming amount of data showing that the best predictor of educational achievement is parental income, Ming's assessment doesn't include that.

If it were possible so simply to concoct a recipe for success, we would all be great leaders by now. But then who would the followers be? Using the historic record is problematic because the data is patchy (the leaders we know about) and a product of the past, so the examples we have are mostly white males. There's no reason to believe that what created success in the last century will do so again in this one. How is success defined? If by money, power or lifespan, Mussolini beats Mozart.

Ming's model of achievement may be subjective, but it is what users of the app buy into when they adopt it. Just like financial forecasts, these heuristics contain an agenda; they might purport to be objective or scientific, but they can't be. Are you willing to sign up for Dr Ming's definition of success, without knowing what it is or where it comes from?

MUSE could be dismissed as just another example of Silicon Valley hype, saying whatever will attract investors and customers. But the hype isn't cost-free. The app can distract parents from their children.[5] Parents ended up feeling a slave to it, rather than learning first-hand about their own child. The more anxious they became and the more time they spent on the app, the less they could read their own kids. In effect, using the product meant that parents were being conditioned to condition their children to behave according to Ming's vague and personal concept of excellence. Apps like MUSE come *between* parent and child at a time when the child would benefit most from attention, time together and eye contact in order to develop mutual understanding. It's no wonder Julia and Mario were aghast at MUSE; they didn't think it would have helped them with their children but might have made a difficult situation worse.

Apps aren't neutral. All technology effectively outsources work from humans to machines, promising purported efficiency gains at the expense of individual knowledge and learning. In the case of MUSE, the rich, if stressful, experience of parenting is delegated to a piece of software. But the automation paradox shows that the less we do something, the worse we get at it. The loss is two-fold: it isn't just that the child gets computer-generated parenting; it's also that the parents lose the complex lessons of uncertainty, delight, anxiety, growth and wisdom that are the rewards of family life. What's the point of having children if they're raised by other people's products?

The failure here isn't exploiting anxious parents – that's been a goldmine for decades. It is treating the child as an object to be efficiently programmed: in other words, to relate to the child as a nascent machine. Implicitly, the app perpetuates a myth that each individual is no more than an aggregation of data and, with enough data, profiles can be drawn up that can fully describe what someone is and will be in the future. This is what astrology has always promised and what personality tests have offered for nearly a century.

Of these, the most popular, taken by some two million people a year, is the Myers–Briggs Type Indicator, developed by Katharine Briggs and her daughter Isabel Myers. Briggs, an ardent Jungian, had been captivated by Jung's concept of types and used them for experiments to study her daughter. Briggs pioneered what Ming adopted with MUSE: she looked to historic leaders to define her frame of reference – incurring, of course, all the same biases.

Initially, Briggs had designed her questionnaire to identify solid marriage partners, but after the Second World War, her daughter repositioned it to place people in the right jobs. The MBTI does what all profiling systems do: asks batteries of questions and organises the answers into types which are supposed to define your personality. And yet the test has no basis in clinical psychology, though it is deployed by most Fortune 500 companies, many universities, schools, churches, consulting companies, the CIA, the army and the navy.

The MBTI test-retest validity lies below statistical significance, meaning that if you test someone more than once, you are likely to get different results.[6] More worrying is that the questionnaire poses binary questions, asking, for example, whether you value sentiment more than logic or vice versa. The question assumes that there is a simple answer to this question, absent of context. Yet in real life, preference is highly contextual: I value logic when purchasing car insurance; I may value sentiment more when choosing to play with my son. Binaries always simplify, often to the point of absurdity, and they polarise what are often complements.

More worrying, however, is the underlying assumption that people neatly fall into one of sixteen types – and that this never changes. In her eye-opening biography of Myers, Briggs and their test, author Merve Emre describes attending an MBTI official accreditation session eerily reminiscent of evangelical prayer meetings. Personality, her fellow participants insist, is innate and immutable, like left-handedness or blue eyes, and they urge her to join in chanting: 'Type never changes! Type never changes!'[7]

This is narrative essentialism at its most crude and static – because we do change over time – just as Jo and Luca did, just as Jacob Dunne did. Experience changes us, flukes, imagination and accidents change us. The complex interplay of personality, work, illness, education, friends, family, history, success and failure will alter who we are.[8] We play with, and add to, our memories and experiences all the time, constructing a myriad of different permutations from them. Most people become significantly more agreeable, conscientious and emotionally stable as they age. But a Myers–Briggs profile encourages us

to think of ourselves as defined for all time along a [...]
dimensions. 'I'm an ENTJ' the name badge says, mean[...]
an extroverted, intuitive, thinking, judging individual. [...]
my fate, all I will ever be – I may as well forget about dev[...]op-
ing whatever other qualities I might have. Small wonder that,
after her immersion in the history of Myers–Briggs, Merve
Emre concluded that personality typing was 'among the silliest,
shallowest cultural products of late capitalism'.[9]

That there are powerful commercial motives for profiling
people is obvious: worth some two billion dollars annu-
ally, the marketplace for personality assessment is swollen
with contenders. After making its name with forecasting
polls, the Gallup organisation moved into profiling with its
CliftonStrengths report. Like the MBTI, this test also asks an
array of binary questions (routine vs variety, heart vs head)
and then algorithmically generates an analysis of thirty-four
strengths. If one of your strengths is that you are a 'learner',
you get to learn that 'It's very likely that you might have a
particular desire for knowledge.' The report is more subtle
and less rigid than the MBTI, with qualities ranked in order of
strength, but few people can resist the implication that those
at the bottom are weaknesses.

When pushed on issues of validity, most profilers concede
that these tools don't have much in the way of predictive
power, they're just useful as conversation starters or to build
a sense of community among common types. In itself, that
might not be so bad – were it not for the evidence that people
tend to believe what they are told about themselves. Telling
a parent, or a teacher, that a child is destined for greatness –
or not – is not a neutral action; it can influence how they see

and respond to their children and what they expect of them. Well understood as the Pygmalion effect, the insight derives from an early experiment where primary school teachers in California were told that a few named pupils were especially talented. At the end of a year, when the researchers returned to the school, they found that, indeed, these children had achieved high marks. The catch was that the children had been chosen at random. The prediction had changed the way the teachers treated the children more subtly than the teachers themselves noticed. (A later experiment with Israeli military platoons showed the same effect.)[10]

How people are described changes the way others relate to them and may create expectations that are unfair, irrelevant or inaccurate. Tell someone that they're bad at maths, lazy or uncreative, and it's amazing how quickly that child conforms to those expectations. Tell an adult that they're punctual, and they start turning up on time. Profiling subtly merges into influence or conditioning, nudging a person's behaviour and self-image in one direction or another.

Or consider the Forer effect. This is the strong tendency that subjects show to *believe* feedback from personality tests, regardless of whether those results are bogus. It is sometimes also known as the Barnum effect because it explains why descriptions which offer 'something for everyone' are nevertheless taken seriously. The Forer effect is regularly cited when discussing why people believe in astrology, infamous for its non-specific descriptions and predictions, so bland that they mean almost anything.

Astrological profiles at the back of fashion magazines may not matter much, but psychographic profiles do. It's bad enough when we invest them with authority; it can be worse when employers do likewise. Increasingly, companies turn to profiling software to facilitate their recruiting: to sift through resumes and match individual characteristics with job requirements. This form of matching is not wildly different from online dating: matching the profile of a job with the profile of a person derived from job applications and sometimes also psychographic tests. It's fast and cheap and up to 90 per cent of employers depend on such algorithms to produce their candidate shortlists.[11] But it's wildly problematic.

In 2014, engineering teams at Amazon began attempting to develop artificial intelligence that could sort through job applications, hoping to meet the furious demand for new hires. By 2018 they gave up and abandoned the project. The AI demonstrated a pronounced preference for men – not surprising since the software drew its profile of a successful hire from a historic dataset. But what defines a successful employee changes over time. Qualities that might have been highly prized last year could be marginal today and irrelevant tomorrow, but neither the employer nor the AI knows in what ways. After several years, the Amazon engineers gave up trying to derive the perfect employee profile from their data and abandoned the project.

Interpreting behaviour is rife with value judgements which are invisible to those making them. According to the tech hiring platform Gilt, frequenting a Japanese manga site is predictive of strong coding skills. There could be a correlation, but it overlooks the fact that women have less leisure time and that manga is mostly a male-dominated pastime. So even the algorithmic scanning of CVs has its problems.[12]

Profiling may also be illegal. As Cathy O'Neil revealed in *Weapons of Math Destruction*, some software implicitly detects whether job applicants may have had a history of mental illness and, if they do, the system rejects them. Asking this question and discriminating on the basis of it is illegal under the Americans with Disabilities Act. You could not ask this question in a face-to-face interview. However, bringing a legal challenge is difficult because the algorithm is protected as a trade secret. What is being assessed within the programs, and what might be determined by implicit or explicit responses, is legally and ethically ambiguous. You may never know what your answers mean or why you were or were not hired. Power lies with those who design and interpret profiles, not those who provide their data.

The more that avid cost-cutters look to this technology, the more problems surface. First, the belief that your capability and capacity can be deduced from their data ignores everything else about you. You are more than data. What data is available is always inadequate, a selective subset of a complex human being. Moreover, results can't be evaluated against outcomes because one large dataset will always be absent: employers never follow up the applicants who *weren't* selected and so never know how many superstars the system mistakenly spat out. This is one reason why even some tech companies, including Google, have rejected such systems.[13] Predicting future performance is impossible, but automating it merely speeds up bias, errors, short-term thinking and flaky assumptions.[14]

Nor does talent exist in a vacuum. Outstanding performers in one part of a company may, when transferred, suddenly fail. At the pharmaceutical company Roche, in a quest for diversity, a 'high potential' executive was moved from Hong Kong to corporate headquarters in Basel. But in Switzerland, he could achieve almost nothing. His bosses considered letting him go but, at the last minute, decided to send him back to Hong Kong – where he flourished once again. Was the cultural difference too great? Had he proved unwilling to adapt? Had no one helped the outsider? The Roche CEO blamed the firm's culture for being insufficiently inclusive. Hypotheses abounded, but what everyone learned is that ability and environment are inextricably linked. As anyone who's suffered a terrible boss will recognise, given the right circumstances, everybody can be made to fail. Because achievement derives in part from context, forecasting individual talent omits half the picture.

Just like economic models, the reductive nature of profiling simplifies what is inherently complex. You need only consider careers like Johanna's and Luca's to appreciate how much hinged on small events and contingencies that neither they nor their parents nor their friends predicted or imagined. Life happened to these children, in the light of which they changed in ways that brought new experiences and perspectives that in turn drove different decisions. Johanna and Luca, like the rest of us, are neither static nor isolated. We live among people, moving across contexts, subject to a vast array of influences, experiences and data, some of which we choose and much of which we don't. In short, we are more than our data.

Profiling and assessment technologies are a cheap, fast way to weed through thousands of resumes. But they pose psychological and social risks. They feed off and look for stereotypes:

simplistic, reductive versions of whole people. As such, they constrain the possibilities and potential of individuals and groups. Stereotyping myself as a Myers–Briggs introvert may make me reluctant to experiment or explore aspects of life that could enrich me. Simplified models of complex individuals encourage us to view one another as objects, types, commodities measured by benchmarks we can't see and did not define.

Writing in the 1950s just as the personality-testing business was taking off, the social critic Theodor Adorno argued that assigning different types to people facilitated their identifying with their own group at the expense of others. What later became known as the 'minimal group paradigm' showed how such categorisation facilitated conformity within one's own group – but also discrimination and hostility against other types.[15] Typing could polarise. Adorno's critique of the profiling business was 'directed against that kind of subsumption of individuals against pre-established classes which has been consummated in Nazi Germany, where the labelling of live human beings, independent of their specific qualities, resulted in decisions about their life and death.' Adorno went on to argue that the very rigidity of constructing types was itself indicative of fascism.[16]

He would probably be aghast today at technologies that not only purport to tell us who we are but try to replace our personality and humanity with nudges, algorithms, profiles that at best interfere with developing self-knowledge and at worst attempt to condition it in the guise of perfectionism. Remembering that technology outsources human activity to a machine should be enough to steer us clear of apps whose ambitious developers hope will produce better humans than humans. Treating each other first as objects and then as groups, mediated by technological interfaces, just makes it cheaper, faster and easier to isolate and demonise one another. Relying on such systems means that we trade judgement for efficiency, reflection for obedience, inquiry for conformity and independence for constraint. Only organisations or individuals that are implicitly authoritarian would arrogate to themselves the right to tell people who they are and what they might become.

***

But if forecasting fails individuals just because they *are* individual, it's reasonable to hope for more success by analysing large human systems and identifying trends. We can't help but see patterns everywhere; it feels a logical assumption that extrapolating from them could reveal how success routinely unfolds. This was, in essence, what Vivienne Ming and the profilers were trying to do when they surveyed successful leaders in the past: draw a profile of achievement from a huge dataset. It's a seductive idea, particularly when coupled with the prospect of efficiency. If only we could glean how complex systems work, then we could invest heavily in productive people, places and things and spare effort on the rest. But that expectation of prediction proves elusive too.

This is particularly frustrating when it comes to scientific discovery. Governments, businesses and institutions around the world spend billions on scientific research. The work takes place within a vast ecosystem, with hundreds of interconnected fields, tens of thousands of researchers and an overwhelming number of published results every year. It works accretively, which is to say that all researchers build on work done before and around them. Everyone wants a return on their investment of time, career and money. So the question arises: how could science be organised to produce more and better results faster? The rhetoric that surrounds the 'war on cancer' or 'fight for the cure' implies that ruthless efficiency will solve complex problems: just double down on what works. The desire is sincere – everyone wants to cure cancer, MS, Parkinson's – but there's a reason why predicting outcomes in science is so often wrong. Science, too, is a complex system.

At certain moments in history, it has become obvious when particular lines of research have become feasible where previously they were not. One example is the Human Genome Project: a vast exercise that became practical when scientific knowledge, technological innovation and computing power all coalesced at the end of the twentieth century. Like pieces of a jigsaw puzzle, it was only when these came together that the genome became describable. Just as the birth of the financial forecasting business depended on the simultaneous advent of trains, telegraph and statistics, periods of breakthrough require that knowledge, technology, resources and human ingenuity align. Everyone would like more of those moments.

But other breakthroughs, like the discovery of penicillin or of cosmic microwave background radiation, exist at the opposite end of the spectrum: big, important discoveries that are flukes, neither predicted nor predictable. Everyone would love more of those too – but they aren't planned; they emerge and are understood only retrospectively. There are also always 'sleeping beauties',[17] big, powerful ideas – such as Mendel's concept of inheritance via the mechanism that we now call genes – that need other notable discoveries before the full import of their thinking is understood. Science has to advance on many other fronts before the sleeper subject can awake.

Across this spectrum – from the expected to the fluke – sits all the rest of science. It makes intuitive sense to imagine that if just some of this could be predicted, science would progress faster and more cheaply. But what principles could inform that process? Where might more investment predictably produce bigger, faster results?

Many propose that science needs to identify its superstars and just invest in them. But there is no profile of the break-through scientist. Great discoveries do come from scientists with a string of breakthroughs to their name, but they also come from newbies and overlooked veterans. There is no correlation between the impact of a discovery and its timing within a scientist's career.[18] What looks like a strong hypothe-sis – such as the Higgs boson – may take decades to validate. In the meantime, do you categorise Peter Higgs as a visionary or a flop? Mendel would never have been selected for his promise – he studied physics, not biology, missed much of his childhood education through illness and regularly failed exams. The Nobel laureate Kary Mullis, the inventor of polymerase chain reaction (PCR) that accelerated decoding the genome, was a self-described surfer pothead whose best idea came during a night-time drive to his beach shack.

If not superstars, could data mining predict where the new hotspots will emerge? Attempts to do so – analysing publica-tion counts, citations, recency, appeal – showed little more than the scientists themselves already knew – after all, it's their job and passion to stay alert to developments in their field. Just as one risk of profiles (DNA or psychographic) lies in oversimplification, so the danger in making science efficient is the risk of inhibiting innovation, marginalising under-represented ideas and discouraging new and multi-disciplinary fields. However society might wish to make scientific progress efficient, the truth about complex systems is that trying to simplify them doesn't guarantee that they become more effective; it risks making them *less* effective. They function best when they are robust, throwing off a vast array of insights whose value may be realised over time. That means they can look wasteful, producing more than what is needed. But when you don't know what's needed, you're safer with more.

A useful analogy here is with air travel. Much in flying is predictable and efficient: you know passengers will check in, their bags will be loaded onto planes, they will want to eat and drink. Those aspects of flying are planned and managed with a beady eye on the efficient use of time, people and money. However, once the plane is in the air, you cannot guarantee with absolute certainty exactly what will happen: whether geese will impact, or a part will fail. Too many factors are at work and beyond control to know for sure what will happen. And because the risk in the air is so much greater than on the ground, aircraft have been designed with more engines and operating systems than they usually need; if one fails, others won't. Robustness, not efficiency, is their protection against the unpredictable.

In a complex system like science, the fundamental robustness of the ecosystem is variety, because it facilitates a rich range of insights and discoveries – like penicillin – whose

84

value can emerge even when unplanned. The big danger in confusing a complex system (like science) for a complicated process (like loading bags on planes) is that, in striving for efficiency and predictability, the robustness of the system, its creativity and ability to withstand adversity, is killed off.

***

Science and counterterrorism might not look like they have much in common, but they do. Both are complex systems where crucial events may be predictable or flukes. Both are full of patterns and total surprises. Understanding such environments and managing them requires the capacity to distinguish between what can and cannot be predicted and tolerance for the ambiguity and uncertainties that lie in between.

Chair of the Wellcome Trust, one of the largest funders of scientific research in the world, Eliza Manningham-Buller has dealt with the complexity of both counterterrorism and science. Her understanding of complex systems developed when she worked in the British security services at MI5 between 1974 and 2007, the last five years of which she served as director general. Of the fifteen terrorist plots that Manningham-Buller faced during her time as DG, twelve were thwarted, including that of the shoe bomber, Richard Reid, and of the 21/7 bombers. Only the four suicide bombers of 7/7 succeeded fully, which means that MI5 had missed something or failed to act in time.

Manningham-Buller knows that while perfect knowledge might be desirable, what matters more is the capacity to take action: 'It's a myth that you *ever* have all the information you need. When I was at MI5, we were always having to make tough provisional judgements based on pinpricks of light against a dark and shifting canvas. Whatever you do, when you make your decision, your knowledge is incomplete. At MI5 consequences could be lethal – but not acting could be lethal too.'

There is no perfect profile of a terrorist because who they are and how they behave keeps changing and adapting. While there are patterns in terrorism, they don't repeat reliably and there is no stable narrative. This is characteristic of complex systems. So tragic mistakes (like 7/7) might reveal information that is helpful next time but it also might not be relevant for years – or ever. Terrorism isn't defined by profiles or patterns; terrorists know that randomness protects them. For those trying to anticipate terrorist attacks, it can feel as though the sides have come off the billiard table and balls can drop off or arrive from anywhere. You don't know how many variables there are, where they may come from, and you can't predict which, if any, will matter.

At MI5, Manningham-Buller required that people *not* tell her what she wanted to hear, but that they find the insights and courage to argue with her, to present alternative points of view in order to assess multiple possible realities. That takes time, of course, and can look inefficient. But in a context saturated with ambiguity, resisting the gravitational pull of certainty remains paramount. Her colleagues say that her tolerance for uncertainty was her strength. 'Make the call too soon, without enough evidence, people are released without charge,' Manningham-Buller insists. 'To do nothing is not an option. Too late and you're calling for hearses. So it has to be a mixture of judgement and how much you need to know to make a reasonable decision. It's a dangerous myth that if you plan enough, if you're efficient enough, you'll always get it right.'

That's why the intelligence services attach probability ratings to their briefings: they know that their forecasts, however scrupulous, are riddled with contingencies, accidents, luck and change. Intelligence officers I know crave critical, independent readers who appreciate that it is impossible ever to provide what Manningham-Buller calls '100 per cent prescience'. Politicians, however, hate the ambiguity in the numbers, seeking to give the public the palliative certainty that only fiction can provide. The probability ratings, just like the colour-coded threat levels Manningham-Buller introduced, articulate ambiguity, reflecting that all information about the future is not equal, comprehensive or conclusive. You get the 'pinpricks of light', but they could mean anything. You only ever get a bit of the picture and have to try to fill in the rest, all the while asking: what is it a picture of?

Staying open-minded to stray bits of information can feel inefficient, disorganised, indecisive, but it is the only way to ensure that decisions are as well informed as they can be. To think better requires more options, not fewer. When Manningham-Buller ran MI5, the number of intelligence operations increased five-fold. This might not have looked efficient, but it aimed to be robust. You have to be alert, she says, to what doesn't fit your preconceptions. Never imagine that you know what will happen. Manningham-Buller tells me: 'About twenty or thirty years ago, the USA made a serious error believing that technology would get us all the information we needed. They thought the future didn't need human intel. It was a big, serious error. It meant that after 9/11, they had no Arab speakers, no local network or knowhow. Of course, it's since been reversed.'

Manningham-Buller and others in intelligence argue that depending too much on technology means that any information that isn't digital data is too easily marginalised. The thought that you've captured all the data is what leads to error. No single efficient process, profile or narrative will prove robust enough for an environment characterised by change. Thinking so gets people killed. Human skills and talents are critical to a fuller picture. The temptation to try to simplify complex systems is how you get them wrong; just like profiling, just like any kind of model, what gets left out or what changes can turn out to be vital. This is why intelligence organisations frequently use multiple teams to examine and analyse the same data: because doing so can tell more than one story. That variety might look inefficient, but it imparts adaptability and responsiveness – essential qualities when you know you can't predict what the future holds.

***

The complex system from which we expect the greatest predictive power is genetics. Ever since we've been able to identify genes and begun to understand how they work, DNA has been seen as destiny, capable of determining who we are – and who we will be. As the Human Genome Project got underway, public excitement positioned DNA as a kind of chemical horoscope: a code for each individual's future.

In reality, it has all turned out to be far more complex than even scientific researchers anticipated. If your DNA is any kind of profile, it is one full of potentials and probabilities but few certainties. There is no gay gene, nor a way to predict an individual's sexual behaviour.[19] Genes do explain hair colour, but even something as simple and heritable as this turns out to be complex, with only red and black hair able to be predicted with 90 per cent accuracy. At least 124 genes determine what colour hair your baby might be born with, and so far nobody knows what predicts some blond hair turning brown.[20] Nearly two million genetic variants determine height.[21] For each of us, just 4 per cent of our lifespan is predicted by our parents' longevity. Heritable conditions such as sickle cell anaemia, Down's, Edwards' and Patau's syndromes, Huntington's disease, haemophilia, Fragile X and cystic fibrosis can be detected through DNA testing, but the DNA can't predict how the conditions will manifest, what quality of life the child might enjoy or how long that life will be. Even here we are dealing with probabilities, not certainties.

This is not just because interpreting the tests for these diseases is difficult. It is also because what happens in your body, in your environment and in your life influences the activity of your genes. This is clearly seen in studies of identical twins, born with exactly the same DNA. If one twin develops multiple sclerosis, then, if genes were destiny, the chance of the second twin also developing MS would be 100 per cent. But it isn't – it is about 30 per cent. Similarly, while the rate of breast cancer among women is roughly 10 per cent, the risk for women who have an identical twin *with* breast cancer is 15 per cent, not a hundred. In his reflections on the human genome, Nobel laureate Sydney Brenner observed that identical twins develop different immune systems. The different experiences and environments of the two individuals, even with exactly the same DNA, are different enough to produce life-defining differences. What happens along the way is life.

Since DNA testing has become easily available to the general public, over 26 million consumers have chosen to see how much of their future might be detectable. Rupert Baines tried the genetic testing kit 23andMe out of sheer curiosity; as a life-long technologist, he was open-minded about what he learned.

'I think what's interesting is what it doesn't tell you,' Baines laughed. 'There were a lot of caveats – likelihoods rather than absolutes. Likely doesn't have red hair. Likely dark hair, that kind of thing.' The most useful thing Baines learned was that he was likely to have a strong response to the anti-coagulant warfarin. That's useful if he ever needs to take the drug, which he hopes he won't.

Baines's test also revealed that he had a 20 per cent higher chance of colon cancer than the population on average. The risk of colon cancer runs at about 4.5 per cent; for Rupert this might mean his risk is closer to 5.5 per cent.[22] He is unlikely to contract the disease but cannot be certain that he will not. Because his grandmother had glaucoma, he has his eyes tested every six months. Learning he actually had a lower than average risk of contracting this eye disease was reassuring, but he hasn't changed his routine.

Rupert's greatest delight wasn't about the future but about the past. Learning that, on his father's side, his genes didn't come from Lancashire but from the Levant, maybe Lebanon, was a surprise. He already knew that his grandfather was a captain in the merchant navy and went to that part of the world with his wife, so this set Rupert wondering what exactly happened there. A cruise romance? A love triangle? It doesn't really matter now, he says, but it is fun to imagine.

'Who it was, how or why,' Rupert reflects, 'we'll never know for certain . . .' And he laughs again.

The revolution in our understanding of genetics has produced huge surprises but also widespread confusion, even among geneticists themselves. An informal audit of three DNA-testing companies showed completely different results for the same DNA sample, largely because each firm uses different sets of reference data.[23] Analysing vast swathes of DNA now makes it possible to stratify people into trajectories for specific diseases, but the biobanks that provide the DNA have limited ethnic and geographic diversity and so may have predictive validity only for those regions. And even the boldest evangelists for genomically determined medicine concede that only 30 to 50 per cent of the risk for many common diseases lies in our genes. Environmental factors determine the rest and some of these are still not well understood. Take, for example, some species of deer that drop off and regrow their antlers each year. When a notch is cut in one antler, you'd expect the next year's antlers to be pristine. But they aren't; they grow back with a notch in the same place. Where and how has that information been stored? No one knows. Epigenetics, the study of all the factors *beyond genes* that determine life, is revealing how much more complex inheritance is.[24] So when you get into the genetic determination of personality, prediction becomes highly problematic.

Some of the loudest claims come from Robert Plomin, best known for his twin studies. In his book *Blueprint: How DNA Makes Us Who We Are*, he makes what he himself describes as a 'sales pitch' for the power of genetics to predict personality. It can, he writes, 'tell your fortune from the moment of your birth, it is completely reliable and unbiased – and it costs only £100 . . . The fortune teller is DNA.'[25]

As sales pitches go, that's impressive. The difficulty lies in the detail. What Plomin means is that no other *single* factor has as much influence as DNA. He is certain that genetics account for 50 per cent of psychological differences – but what about the other 50 per cent? Collectively the other half has equal influence – it's just that those influences are varied, diverse, random and unpredictable. So while taken altogether they are just as important as DNA, they're more difficult to study and to measure.

Plomin is a loud voice in the genetics world, though not without his critics. A psychologist, he focuses on personality: everything from the Big Five traits (neuroticism, extroversion, openness, conscientiousness and agreeableness) to bipolar disease and schizophrenia. But these characteristics aren't detectable by biological tests; they can only be determined through observation and assessment. Scientists have already raised concerns that statistics now risk overpowering biology, and they risk even more uncertainty when there's little established physical biology to study, only observed behaviour.[26] Nevertheless, even while acknowledging that everything else constitutes the other half the story, Plomin still insists that personality is defined by DNA. As a researcher, he's drawn to the factors he can measure, but this makes him as in love with his Big Idea – the genetic determination of personality – as the founding fathers of forecasting were in love with theirs.

Analysing his own DNA, Plomin discovered that he had a high probability for schizophrenia. He's puzzled because there is no evidence of schizophrenia in his life nor any history of schizophrenia in his family. But the DNA analysis leads him to wonder whether it explains his need for a highly structured, scheduled working life. This is a marvellous example of the Forer effect in action: told something is true, he starts to redefine himself in the light of the new knowledge.

Plomin frequently asserts that 'Prediction is the *sine qua non* of prevention . . . an early warning system.'[27] But what might Plomin's parents have done with this knowledge? Would the pregnancy have proceeded? Perhaps his parents would have enrolled him in trials of prophylactic anti-psychotic medication at the age of fifteen, but whether the drugs would have advanced or destroyed his academic promise is unknowable. Or, noting his predicted high level of educational attainment, his parents might have hesitated, worrying that acting on one prediction might undermine the capacity to fulfil another.

The discovery that DNA can predict school achievement thrilled Plomin. His own predicted academic achievement was so extravagant, he confessed, as to be 'embarrassing'.[28] But what is the value of this prediction? He argues that it would make parents and teachers of failing kids more understanding and forgiving, less likely to blame the student for their failure. But that risks stereotyping and giving up on the child, or provides the perfect excuse for rationing: why bother investing in struggling students whose DNA says they'll never get that PhD? Or the reverse: the smart kid's going to do well anyway, let's send the less well-endowed sibling to a really great school and provide extra tutoring!

We should never forget the other 50 per cent of the equation. The genetic capacity for a PhD isn't negligible, but it is not a guarantee of getting one. High levels of predicted educational attainment count for nothing if the promising child in Syria or Venezuela hits school age just as the education system falls to pieces, or their parents can't afford the bus fare to less violent schools or older kids are made responsible for childcare.[29] For Johanna, the absence of educational qualifications said nothing about her intellectual capacity but everything about other factors: her illness, an unfriendly school. Just because those environmental factors are impossible to predict doesn't mean they don't matter.

Ever since Renner and Rosenzweig first pioneered research into neuroplasticity, we've been able to see physical evidence that the brain's capacity changes according to the richness (or poverty) of the environment in which it develops.[30] And what does educational attainment actually mean? It can't be seen under a microscope but is defined by bureaucracies that codify what it means to be educated. That changes over time; on its own educational attainment predicts nothing more than further academic achievement. Good grades are helpful but don't, in themselves, predict success in life.

Confusingly, Plomin concedes that 'genetics is not a puppeteer pulling our strings. Genetic influence means just that – influence, not hard-wired genetic determinism.'[31] However random, complex and hard to measure the other 50 per cent of the equation may be, it makes a significant difference to what the future holds. Rich parents, a house full of books, being able to breathe clean air, to have breakfast and to get to school, having neighbours who can help with homework or a friend who shares a passion for sport: any of these – or none – has a profound and real impact on life outcomes. A parent's decision to move their family to a different country provokes exposure to new experiences which prompt different ideas and choices – all unpredictable because there is nothing in the parents' or the child's DNA that predicts the move, the exposure or the subsequent decisions. If Plomin at times seems confused and contradictory, it is because the evidence is confused and contradictory: the DNA matters, but it isn't the only thing that matters. And what might change your life could be predictable – or not.

The uncertainty and ambiguity implicit in DNA data are hard to explain, to understand or to use for rational, safe decision-making. I've watched well-trained genetic counsellors struggle as they've guided educated, mature executives through the complex data that goes into polygenic scorings. Though they all sought to understand the consequences of the genetic information, the day ended with the audience dazed and confused by just how uncertain it all remains. Mark McCarthy, a geneticist at Oxford University, worries that 'there aren't enough genetic counsellors on the planet' to manage the subtle interpretations of polygenic scores.

But, as always in the world of forecasting, there's money to be made from commercialising prophecy and imbuing it with moral urgency. Both Plomin and Anne Wojcicki of 23andMe believe it is a parent's duty to 'arm themselves with their child's blueprint'.[32] Duty to whom? Plomin's big idea and Wojcicki's big business trivialise the danger of emphasising what's certain – the score – over and above what's uncertain – the other half that represents life. Stereotyping, rationing, discrimination, passivity, surrender: these are the very real risks produced when overstating the foresight afforded by DNA.

What should be done with this knowledge? More deliberative voices than Plomin's should be heard. Where Plomin gets excited by the prospect of 'precision education' that would tailor schooling to genetic potential, he's loading the dice: amplifying with environmental contributions what the DNA shows as merely probable. He doesn't contemplate the decisions that might be made by the parents of a foetus demonstrating a high risk of schizophrenia. And like most clever people, he's markedly more interested in opportunities for the fortunate than danger for the unlucky.

But ever since Darwin described evolution, researchers into inheritance have been tempted by the prospect of the perfectibility of human beings, by amping up strengths and reducing weaknesses. Francis Galton (Darwin's cousin) posed the incendiary question: 'Could not the undesirables be got rid of and the desirables multiplied?'[33] He coined the term 'eugenics' and in 1869 wrote: 'The time may hereafter arrive, in far distant years, when the population of the earth shall be kept as strictly within the bounds of number and suitability of race, as the sheep on a well-ordered moor or the plants in an orchard-house; in the meantime, let us do what we can to encourage the multiplication of the races best fitted to invent and conform to a high and generous civilisation, and not, out of a mistaken instinct of giving support to the weak, prevent the incoming of strong and hearty individuals.'[34]

The language of efficiency is unmistakable: life is much simpler, and more predictable, if the complexity, anomalies and flukes can be managed out of it. For decades, eugenics attracted a large and distinguished following from all parts of the political spectrum: Beatrice and Sidney Webb, Maynard Keynes and H. G. Wells believed that human 'stock' should not be diluted by allowing 'detrimental types' to have children. Bertrand Russell proposed that the state issue colour-coded 'pro-creation tickets' defining who was and was not allowed to bear children. Sterilisation, segregation and incarceration were all proposed as means of eliminating those deemed to be 'social rubbish'. Writing to Prime Minister Asquith, Winston Churchill warned that 'The multiplication of the feeble-minded is a very terrible danger to the race.'[35] The mother of the Myers–Briggs Type Indicator couldn't have agreed more: 'Multitudes of people are utterly worthless or worse than worthless, having no just claims whatsoever upon the civilisation which they burden with the dead weight of their existence.'[36]

Eugenics first moved from theory to practice in the United States. In 1923, the German geneticist Fritz Lenz observed that 'Germany had nothing to match the eugenics research institutions in England and the United States.'[37] In 1927, the US Supreme Court upheld forceable sterilisation when Judge Oliver Wendell Holmes argued in *Buck v. Bell*: 'The principle that sustains compulsory vaccination is broad enough to cover cutting the Fallopian tubes . . . Three generations of imbeciles are enough.'[38] In parts of the US, forced sterilisation – of uneducated girls raped by older men, epileptics, those with low IQ and those deemed too 'feebleminded' to raise children – continued until 1977. Poor, uneducated and black Americans were disproportionately affected.[39]

The advent of genetic testing in the 1970s brought eugenics back to life as 'newgenics': the use of prenatal screening and abortion to introduce some element of choice into having a baby. There were important differences: prenatal testing and selective abortions were performed with no state mandate and no centralised legal definition of fitness or unfitness.

The advent of IVF introduced the idea of 'procreative benevolence' that enabled parents to test which of their four embryos looked most promising and choose only those for implant. Many found (and still find) that reasonable.[40] Giving choice to individuals rather than to the state preserved variety and while some nations (such as Japan) preferred girls to boys, others (such as India and China) chose boys over girls. In 1980, a millionaire sunglasses entrepreneur, Robert Graham, opened a Repository for Germinal Choice that called for elite sperm from men of the highest intellect (preferably Nobel laureates) to be inseminated into intelligent, healthy young women. His 'genius bank' was widely ridiculed and, before it was disbanded, seems to have produced just fifteen children, none of any distinction.[41]

As the mapping of the human genome progressed, the possibility of 'improvements' moved from the level of the whole person to the level of the gene. This progress has taken two forms. The first, gene therapy, involves the manipulation of genes to treat major illnesses. These alterations last only one generation and are not inherited by future offspring. But the second form of genetic manipulation, known as 'germ line gene therapy', does pass to future generations. Editing the genome of an egg or sperm, through CRISPR (clustered regularly interspaced short palindromic repeats), offers the possibility of permanent genetic change. Some argue for efficiency: why not improve the quality of the future human genome through selection or editing? Others are deeply uncomfortable with the prospect and consequences of reducing genetic variety.

In 2015, recognising that a fundamental turning point had been reached, genetic researchers called for a moratorium on the use of gene-editing and gene-altering technologies. CRISPR genomic editing had potential that neither old-style eugenics nor newgenics ever had: the ability to add or subtract information to the human genome. Francis Collins, who had helped to lead the Human Genome Project, was alarmed: 'This reality means that germline manipulation would largely be justified by attempts to "improve" ourselves. That means that someone is empowered to decide what "improvement" is.'[42] In 2018, a Chinese researcher horrified the scientific world when he created the world's first gene-edited babies, a pair of twin girls. He subsequently faced criminal charges as the Chinese government rushed to develop new gene-editing legislation.

This new science poses two fundamental questions that dog all those trying to determine the future through DNA. First: who decides what is eliminated or amplified? Do we return to state-mandated definitions of improvement, as we saw in the Third Reich and in North Carolina? Or does the market decide, with greater choice ceded to the wealthy, making inequality not merely economic but also biological and heritable? Historically, both markets and authoritarian regimes have demonstrated an insatiable appetite for eliminating variety.

The idea of the perfected world, from which all difficulties and anomalies are removed, is a persistent one, attractive to individuals who feel they already have what it takes, and repellent to those who see in our diversity and interdependence the foundations of adaptive, creative and sustainable societies. Watching the resurgence of eugenics, Victoria Brignell wrote a series of articles exploring why it feels so disturbing. A professional researcher, she strongly identified with those who might be edited out. Left paralysed from the neck down by a spinal tumour, she is looked after, day and night, by carers. She puzzled over the allure of perfection, finding it homogenous and dull. 'Do we really want a society where, for example, everybody is equally good at maths – so we don't need each other's help?' she asked. 'Where we don't need each other because we're all perfect in all the same ways? Society celebrates independence but without dependence, there *is* no society. Or any diversity . . .'

Removing flaws might reduce uncertainty, but doesn't it also risk reducing variation in the population? Variation and mutation make evolution robust over time. Not knowing which qualities and traits the future will need, why increase risk by *reducing* the broad spectrum of human talents, insight and capacity in our species? Concentrating on strengths today would constitute a big, dangerous bet, the consequences of which we can't even guess.

Over the past 100 years, turning to models, data, history, profiling and DNA have thwarted our hunger for certainty. All predictive models are reductive. And so, subtly, we have moved from trying to forecast the future, using theories and data, to trying to influence it, using salesmanship and propaganda. We have now reached a stage where, instead of coming to terms with uncertainty, companies intervene to eliminate it. Rewards (air miles, discounts) and punishments (higher prices, being expelled) condition their customers to converge on some choices and turn away from others. Defeated by the ambiguity and complexity of human life, many now think it will be easier and more profitable to reduce free agency than to predict it. This is the thinking behind Amazon's anticipatory shopping patent.[43] Instead of customers making their own decisions, Amazon decides for them, sending what they want before they know they want it. It is, as one commentator noticed, one more step towards cutting out human agency altogether.[44]

Pervasive monitoring devices – smartphones, wearables, voice-enabled speakers and smart meters – allow companies to track and manage consumer behaviour. The Harvard business scholar Shoshana Zuboff quotes an unnamed chief data scientist who explains: 'The goal of everything we do is to change people's actual behavior at scale . . . we can capture their behaviours and identify good and bad [ones]. Then we develop "treatments" or "data pellets" that select good behaviours.'[45]

MIT's Alex Pentland seems more interested in enhancing machines than human understanding. He celebrates the opportunity to deploy sensors and data in order to increase efficiency and to impose 'a quantitative, predictive science of human organisations and human society'. Without any apparent irony, he proposes 'social efficiency both as a design goal and a metric for the design of social network systems', urging us to build 'social network systems' as wondrous as the 'rich legacy' of our financial system.[46]

This is a eugenics mindset, applied to everything we do and everything we are. With CRISPR, would-be forecasters crossed the line into casting the future. This transition – from information to intervention – could not be more profound or challenging. In many ways it acknowledges that the future cannot be foretold. Economic models aren't fully successful. Narratives prove misleading and history doesn't repeat itself reliably. Profiles of individuals or systems cannot overcome the ineradicable uncertainty of the complexity of life. For those determined to master the future, the only recourse is to force-fit a standardised model of a predictable reality onto a world that remains complex and rich but unpredictable in all its individuality. The appeal for large corporations is that doing so is hugely profitable. The temptation for us is the allure of a life that is convenient, predictable and certain. No longer overwhelmed by choice, our decisions get edited for us, day after day, as surely as CRISPR edits human potential.

So we stand now at a crossroads. Can we live with the fact that neither professional forecasters, nor historians, nor profiles, nor even DNA can untangle the systemic complexity, uncertainty and ambiguity of our lives? All of our ancestors did so. Or is a more predictable life – calmer, easier, with less fear of error or surprise – too tantalising to reject? The price of certainty is high: surrendering to a limited experience of life, designed by individuals and corporations who do not know us, whose interests are not ours. In this condition, convenience is passivity and choice obedience. In our hunger to know the future, is the alleviation of doubt and uncertainty sufficient reward for the loss of agency, of autonomy?

All of the advocates of eugenics or fully efficient social systems are eager to demonstrate their advantages: less suffering, less waste. They are reluctant to spell out the risks, which are not just conformity, injustice and authoritarianism b[...] loss of social connection and diversity. In Pentland's uto[...] where every bus arrives on time and medical appointmen[...] are magically scheduled just before you get sick, nobody needs anyone else. We don't need compassion, generosity or trust because everyone is taken care of by a system. In this picture of predictable lives, there are no flukes, no happy (or unhappy) accidents. And with everyone equally dependent on the same system, this vision contains little diversity and no capacity for robustness, even though we know that this is what gives evolution the capacity to adapt. As such, a world in which we are all reliant on an invisible system we don't understand seems the most dangerous response to uncertainty ever devised.

Every generation of human being has lived with uncertainty and unpredictability; that's how we developed the staggering human capacity for invention, discovery, improvisation and creativity. Our ability to invent and explore came from necessity, not comfort. It's been in the interstices of uncertainty that we have found and used freedom. As Eliza Manningham-Buller found, trusting a single approach is always dangerous, but living with incomplete knowledge doesn't leave us useless or passive. Just because perfect success isn't possible doesn't mean we should all become Galton's sheep on Pentland's well-ordered moor. While we can never render complexity simple, we could embrace it as an adventure, calling us to investigate the infinite permutations of life that it contains. Surrendering agency, action and adventure for convenience is a miserable bargain. In an uncharted world, who is content to be left hugging the shore when we could use our freedom to explore?

PART TWO

WHAT WOULD YOU DO IF YOU WERE FREE?

CHAPTER FOUR

NO AVAILABLE DATASETS

What do you want to be when you grow up? Most of us faced that question in childhood, on leaving school or university. What did we do then? Like Johanna and Luca, we tried things. A niece, after a year in PR, decided to go into family law. A nephew, after a year in law, went into human resources. A doctor who found she didn't much like patients moved to research. A musician went back to school and trained to be a physicist.

What was everyone doing? Experiments. They had hypotheses – 'I think I'd love being a doctor' – and tested them to see if they were true. When they were, something was learned; when they weren't, something else was learned. While we try to imbue our decisions with confidence, in reality they're all just hypotheses that may be proved or not. The great advantage of experiments is that they stop you being stuck; they're one way to prototype a future we think we want.

You could say that experiments are how we learn everything. We try to stand up, fall over, recalibrate and next time find we can teeter for a second or two. Keep at it and mastery emerges. Misbehave and feedback provides evidence that throwing food is a poor means of securing affection. That life, work, love, politics are more complex than rules-bound games makes experiments more valuable, not less. They allow us to see how the systems we inhabit operate. Since we can't see the whole of complex systems at once, trial and error is how we probe them to find out what works. The key quality of experiments is that we don't know what will happen; if we did know, they wouldn't be experiments. So they both spring from uncertainty and are a creative response to it.

The first half of *Hamlet* is a vivid, excruciating demonstration of this idea. A ghost tells Hamlet that his uncle murdered his father. But is the ghost reliable? Real? Is the information true? What if it isn't? What if it is? Ambiguity paralyses Hamlet. What should he do? He does experiments. Putting on a play – 'The Mousetrap' – is an experiment. When Claudius explodes with rage, evidence mounts that he is a murderer. But the evidence is still ambiguous; vengeance is justified only if he can find incontrovertible truth. When Hamlet opens a private letter from Claudius to Rosencrantz and Guildenstern, he is conducting another experiment, testing the good faith of all three men. Reading that the king has sent his two friends with a letter commissioning the King of England to kill him, Hamlet finds the certainty he needs. Now he can act.

The driving tension of the play derives from uncertainty: from Hamlet's agony in not knowing who he can trust, what version of reality he can believe, in his search for action that will honour his late father and himself. The play's genius lies in its capacity to show us that this is how we live our own lives – not because our fathers have been murdered but because we all agonise over choices we feel inadequate to make. When will I be certain enough that I want to have a family? How can I know whether I will like working in Japan? When I see degradation and injustice in the world, what can I do to stop it? Our future hangs on how we answer those questions. We need to know more, so we do what Hamlet does: we experiment.

***

Growing up on her father's small Devon farm, Rebecca Hosking didn't feel that she lacked companions. Surrounded by wildlife – robins, bugs, bees – who were both pets and company, she always felt most at home in nature. Studying photography gave her an excuse to get outside and wander. Now in her early forties, Hosking's weathered face shows she has spent most of her life outdoors; it's when she pulls the thick, curly blond hair away from her face that you notice she's beautiful. But chiefly the impression that sticks is one of tenacity, a rugged determination not to be daunted by stiff challenges.

In 1999, after completing a degree in photography, her teachers encouraged her to apply for a coveted BBC bursary, working in the Natural History Unit. No woman had ever won it before, but Hosking did. Two years later, she was a producer, travelling the world shooting the documentaries that made the NHU so successful. Not all directors wanted to travel the world with a woman. Many were sceptical that Hosking could cope with carrying heavy film gear and tripods. She proved them wrong. After six or seven years working on David Attenborough films, she had disproved the naysayers but was severely disillusioned by what she had seen in the wild.

'In all of these projects,' Hosking recalled, 'we'd go past horrific ecological devastation. Huge monoculture farms. Dead zones where you can't film. Climate change was seen as an annoyance, getting in the way of film shoots and messing up our schedules! A great subject staring us in the face – seen as an annoyance. I just got more and more cross.'

Hosking appreciated that she was in a privileged position: she had resources (her expertise, access to audiences), she had real passion for the environment and could see there was a crying need for something to be said about its spoliation. The BBC agreed to commission her film about Hawaii, but it wasn't showcasing the glorious wildlife; it was about the ruination of the ocean caused by plastic. 'I sold it as beautiful people saving animals,' Hosking said. 'But I didn't say what they were saving them *from*. The series producer knew. He kept telling me: you have to tell the series editor that every marine animal seen on screen would be shown choked in plastic, ingesting plastic . . .'

Hosking's hypothesis was that if audiences could see the horrors she had witnessed, they would rise up and demand change. But when the film aired, nothing happened. Her hypothesis wasn't proved. What she learned was that people watch TV and carry on as usual. She went home severely jaded. Her achievements now seemed superficial, pointless. Alone in her small flat in Modbury, south Devon, Hosking wondered: why hadn't people responded? Perhaps they didn't know where to start. What if she started by persuading her village to go plastic-bag-free . . . ?

Friendly with the local deli owner, Hosking floated the idea with him and gained her first supporter. The art gallery owner thought it was a fantastic idea too. The butcher was supportive but asked what he was supposed to do about meat juices. If she could find a decent substitute, he'd go along with her. Six weeks later, all of the local independent shops had agreed to support her plan. She called a public meeting to confront the big retailers, challenging them to support the campaign and they did, promising to give every household – 1,500 people – a cloth bag. The night before the launch, every householder got their bag through the letterbox, with a note saying: from Monday, we are not going to be using any plastic bags in the village. If her film couldn't change the world, Hosking hoped that she could at least change her little village.

She was wrong again. The world's media got wind of the story and arrived en masse on her doorstep. *The Guardian* picked up on it first, then other newspapers. Then, she said, it went stupid: CNN, Sky, Russia Today, NBC, Chinese TV crews, Canadian, French. Chinese officials presented Hosking with a cloth bag that said: Our Province follows Modbury! They had banned bags overnight. Hosking asked them how many people live in their province. It was 32 million.

In 2007, the year of Hosking's experiment, Botswana, Ethiopia, Belgium, Rwanda and China all either banned plastic bags, imposed a levy, or introduced laws requiring bags to be bio-degradable. In China, bag usage fell by between 60 to 80 per cent. In Ireland, it fell 90 per cent. In the United States, bans were local, by state or city, but around the world the trend has continued ever since.

Why did Hosking's documentary experiment fail when her second, small-scale one was so successful? Why did the BBC's 2017 film on plastic pollution in the ocean go on to make an impact, where hers had not? She will never know. But it is characteristic of complex systems that small actions can make a disproportionate impact. You just don't know, won't know, until you try. Experiments are how you explore the ecosystem, the boundaries of which you can't quite discern.

As individuals, organisations and corporations confront enormous problems – inequality, disease, injustice, technological disruption, environmental degradation, climate change – it's become fashionable to seek to define theories of change. What makes people and institutions abandon old bad habits and acquire new, better ones? How should huge companies and institutions change to secure their future? Investors and participants demand a theory of change that promises to contain or define their risk. But the test of a good theory is that it can predict – and what we know about complex systems is that, while aspects of them may repeat, they are inherently *un*predictable. So theories of change in highly dynamic systems might purport to offer certainty, but often prove illusory. The value of experiments is that they accept risk.

Hosking's experience reveals useful principles. She made no promises – if she had, she would have got them wrong. But she came to the problem with three assets: need, resources and passion. She knew that there was a demonstrable need for a change in consumer behaviour. She had resources: her knowledge, her media experience and her relationship with the villagers who trusted her. And she had passion for the subject – essential if she was going to have the resilience and energy needed to bring the project to life. If you think of those three assets – need, resources, passion – as a Venn diagram, where they intersected was where she took action.

Experiments are pragmatic ways to test out the future. But to have real impact, other people must know about them and be able to contribute. Hosking was lucky that the world's media amplified the impact of her experiment; without them, she'd have had to satisfy herself with a small victory. Because complex systems involve so many factors, experiments reveal more by bringing together a variety of influences, players and perspectives. As a consequence, they demand high levels of diplomacy and collaboration.

Wolfe's Neck Farm is a 600-acre site on the southern coast of Maine. A wild and rugged setting, the casual visitor might imagine that it is nothing more than another untouched beauty spot of the kind that has made Maine famous. But for nearly sixty years, it has pioneered new forms of agriculture. As early as the 1950s, the farm produced organic beef. Today, under the more illuminating name of Wolfe's Neck Center for Agriculture and the Environment, this small, remote farm is hosting some of the most ambitious experiments in the world.

No one involved in agriculture can escape concern about climate change. As Fiona Wilson, chair of Wolfe's Neck, explains, farming is responsible for about 14 per cent of the world's carbon emissions. Much of this stems from over-tilling the soil, which both sends carbon into the atmosphere and destroys the soil's natural ability to sequester carbon. 'So there are two pieces to the puzzle,' she says. 'Stop doing harm – and start thinking about how you could use soil to increase carbon storage, help stabilise the climate and improve food security.'

Wolfe's Neck couldn't contemplate such ambition alone. It works with Stonyfield, a commercial yogurt producer completely dependent on the dairy industry, which makes climate change a threat to its business. The company decided to work with Wolfe's Neck on a series of experiments designed to improve soil health and to disseminate successful learning across the industry as a whole.

'If we can improve soil health, we improve yield and water retention,' Stonyfield's director of organic and sustainable agriculture, Britt Lundgren, explained to me. 'We might even be able to use soil to sequester carbon and pay farmers to do so.' The shared goal of multiple experiments is to make Wolfe's Neck the world's first carbon-zero dairy farm – and, by collecting and disseminating enough data along the way, to teach the industry as a whole how to do likewise.

Bringing together an independent non-profit (Wolfe's Neck) with a food company (Stonyfield) hasn't been straightforward. Originally Stonyfield was owned by Danone, a global firm with a large environmental research fund. But when a corporate merger required that Danone sell off Stonyfield, Lundgren and Wilson had to find new funding and partners for their experiment. Ensuring that the work stays on track, that all partners get from it what they need and, as Wilson puts it, 'that shit gets done' is no small undertaking. Her collaborators -- dairy farms, food companies, the United States Department of Agriculture, several universities and tech companies – all have their day job to do too. In reality, these kinds of projects take immense co-ordination.

This isn't even Wilson's job. An academic, she works full-time in public policy, social entrepreneurship and sustainability at the University of New Hampshire. But for the experiments to progress, Wilson has to keep the farm, the yogurt company and the ecosystem of Maine dairy farmers working together without losing focus or discipline. The ambition – the world's first open-source ecosystem to address soil health and mitigate climate change – is a big one. But even when the stakes are high and success is in everyone's interest, unless there is glue, it doesn't happen. 'The physical science is just the first issue,' she says. 'The experiment is: can you create behavioural change by getting large swathes of farmers to adopt what we learn? That's the experiment. Can we do it at Wolfe's Neck and then make new agricultural knowledge available to everyone everywhere on an open-source platform?'

Wilson is a gifted diplomat and communicator with a successful business career in advertising and technology. She's low-key and unpretentious. Citing the work of Michael Porter, she argues that for individual experiments to make a collective impact on any ecosystem requires a backbone: a person or organisation that keeps the work on track. Part of that role also requires that, when experiments appear to fail, they don't stop. 'There's a wonderful example of a programme to reduce teen substance abuse in Massachusetts,' Wilson recalled. 'At first they trained parents to train others how to spot and deal with the problem. But after three years, they saw no improvement. So they tried something different. They'd seen research showing that kids who have regular family dinners were at less risk of substance abuse. So they focused on that message and, for the first time in seven years, they saw risk factors decline.'[1]

As the 'backbone' of the Wolfe's Neck experiments, Wilson has to keep the farmers, the USDA, Stonyfield, General Mills, the Foundation for Food and Agriculture Research, seven universities and several technology companies communicating, honouring their commitments to each other, sharing what they find. If results disappoint, the group will need to design new approaches. All of the experiments demand clear metrics to demonstrate their validity and meaning. And the data must be compelling enough to make others wish to follow suit. After all, experiments in isolation may yield great results but have little impact if nobody knows or cares about them.[2]

But, as Wilson explains, the difficulty of managing collaborative experiments is worth the hard work because they are one way that small organisations like Wolfe's Neck make a big difference to the world: 'It's a huge experiment,' she says, and she sounds nervous. 'This is bleeding-edge stuff, involving technology and human behaviour. Both those things are pretty unpredictable. But you have to start where you are.'

Wilson knows that the Wolfe's Neck experiments can never be enough on their own to halt climate change. She is a walking encyclopaedia of other initiatives – from manufacturers to utilities companies, from global multinationals to small startups – tackling the same fierce problem. Her work doesn't compete with those but compliments them. Government initiatives, the Global Development Goals, the Paris Accord: these all help. But when it comes to complex threats, waiting for the perfect grand masterplan is risky. If it arrives, it could be too complex, inadequate, wrong – or simply too late.

But traditional management is addicted to masterplans. However much executives claim to want and to support innovation and so-called 'transformation', much of their enthusiasm runs tepid to cold. They want safety and certainty, not the creativity and risk that come with experimentation. The irony is lost on no one: the more they demand certainty, the more they constrain their chance to map a safer future. Nowhere has this constraint been more obvious than amid the bloodbath of retail, where companies seem to have taken to heart Hilaire Belloc's line: 'always keep ahold of Nurse/For fear of finding something worse.' So afraid are they of failure that executives plan shop closures and layoffs with meticulous efficiency – while failing to be inventive enough to keep those businesses alive. Market analysts may call this creative destruction, but it's hard to find much that's creative about it. Experiments and innovation are almost nowhere to be seen.

In part this is a classic competition problem. In Amazon, traditional retailers face a common threat. They all struggle to survive against a tax-free competitor who can afford to sell goods unprofitably, and whose long game is to put traditional retailers out of business. But companies like BHS, Next, Debenhams, House of Fraser in Britain and Sears, Macy's, Rockport, PayLess, Nine West and RadioShack in the US have all competed against each other for so long that they find it near impossible to work together effectively, even against a common enemy. They're so accustomed to competing on price that they can't kick the habit, so now they cut prices, costs and jobs so viciously they can scarcely survive – and, in doing so, their stores and malls now manifest the same scrawny mien of austerity. Success in this context could mean being the last store left standing – but what kind of future is that? Behind the scenes, rigid board structures, legacy homogeneity and all the paraphernalia of management planning leave these businesses paralysed, waiting for the past to return. Their competitive isolation has left them poor at building the collaborative networks and adaptive partnerships that experiments with impact.

Individually, a few companies have proved imaginative. The John Lewis Partnership is culture derived from the company's structure in which every employee is an owner. Working together as 'partners' in a somewhat federated structure could, perhaps should, encourage the entire workforce to generate and act on their own ideas. That sometimes happens. Head of Diversity, Inclusion and Wellbeing Yulia O'Mahony described experiments aimed at improving the health and motivation of partners that had been initiated by local branches and taken up by other stores across the partnership. 'When asked what they wanted to do, people told us: we want to get healthier. So we have Leeds Wellbeing Warriors and Sheffield Health Geeks. They started this movement that has grown to ten branches. What was interesting was seeing how powerful it can become. It wasn't entirely laissez faire — we had parameters and objectives because we also have a duty of care. But creating this gave them a real zest for life. Silly things: wake up/shake up in the morning, five minutes of star jumps, blasting fun music before opening every branch. The buzz in the branch changed, you can feel this energy. Everyone connected and became more of a team. It was all about creating an atmosphere to be human.'

In the autumn of 2017, the company opened The Residence, a fully furnished in-store apartment where shoppers could dine and stay overnight. Incorporating all the latest technologies, it was a chance for consumers to see how a thoughtful use of new software and the Internet of Things might work in a home. Queues to visit the apartment went around the block, with a huge waiting list for overnight stays.

On a separate front, O'Mahony and her colleagues have initiated a training programme to help staff become better listeners – both to their customers and to each other. Working in partnership with the Samaritans, the goal is to address the epidemic of mental illness that has become apparent across UK workplaces.

O'Mahony's colleague Sophie Birshan said that, while people have embraced the idea of experimentation, this is easier to do online, where digital development makes the standard testing and tweaking so easy. Offline experimentation, Birshan concedes, is harder. In part, this is because, for a real-world experience, some capital is required. And while local experiments sometimes seem to yield results, without a champion they fail to spread.

'A year ago we looked at the staffing schedule at our Kingston branch,' Birshan told me. 'They'd brought in some new ways of working and we could see a marked improvement in customer happiness scores. But we couldn't absolutely prove the correlation.' You might think that the example alone would be worth at least trying in another store. But without absolute, demonstrable proof, the idea wasn't tried elsewhere, thus ensuring that the correlation couldn't be found – even if it was there. Birshan calls this a deep, systemic industry trap: we can't do the experiment unless we are certain it will work. But we can't know it will work until we do the experiment. And in the meantime, there's a tension between experimentation and business as usual (BAU) that must be attended to – even though that alone definitely *won't* work. Real experimentation can't get started without a frank acknowledgement of just how much isn't understood.

John Lewis is an unusual company, insofar as the first line of its constitution boldly states that it exists for the happiness of those who work there. Its remit is strikingly different from publicly traded, private or family businesses. But the company's ambivalent embrace of experimentation reflects how profoundly the move to complex systems has unsettled traditional ideas of management. Many retailers like John Lewis have devoted years to so-called 'scientific management' aimed at improving competitive efficiency. Algorithmic task assignments directed employees as discrete units, hoping that more work would get done by fewer people. Today, in private, most acknowledge this was a disaster. Even relatively simple businesses like supermarkets and department stores have to be prepared for the unexpected – the toddler who knocks down a display, an inexplicable run on coconuts. Being too efficient reduces the capacity to respond. Trying to run the business on algorithmic prediction demoralised the workforce, annoyed customers and did nothing for profits.

Where companies used to operate in three stages – forecast, plan, execute – in theory now they can't because forecasting has become so difficult. But organisations still go through the three stages (independent housing associations are required by law to present five- and thirty-year plans), not because their executives believe that these are accurate – in private, they roll their eyes – but because old habits die hard, you have to start somewhere and an old broken system offers security, however false.

Have decades of strategic planning left companies paralysed, unable to explore without a map, incontrovertible data or rock-solid guarantees? Are firms now like travellers who daren't stray outdoors without a GPS, afraid they might lose their way? Yulia O'Mahony is starting to think that traditional market and management mindsets erode the willingness to try: 'I'm Russian and I grew up in the Soviet Union and observed a failed social experiment, so it's ironic for me. What I saw where I worked before at Bain [the management consulting company] is similar kinds of structures of function-aries – *nomenklatura* – that perpetuate old regimes that want to be idolised and idealised: lots of deference to the past, lots of loud loyalty. Of course they dream of radiant futures . . . but they won't try to make them. I don't know how much is fear of loss, fear of risk. Is the fear of failure greater than the hope for the future . . . ?'

Everyone I've talked to within John Lewis loves the company and embraces the idea of experiments. But executives easily become mired in what Fiona Wilson would call 'the day job' and nervous of trying something they can't prove ahead of doing it. Everyone complains of how centralised the company is and wishes that there was more freedom at a local level. Is that because there *isn't* more freedom – or because what freedom that is there isn't being used? John Lewis is not exceptional in its caution; most businesses I know pay lipservice to innovation while, in fact, visibly lack the creativity or confidence required to do it. Most use the cliché of a burning platform as their alibi: until life is even worse, they can't find the will, or win the mandate, to experiment. I'm reminded of the dancing bears of Bulgaria, trained to dance for humans and who, even after they were liberated from their labour and set free in a park, still danced. Witold Szabłowski, the Polish writer who described their fate, likened the bears to the populations of Poland, Albania, Ukraine – people whom he saw were 'nostalgic for life under tyranny'.[3]

'Lots of people have only ever known control, so they think change has to come wholesale from the top. Life is a lot easier when you think the system locks you in,' is how Oliver Burrows describes the push to experiment versus the pull of the status quo. 'So I've been quite deliberate, provoking people to challenge the constraints they work under, to ask if they're real or meaningful – or just an excuse for keeping life simple.'

Burrows is scarcely your traditional picture of a revolutionary; he is the chief data officer at the Bank of England. His department of 150 already processes over a billion pieces of data a year. But he knew that the workload was bound to increase. A tougher regulatory environment now demands more data, analysed with increasing granularity. Resources wouldn't increase in proportion to workload, and just making people work harder wasn't a sustainable strategy. So how could the system cope with the demands he expected to be made on it? 'People look at the bank and assume it's very hierarchical,' Burrows reflected. 'But when I dug into the governance, I found it was incredibly permissive. At my level, we all have quite a lot of freedom to decide how we achieve our objectives, but it is a social norm *not* to use it. There's more constraint in the head than is real.'

A loose-limbed, wiry economist, Burrows was excited by the idea of experiments that could loosen up the hierarchical culture of his organisation; he hoped it would create smarter ways to work better. If nothing changed, then tension and stress would just escalate. So why not experiment with different ways of working? What he didn't do was sit at his desk and try to map out a new organisation. Instead, he called for volunteers and for ideas. This was an experiment in itself, one that showed him how much more appetite there was for innovation than he'd expected. People were inspired by the prospect of inventing change, rather than having it thrust upon them. Together, they mapped out twelve experiments, some of which worked and some of which, Burrows shrugged, didn't. 'I made the decision to open up our senior management meetings to anyone who wanted to sit in. At first, lots turned up, but over time they drifted off. Turns out: it wasn't all that exciting! We made the annual appraisal process a lot more participatory; that worked really well. Some very technical coding projects were suggested that nobody in the management team would ever have thought of, or been brave enough to do. They tried them and they worked! I'm really proud of that.'

But the big win, Burrows found, was that he started sourcing lots of strategy ideas from the bottom up. In the past, people had thought strategy was the preserve of management types – which meant: not them. But Burrows found an unexpected source of new ideas. The bigger experiment for Burrows had been to test how much freedom and power he had within the Bank and in his own mind. What had stopped him in the past? Fear: the sense that he needed certainty before he could start. What his experiments showed him was that there was more give in the system than he had imagined. What trapped him was more imagined than real. The simple act of doing experiments revealed territory he didn't know was his.

***

Caught between uncertainty and ambiguity, it's easy to fall into the trap of imagining that the only way to solve hard problems is to start with a clean slate. When I was at the BBC, I recall executives arguing that the best way to confront change would be to build a parallel Corporation and, when it was ready, turn it on and turn the old one off. It is what the Irish might call a 'you can't get there from here' problem that usually becomes the alibi of inertia.

That doesn't mean that fresh systems are entirely fanciful. When Jos de Blok worked as a nurse in the Netherlands, he became frustrated and downhearted by what he experienced as the industrialisation of healthcare. Every level of service had a code and the average nurse had to deal with ten different codes each day: personal care, personal care extra, personal care special. It needed an expensive bureaucracy and, de Blok said, it meant that people – patients – were being treated 'like apples on a farm: just picked and packed off'.

He had trained as an economist but was drawn into nursing by his two brothers. They were both homecare nurses, a profession whose work is the core of the Dutch healthcare system because, in general, patients get better faster at home. But after several years, de Blok felt that the recent introduction of so-called modern management methods – key performance indicators, targets, 'productisation', metrics and efficiencies – had made the work complex, expensive and meaningless.

De Blok introduced the Dutch healthcare minister to twelve nurses who talked about their experiences in industrialised medicine. It was, he said, an emotional session, with tears running down the minister's face as she heard how bureaucracy forced nurses to treat their patients like objects. She asked de Blok to come to The Hague and explain to the government his principles and his idea for an experiment. What he proposed was creating a team of just twelve nurses whose only instruction was: do what's right for the patient. That was it.

Central to his proposal was an important distinction. In homecare nursing there were two parts to the work: first, getting the nurse to the patient. That was simple and should stay simple; it didn't need an ornate bureaucracy. The second part is helping the patient recover. That's complex, because no two patients are identical and the work cannot be predicted or prescribed. That part should be left to human beings.

When the accounting firm EY audited the experiment, they showed that, with de Blok's approach, patients got better in half the time. When the experiment was expanded, costs were 30 per cent less than the traditional approach. A single, simple experiment had proved a revelation and kickstarted a revolution.

When asked what about the experiment had surprised him, de Blok's answer was succinct. 'I never imagined it could be so easy to make such a huge difference so fast,' he laughed. Since then, de Blok named the company Buurtzorg (which simply means 'neighbourhood care') and, with 10,000 nurses, it now provides approximately two thirds of all homecare nursing in the Netherlands. The success spills over into the rest of the health system: emergency admissions are reduced by a third and admissions tend to be shorter. EY estimated that €2 billion would be saved if the whole of the Netherlands adopted the system and that, if scaled to an American population, savings would be $49 billion. In the future, de Blok expects hospitals to get smaller as the need for them shrinks.

The success of his experiment makes it hard now to distinguish between what de Blok knew at the outset from what he and the nurses have learned along the way. But principles emerged. Separating the ineradicably complex (patient care) from the merely complicated (assigning nurses to patients) radically reduced costs and enhanced motivation and meaning in the work. Though both aspects of the work are necessary, they don't have to be run the same way.

I spent a day visiting patients with Ani, a Buurtzorg nurse. With one patient, she spent just a few minutes, because family members were there and the patient was doing fine. With another, she spent nearly an hour; the patient had recently lost a close friend and was distressed. Ani is part of a team that looks after forty to fifty patients. All their notes, treatments and schedules are shared via tablets, so that, covering for each other during holidays or illness, they can retrieve any information they need. The team also decides where or whether to have a team office, to hold meetings and what expenses to allow. They share a team credit card so everyone can see what team funds are available and can decide how to use them. Often, they are spent on the team's own experiments.

When making decisions for their team about schedules, patient care or new treatments, Buurtzorg nurses aren't aiming for perfection. They know too much of life to expect that. Nor do they seek consensus, because that may be impossible; there may simply not be a perfect solution. So if no one has a principled objection to a proposal, it can be supported. That way, if it turns out not to work, the topic can be revisited without recrimination. Trial and error is how Buurtzorg and its nurses learn. Without a fear of failure, better ideas and experiments emerge.

More recently, de Blok experimented with the insurance companies that pay for the nursing, trying to create a contract simpler than the current hundred-page monstrosity. They got it down to six. The police and fire services asked if a Buurtzorg approach could be applied to their work. He tried and failed because, he says, the systems are too centralised. But he is working with neighbourhood schools where there are closer parallels with nursing and where the relationship between students and teachers is ripe for an overhaul.

De Blok's guiding principles – separating the simple from the complex, acknowledging humanity in work and a focus on outcomes before cost – have inspired healthcare systems around the world. Many of the Buurtzorg nurses are slightly amazed to sometimes find themselves in Thailand or Japan working alongside local nurses to see how these principles can be adapted.

De Blok didn't try to second-guess the outcome of his experiment. He didn't predicate future decisions, strategy or structure on information he didn't have yet. Instead, he started with his idea of the best, of what mattered to the people who mattered most: the nurses and their patients. Similarly, when Brian Chesky founded Airbnb, he had only the loosest idea of what his company could or would become. He did what most business people do: he talked to customers. But he didn't ask them about the existing products or make them fill out dreary surveys. Instead, he interrogated them about their fantasies. What would a six-star experience be for a customer? To be greeted with a bottle of wine and nice toiletries in a great place to stay. A seven-star experience? A host who knew you liked surfing, so had booked lessons, or knew you liked Vietnamese food so had reserved a table in the best restaurant in town. Like de Blok, Chesky sought to understand what the best might look like. That way, he said, you get away from marginal improvements of something fundamentally inadequate.

It's comforting to argue that entrepreneurs like Chesky have it easy because they start small. That defensiveness yields to awe, however, when looking at a newer, bigger experiment in the United States, home to the world's most expensive healthcare system. Less well known than its exorbitant cost is the level of dissatisfaction among American physicians: after ten years of practice, 50 per cent of doctors say that they would get out of medicine if they could.[4]

One who has persisted is David Ring. An orthopaedic surgeon at Massachusetts General Hospital, David was a model of a modern medical man: tall, dark, handsome, powerful and a Harvard professor. But his work kept throwing up questions he found harder and harder to answer. Why were patients persuaded to accept ineffectual and expensive medical procedures? Why were medical mistakes the third largest cause of death in the United States – and why, when doctors made them, were they urged to deny and defend their actions? Why was it so hard to have a decent, straightforward conversation with patients? An outspoken critic of the role that money plays in medicine, he found the fact that hospitals could do well by serving people so badly unacceptable.

Ring wasn't alone in asking these questions. The struggle to pass Obamacare, an inadequate solution that was the first politically acceptable proposal for fifty years, had left most professionals in the industry jaded, cynical and resigned. That it had had to be defended, not enlarged, only made matters worse. Experiments? The whole system felt like a failed experiment – bloated, corrupt, too big, too old and too complex to change.

But in 2009, just a year after the worst financial crisis since the Great Depression, the University of Texas decided to found a medical school. In 2012, the University Regents allocated $25 million of annual funding and $40 million to start recruiting for the project. More remarkable still, the citizens of Travis County voted to increase their property taxes specifically to fund improved healthcare for all of its citizens. In 2013, the Michael & Susan Dell Foundation pledged $50 million to the school. In a city that was economically the most segregated in America, the dream now was to make Austin the healthiest.

The new dean, Clay Johnston, came from California to launch the school for one reason only: to reinvent American healthcare. Unlike Silicon Valley salesmen, he didn't pitch the vision that the only way to do that was by eliminating doctors and replacing them with machines. Current models of healthcare fail because they don't focus on keeping patients well. He hoped, he said, that 'Starting from scratch, we can design a medical school that empowers doctors to work collaboratively *and* embrace new technologies *and* perform cutting-edge research. All of that *together* is how you serve patients better.'

From its opening in 2017, the school had a contract to serve the uninsured. It will have to prove, ultimately, that its services are so good that other health insurers will want to join in. That's a huge experiment in itself. But for now, Johnston's goal is to prove that he and his team can deliver better healthcare at a better price by focusing only on what matters: patient outcomes. That goal might seem self-evident, but achieving it requires challenging every orthodoxy, every tradition, every assumption.

Austin isn't an easy place to start. Most of the uninsured live a long way from the health centre, so seeing a doctor can require expensive travel and time off work. When Ring arrived, a waiting list of 2,000 patients greeted him, all needing to see a hand surgeon. The wait for a neurologist, dermatologist or orthopaedist was even longer. The hospital contract allowed for video consultations and Ring hoped these would help him reduce the list more quickly. But he was wary. He already hated how often consultations felt like transactions and worried that the technology would exacerbate that problem. But he was willing to experiment.

'Most consultations give the doctor all the power: *my* time, *my* place, *my* office, *my* fifteen minutes – and then you're out,' Ring explains. 'This time, the whole idea was: to help you, I'll come at *your* convenience, just text me! We can talk in your home, on your laptop. It's about you. It's more relaxing. You can spend time setting up the camera, we can build some rapport. It's like a house call and it feels more like a relationship. It's surprising, because the average person might think this was cold. But it isn't, because it levels the hierarchy.'

On one occasion, he phoned a patient whom he knew he couldn't diagnose or treat over the phone. But he reasoned that he could get a conversation started and maybe be helpful. At least she wouldn't feel abandoned. When he called, she gave him an earful: '"You make people wait, how dare you?" "You're right," I said and let her vent,' Ring remembered. 'Then I asked her to describe what was happening with her hand. I explained what the options for treatment could be. One option was an aspiration that I didn't think was the right treatment, but she needed to feel that she had options, that something could and would be done. She had started off just being *so mad* at me! But by the end of the call, she was apologising and promising to come in. And she said, "The first thing I'm going to do when I come, I'm going to hug you."'

Two weeks later, the patient came into Ring's office and she hugged him. Then they sat down to discuss her choices. It had helped her to have had time to discuss her decision with her family. She had concluded she didn't want the aspiration but would be happier with a simpler procedure that Ring did there and then. When she left, she turned to Ring and said: 'Well done!'

Ring had hoped that calling the patient directly would disrupt the hierarchy implicit in the doctor–patient relationship, and it did, but in ways he hadn't expected. He hadn't anticipated being screamed at, or that absorbing the patient's ire would prove valuable in building their relationship. But his bigger discovery was that for the patient to have time between the call and the appointment – time to do her own research, to reflect on her choices with her family – led to a better decision that the patient felt was her own.

The insight that power leads to poor and expensive decisions has had a huge impact, not just on the way doctors work but on the entire design of the hospital. One of Clay Johnston's many experiments has been to create a companion Design Institute for Health charged with co-creating simpler, better systems and a better environment for patients and doctors alike. Most hospitals have waiting rooms but, to Stacy Chang and Katherine Jones at the institute, these felt like factories, pushing bodies along a conveyor belt where each encounter was a billable event. Sitting in a holding pen full of sick people was demeaning, depressing and frightening, and set up the relationship between doctor and patient for failure. Why not reverse the power equation and give ownership of the exam rooms to the patients?

The idea of handing over control disturbed a few physicians, but it confounded all the architects. They argued that every hospital had waiting rooms. But Dell was set up explicitly *not* to be like all hospitals. The architects offered to simulate patient flow using analytics software to show how useful waiting rooms could be. But Chang and his colleagues rejected the offer because there was no alternative to use for comparison. They had to do the experiment themselves because, as Chang said, 'The future has no available datasets – there was no evidence one way or the other about *no* waiting rooms . . . !'

The waiting room fight lasted for two and a half years, with architects deeply uncomfortable doing something new and the Dell team determined that experiments were what they had come for. Chang worked through the logic: poor decisions derive from anxiety; anxiety comes from a lack of control. If you reduce anxiety by giving control to patients, they will make better decisions. If, rather than intimidating authorities, doctors could be seen as experienced guides, then the relationship between doctor, patient and caregivers could change outcomes. Changing the patient experience is part of the treatment. Creating individual 'care rooms' controlled by patients, in which they could sit with friends and family, could reduce stress, enhance doctor/patient relationships and produce better choices which would lead to better results.

Along the way, new issues arose — what if the patient got lost? What happened if they arrived hours ahead of time? — but were resolved. Chang and Jones even managed to replace intimidating examination tables with sofas and chairs that could convert to tables if needed — because in so many cases there is no need to put the patient in so exposed a position.

When the clinics opened in 2017, patients went directly to their care rooms, where doctors, nurses, social workers — the whole integrated care team — came to them where they waited in calm, social surroundings. The geography of the experience put the patient in control.

David Ring now spends most of his time on his feet. Knocking on the door, he entered a care room to meet with a Hispanic woman with carpal tunnel and trigger finger. She had tried treating both with steroids and now worried that she had killed her dog; she wept as she explained that a neighbour had told her steroids increase the rate of infections. Ring reassured her that she wasn't responsible for the dog's death. Then he went on to explore treatment options: an injection or an operation. He thought the operation would be preferable because it would make her feel better immediately. But her family members had said that carpal tunnel surgery doesn't work, so Ring explained the circumstances in which it does and doesn't. All this time, the injection was on view so that she knew it was always an option. Ring sat level with her, eye to eye, not behind a desk, and spoke Spanish. He held her hand gently, asking about numbness and tingling. They laughed together. She chose the surgery.

The next patient had a ganglion cyst. Accompanied by her son and a friend, they sat in their care room as Ring examined her hand. The cyst was quite noticeable and she wanted it removed. Ring asked her if she knew what it was. She didn't, so he explained that it was joint fluid, that most people get them, they're entirely benign and go away eventually. Ring is alert to the possibility that the problem might not be orthopaedic and so he asked her if it was painful, because these cysts shouldn't be. If she had had pain, he would not want to operate because it wouldn't help; the real problem would have to be elsewhere. But no, it wasn't painful.

'Tell me what you're thinking,' he said.

'I want it out,' she replied.

'Okay,' he said, 'we will remove it in a month.'

He wanted to give her time to think about it because, given time to reflect, 80 per cent of people cancel the unnecessary surgery. In a more traditional setting, Ring would make more money from the surgery. Here he doesn't. His only interest is in the patient making what feels to her to be the right decision.

Another patient, in another care room, had fallen and hurt her shoulder while running for a bus. Ring took his time finding out where she worked, what she did, how she had managed to dress herself; he wanted to understand how much help she might get at home too. He never left her side but x-rayed the shoulder himself and, as he did so, pointed out where it had been broken. Then he fitted her with a sling and demonstrated an easy way to get dressed next morning. She had come in rattled and wound up; she left beaming and calm.

In the central area between the care rooms, nurses, nurse practitioners, psychologists and social workers hover, moving from room to room, conferring with their colleagues about patients. Ring talks to one about the difficulty of working through translators and how much subtext gets lost, how patients sometimes simplify what they're saying. Communication is a central subject at Dell. Better questions mean Ring learns more and faster about the lives his patients inhabit, which may influence their choices and recovery: 'We've been working with psychologists on the best questions to ask,' Ring explained. 'I used to come into the room, introduce myself, and say: "How can I help you?" But the immediate response is always: "Oh my aching . . ." It's too quick. There's no time for rapport. We thought: what if we started with a positive question? Who are you at your best? What things do you love to do? What makes you laugh? You learn so much more about the patient and their life that way. When doctors ask: "Is there anything else you want to talk about?", the answer is always no. But if you ask: "Is there *something else* you want to talk about today?" and there is, you'll find out.'

Erin Donovan is a communication academic who works with Ring and his colleagues. She appreciates that medicine is saturated with uncertainty and anxiety and teaches her doctors and students to understand concepts such as tolerance of ambiguity.

'My experience is that natural science students do not have high tolerance for ambiguity and don't understand why some people do,' Donovan says. So she teaches a seminar on uncertainty management. Some students experience uncertainty as full of hope and opportunities, others as danger and risk. Her students learn why a patient won't ask a scary question or might not call back for test results. More positive interactions help patients to remain hopeful and open.

Doctors are often unfairly pilloried for being poor communicators, Donovan observed. But when you measure and price every minute of each interaction, hoping to increase efficiency, communication takes the first hit. In many American pharmacies, a red light flashes if prescriptions aren't filled fast enough, so of course pharmacists make mistakes. The same is true for conversations: the more doctors consider the financial cost of every minute, the more mistakes they make.

At Dell, doctors, communicators and designers are experimenting together, exploring and devising what they call 'interpersonal medicine'. This approach isn't about being nice; it acknowledges that improved human relationships between doctors, patients and caregivers is associated with a 19 per cent gain in patient adherence to therapies and improved outcomes. It recognises that a patient is a person, not just a body; there is more to medicine than data and statistics and the next big leap in medicine depends on making healthcare interactions more human.[5]

Dell is full of experiments underway and planned. The old hacksaws that surgeons still use have now been replaced by a cold laser tool designed at the hospital. Dean Johnston hopes consultations can be documented using voice recognition software. Self-care websites are prototyped along with new systems for catching opioid overuse early. Informal caregivers are included in every conversation. They are educating family doctors about when MRIs help and when they don't. Experiments continue into community impacts on health. The goal is to experiment, learn and build out only what works. One consequence of this principle is that, just like de Blok's Buurtzorg, experiments start low-tech – paper prototypes, white boards – to ensure that the human element remains front and centre and that snazzy technology doesn't get in the way.[6]

There are so many experiments going on at Dell that it can be hard to see how the day jobs get done. But the day job *is all* experimentation, each consultation an experiment in doing one thing better. There is no organisational chart yet. Johnston wants to get Dell's culture right first before imposing a structure. The experiments are designed to allow the structure to emerge, just as they drive the design of tools. So far, Johnson's organisation sketch looks more like a web, designed to enable people to move in and out of collaborative experiments with ease, unhampered by departments, hierarchies, siloes and functions. That way, he hopes, new projects can start quickly, people come together easily and, if the project proves unproductive, everyone can move on to the next challenge. It's a complex skein of questions, experiments, learning and improvement in real time on real patients leading real lives.

The big overarching hypothesis at Dell is this: if you change the power relationship in medicine by putting the patient in charge – not the doctor, not the infrastructure, not the technology salesmen or the insurance companies – you will get better, more affordable and more sustainable outcomes. It's a big bet, expressed and explored through hundreds of experiments because there's no other way to find out. Johnston, Ring, Chang and all their colleagues have a lot going for them: with US healthcare seen as an extravagant mess, they have the mandate that comes from a failed system. They have the enormous privilege of starting with a clean slate with the active support of the community they serve. Already they can demonstrate that Dell produces better care, at a lower price, with a better experience. Because the funding comes directly from citizens' property taxes, there is a tight coupling between patients and the hospital. They succeed together or not at all.

***

It can be tempting to argue that you can't change the future without that neat, blank slate. It's a seductive idea and often a dangerous one. In software development, there's always a moment in bug fixing when the number of errors seems so overwhelming that the cry goes up: wouldn't it be better to throw this code out and start again? The implicit belief, of course, is that *this time* we will write it flawlessly, this time we will get it right. It never works that way; the fresh version just has different bugs, different problems. Perfection is an illusion.

Similarly, many have been tempted recently to look at democratic institutions around the world and condemn them as impossible to change or to reform. Time to throw them out and start again. Those behind such arguments make the same error as the rookie software coder, envisaging their idealised future blissfully empty of error, violence and recrimination. Their sense of crisis isn't misplaced, but a crisis isn't the moment to give up on experimentation. It's the time to start.

Ireland in 2008 didn't look a promising seedbed for anything new. Even in the context of the global economic crisis, failure in Ireland was extreme, as all of its major institutions had failed at once. Bank failures brought the economy close to collapse and, when the most unpopular government in the country's history signed a punitive bailout agreement, democracy seemed moribund too. Those who had caused the banking crisis went largely unscathed while the rest of the bewildered populace were left to pay for their recklessness. At the same time, the Catholic Church, which underpinned all of civil society in its running of churches, schools and hospitals, was revealed as an abject moral failure, guilty of perpetrating and covering up the abuse of children, the historic illegal sale and burial of babies and the exploitation of young women. With the failure of the banks, the government and the church, the survival of a democratic society suddenly seemed fragile.

That concatenation of crises lured David Farrell home. He'd been teaching politics at the University of Manchester and knew how badly Ireland's institutions needed renewal. He and his colleagues believed that the rich, recent history of democratic experiments could be helpful. In 1994, the American political scientist James Fishkin had conducted his first experiment in what he came to call deliberative polling. He brought together a representative sample of the British population, provided them with fair, impartial briefing documents on current topics, such as crime, and asked participants to discuss and debate them. His experiment tested several things: how a random national sample would interact, how seriously people would read and consider their materials, how civil (or otherwise) the discussions would be and, crucially, how far anyone would change their minds.

'And it worked beautifully,' Fishkin says. 'The sample was representative. The discussions were civil. They had knowledge gain and there were coherent and identifiable changes of opinion that were statistically significant. So the big thing I learned is that, while my colleagues in political science mostly think that the public is stupid and easily manipulable, it's not stupid.' Since then, Fishkin has conducted over one hundred such polls around the world, all showing that such public discussions can be an effective way to enlist citizens in political issues of consequence: budget priorities, voting reform and constitutional amendments. These experiments encouraged Farrell and his colleagues to launch one of their own.

But in arguing that Ireland needed a similar device, called a citizens' assembly, David Farrell and his colleagues anticipated opposition – and they got it. Ireland already had a parliament; people are too daft. Such projects worked elsewhere but that didn't mean they would work in Ireland; why trust ordinary, uninformed citizens? But they kept pushing and, in 2011, the Labour Party and Fine Gael formed a coalition government that included a promise to hold a convention of citizens – one third politicians, two thirds ordinary citizens – to explore amendments to the constitution. The new government made no promises regarding the outcome, bar a commitment to respond formally and debate any recommendations in the Oireachtas, the Irish parliament. It was an experiment in democracy that went largely unnoticed except by cynical journalists who were convinced it was just a fig leaf – a pretence at action.

The outcome surprised everyone. Of the many sane, coherent recommendations emanating from the convention, one proposed a referendum on the legalisation of same-sex marriage. On 22 May 2015, the referendum was held and approved by a clear majority: 62 to 38 per cent. Those who had participated in the convention believed it should be continued as a valuable and important addition to democracy, but Taoiseach (Prime Minister) Enda Kenny disagreed, declaring it the kind of exercise applicable only to the lifetime of a single parliament.

But by 2016, another coalition government – Fine Gael and independents – again found citizen deliberation a useful way to sidestep intractable social issues on which the electorate demanded action. Few politicians and no political party wanted to take a public stand on the subject of abortion: the topic was simply too toxic. Once again, the idea of consulting ordinary people was derided and Enda Kenny pilloried by all sides for 'kicking the can down the road', or using the device of a citizens' assembly to sidestep action.

On the day she returned from maternity leave, the civil servant Sharon Finegan was assigned the task of managing the assembly. Her colleagues warned her not to touch it. The issue and the process were too risky. 'I was warned,' she said. '"You'll be personally attacked." "It could damage your career." I took a different view – I thought it would be incredibly interesting. And if it was to be done, I thought it should be done well and I thought I could do that. I thought it would be an enormous challenge.'

A lot was in play during this experiment. Nobody knew whether the assembly's deliberations would be useful or if their conclusions would be accepted as legitimate by politicians or the electorate. Not everyone was convinced that such thorny issues could be understood by ordinary people. Would the assembly strengthen democracy or merely reveal how impotent and irrelevant it had become? At a time when politics seemed increasingly driven by ego, vanity and corporate interests, and when the binary nature of elections grossly oversimplified every issue, commentators and citizens speculated about what good a bunch of barmen, parents, electricians, nurses and truck drivers could do.

Finegan had a huge job. The assembly required ninety-nine ordinary citizens who were an accurate reflection of the country's demographic. They would be asked to sacrifice twelve weekends over a period of eighteen months, during which they would come together just outside Dublin to listen to a series of presentations by lawyers, academics, doctors and advisors on four topics: abortion, the ageing population, parliamentary term limits and climate change.

This time, no politicians would take part; it was to be an assembly of ordinary citizens only. The earlier experiment had suggested that professionals might dominate discussions – and the politicians were eager to keep their distance. At the request of the chair, Supreme Court Justice Mary Laffoy, an expert advisory group assessed and prepared every expert who presented to the citizens. At the end of each meeting, members were surveyed to see if they had got all the information they needed. If they wanted more or different input, Finegan's team of four sourced it. Those procedural changes to the experiment paled in comparison to the big change: overwhelming public scrutiny.

'From the very beginning, the chair was obsessed with transparency,' Finegan recalls. 'We had to do everything with utter transparency and clarity, otherwise we'd always have to justify everything we did.' So every session was filmed. Every presentation, every paper was put online, in English, Irish and in sign language. The whole country could watch and contribute by submitting their own views and arguments. But the full burden of the work fell on the group of citizens, recruited door-to-door to reflect the demographic of the Irish population. Few had heard of the assembly or knew exactly what would be required of them.

The assembly opened at Dublin Castle with a welcome from Enda Kenny: 'We chose to go about our business this way so that as a nation and as a society we could move from a position of contention, even of contempt, and find in valuable consensus some common co-ordinates in a matter so privately and publicly tender.' But unlike many grand opening ceremonies at which heads of state preside, Kenny didn't just say his fifteen minutes and leave. He stayed and listened as Justice Laffoy set the tone for the next eighteen months with an introduction that was pragmatic, straightforward, wry and punctual. The next day, the members were treated to a masterclass on ethics: what they are, the role of disagreement, the meaning of decisions and their impact on others unknown and unseen. Members left impressed, serious, intent.

Few assembly members appreciated what they had let themselves in for: eighteen months of some of the most intense work and homework they'd ever done. Briefing documents. Presentations. Discussions. Debates. Hundreds of hours of work – even before they met for weekends in Malahide. Like many of his fellow members, ventilation technician John Long worked long days Monday to Friday, then came home to fifteen lengthy briefing documents to be read before the weekend. He didn't want to be sitting at a discussion table unprepared, so he took his new work seriously. He enjoyed meeting so many different people from all walks of life and learned to listen keenly: 'You'd be sitting round the table and someone would say something and, gee, I'd never thought of that! They came at it from a direction I'd never have thought of, whether I agreed or not! You come along with this big arc – the *way* and the *reasons* you'd never think of yourself . . . Some of the sessions were head-melting, there was so much legal, medical information. But the process – the roundtable discussions, the Q&A. At the end, you understood.'

Barman Peter Patrick said he had no idea how important the work was until the end. But nothing about the process intimidated him. 'I am a relatively quiet person in the group,' he said. 'But the facilitators ensured everyone's voices were heard. It could get slightly heated but you could always ask questions and overall there was real respect for every point of view. Some had strongly held views but still there was total respect . . .' Patrick appreciated Sharon Finegan's secretariat. They ruthlessly excised jargon from papers and presentations and made it easy for any member to ask questions. Another member, Deirdre Donaghy, felt that the insistence on straight-forward language made it comfortable for people to challenge each other in debate in a way that was reasonable and respect-ful, without grandstanding or point-scoring.

Over 13,000 members of the public made submissions regarding abortion, over a thousand on climate change. The process rejected lobbying organisations and pressure groups but welcomed those with first-hand experience or non-aligned expertise. For the hard-working secretariat and for the ninety-nine members, the experience was unforgettable – a source of intense work, new friendships and huge learning. Understanding how far behind Ireland was on climate change forced theatre technician Oisin Heraghty to re-examine how he lived his own life. Given facts about the country's ageing population made him consider choices and consequences he'd never thought about before. Being given reliable information made him more thoughtful.

Although they had the other topics to consider, the nation as a whole remained transfixed by the way in which deliberation of the eighth amendment (on abortion) played out. The assembly's radical transparency didn't extinguish the firestorms that typically accompany any discussion of the subject, but it did counter it with non-partisan speakers, documents and a wide range of perspectives. The spill-over of information and argument – much of the assembly's work was replicated by coverage and debate on RTE, the national broadcaster – connected the public at large, enriching what became a national conversation.

On 23 April 2017, the assembly voted 64 per cent in favour of a referendum proposing the liberalisation of abortion up to twelve weeks. According to Finegan, the perceived wisdom in political circles was that this was so far from public opinion as to be useless. Media headlines concurred, asking how on earth this extreme view could be watered down to make it palatable to the population. Had he been asked the night before the vote, Farrell told me, he'd have said that the referendum would be lost. But it wasn't. On 25 May 2018, in an almost perfect mirror image of the assembly, the electorate of Ireland voted by 66 per cent in favour of legalisation.

Not everyone, of course, was happy with the outcome of the referendum. But everyone accepted its legitimacy. For David Farrell, the result had been a cathartic moment in Irish history, a time when citizens saw that they could learn, work and live together even amid disagreement. Assemblies weren't, he insisted, a substitute for parliaments, but an important and valid addition. 'Right now,' he said, 'we have ongoing crises across the world: climate change and a populist challenge to democracy. This is the perfect time for us to adapt these devices to take charge of the debates on immigration, multi-culturalism and let the mainstream political class engage in debate with their citizens. I think this device is perfect for those big ideas to be tackled and explored so that the people feel involved in their own future.'

Judge Laffoy produced a thoughtful report with recommendations for improving the process. The time commitment had been extreme; one item at a time would be less exhausting, with a minimum of two weeks' deliberation for each. Members should serve for a maximum of six months and Parliament should consider paying them a modest stipend. The experiment wasn't over; there was still opportunity for improvement and discovery.[7]

Sharon Finegan had plenty of ideas, too, about how to improve the process but, for the time being, was happy to be going home to have another baby. Her greatest praise went to the members for their hard work, their dedication, their sense of efficacy: they knew that their work mattered and they took it seriously. On the day that the assembly had been launched in Dublin Castle, she had listened as Michael Manning, the chancellor of the University of Ireland, warned the newly minted members that their deliberations would test them to the full, but believed that they already had what they most needed: 'You come here as free citizens, bringing with you your own life experience, your own sense of duty, your own values and insights . . . The great quality you bring to this process is your freedom to be yourselves.'

'It actually works,' Peter Patrick reflected. 'I just came back from Berlin and I went down to where the former SS head-quarters was. Looking at it, I thought how quickly a country can change. Democracy can just disappear because something that isn't democracy takes over. You can just get rid of people, livelihoods. So you have to keep working on democracy, because countries can change very quickly. It made me realise how very fragile we are.'

**

We start to map our future when we dare to experiment with the present, when we don't make ourselves hostage to the past or to the salesmen of determinism and machines. Experiments are how we explore ecosystems, feeling out their contours and boundaries. Whether in individual careers, startups, businesses or nations, these experiments share vital characteristics. They have a mandate, a reason to be. This stems from a shared awareness that the status quo is inad-equate or in danger. Effective experiments aim at practical learning, with no one trying to second-guess the outcome. They aren't binary or final, but a healthy means of exploration. They're real, in the world where practical outcomes matter to the curious people who conduct them. They should be adjusted and refined with the ease and flexibility that volatile times, imperfect people and systems demand. They must be defined enough to be meaningful. Measurement matters, but an obsession with metrics will constrain thinking and reduce learning. And measurements mustn't become targets because, when they do, the experiments are easily gamed or hijacked, making them unreliable and unproductive.

Passion. Need. Resources. What else do good experiments require? They need backbone, someone who cares enough to – as Fiona Wilson of Wolfe's Neck Farm said – ensure that shit gets done, that momentum is maintained and ambition isn't compromised. But perhaps more than anything else, they need open minds and, within organisations, the freedom to transcend hierarchy. If we want to map the future, we start by acknowledging that we don't know all it holds, that everyone can contribute, but no one knows what we will find. With simple language, an absence of power and entrenched interests, alertness to weak signals and small insights, we start to delineate the contours of what lies ahead. Instead of abdicating the future to those who know no more than we do, experiments are bolder, enlisting every kind of imagination in pursuit of more options. They show us what we miss when we cling to the shore, pinioned by forecasts or orthodoxies, doubt or fear. Each new insight adds detail to pictures of the future as they start to emerge.

CHAPTER FIVE

GO FAST, GO FAR

If you want to go fast, go alone.
If you want to go far, go together.

— AFRICAN PROVERB

One morning in 2010, Alberto Fernández woke up to discover that his world had changed. Nine men were hanging from a bridge over the highway that led to Monterrey, Mexico, where he lived. In later days, executed bodies were found around the city. People he knew were hijacked and killed. The homicide rate increased by 650 per cent in one year, kidnapping by 293 per cent and violent robbery by 392 per cent.[1] He had to buy a bulletproof car. His sister, married to the president of the country's largest newspaper, had to leave the country. The biggest problem, Fernández reflected, was apathy; it was so much easier to blame others than to take action.

Fernández is one of the most successful businessmen in Mexico. A serial entrepreneur, he has started, run and sold telecommunication businesses, a construction company, restaurants, a beverage business. He could see that the sudden eruption of violence signified attempts by drug cartels to infiltrate one of the country's wealthiest, most modern and industrialised cities. Everything Fernández prized – his family, his home and community, his companies and his employees – was under threat.

His instinct was to do something, to act where passion, need and resources intersected. After thinking about the violence, and the apathetic response to it, Fernández concluded that a fundamental failure to believe in the rule of law was what allowed violence to flourish. That was where he needed to intervene. 'This is not a sexy topic!' Fernández concedes. 'Eighty per cent of people said they would break a law for personal benefit; seventy per cent said they wouldn't do anything about conflict; young guys said it isn't worth being honest. We were silent accomplices. With no rule of law, there's no social mobility. With no rule of law, there's no security. Without law, there's no development. For me, that's what the crisis of 2010 was about. We had a huge crisis and we had to stop whining and start doing. Otherwise we are part of the problem.'

Fernández decided to found an organisation to promote the rule of law. After consultants delivered a fancy, complicated marketing strategy, he turned to his cleaning lady, explained the concept, and found that her way of describing it got to the heart of the matter: *hagamoslo bien*, which, roughly translated, means 'let's do it right'.

Fernández's prominence in the community allowed him to reach out to anyone and everyone who mattered. All of the churches backed him. Both universities. Community leaders. Businesses. Schools. A world racketball champ and both the city's rival football teams: popular heroes whom everyone would listen to. The coalition started to research and experiment. Online courses reached 14,000 people. Activist workshops. Negotiation workshops. Workshops for parents. Street festivals. Courses for *evolucionarios* in corporations, the fire department and the police. Family rallies. Students led programmes to eradicate cheating at university. A huge campaign against texting while driving. Major employers such as OXXO (the Mexican equivalent of Walmart) began redeveloping public spaces to encourage transparency and safety. Educationalists worked at integrating ideas of trust and trustworthiness into the curriculum.

Tall, trim, slightly balding, Fernández looks every inch the corporate citizen. But if you have in mind a stereotype of a business leader or entrepreneur, he won't fit it. As we drove around Monterrey, his conversation wandered. A love for the poetry of Pablo Neruda. The art of Banksy and the power of graffiti. The architecture of Tadao Ando and the technical demands of building with reinforced concrete. A passion for Shakespeare. The importance of carpooling. The genius of Issey Miyake. Studying at Georgetown University. But the *leitmotif* was consistent: how to provoke change. As Fernández put it, 'it's not a question of changing the landlord but how to stop being a dog.'

By 2018, Fernández's passion for the rule of law was unabated, refuelled by success. The number of people who'd said that they would break the law if they could had fallen to 28 per cent. But a mind as energetic and complex as Fernández's couldn't be satisfied by survey data. Violence had receded from Monterrey but remained a looming threat. In 2014, forty-three teachers and students in the southern state of Guerrero disappeared, later found murdered, the police unable or unwilling to help. Each year, corruption costs Mexico between 2 and 10 per cent of its GDP.[2] There had to be more he could do. So, when colleagues approached him about scenario planning for the future of Mexico, Fernandez didn't quite know what that would entail, but he was definitely up for it.

***

Scenario planning was pioneered after the Second World War by the Rand Corporation and the American military. As a process, it grew out of an understanding of complexity and the recognition that it is never possible to identify all the forces at work that will define the future. This makes traditional planning dangerous: it will always contain too many assumptions to be reliable and risks offering certainty where none exists. The best one can do is to identify a plausible variety of futures and interrogate them for implications and consequences. The military still deploys a variant of scenario planning today. It has to, because it functions across multiple time zones: the immediate present, the near future and the distant future, decades out.

The British military uses scenario planning, too. If experiments reveal immediate internal features of a complex system, scenarios explore where the internal organisation meets the external environment, where uncertainties lurk beyond anyone's control. This kind of planning is designed to identify and test how and where the future and the present meet. Chief of the Defence Staff General Sir Nick Carter previously served as Chief of the General Staff in the British Army. In that role, he confronts two competing demands: his organisation must be ready to respond at a moment's notice, but he must also plan today for the fighting force Britain will need twenty-five years from now: 'You have to distinguish between determined strategies and emergent strategies. Because the future is inherently unpredictable, a determined strategy won't be successful. We think that the future emerges and therefore we can only really take one step at a time, building alliances and hedging opponents' behaviour along the way. But you need scenarios to get a general idea of what parts of town you're aiming at and to check your steps are in the direction of your ends.'

Reconciling the tension between the internal, immediate demands of the army and the external realities of the world in which it operates, scenario plans must separate predetermined certainties (the army has these capabilities and resources) from uncertainties (where the army might be called to intervene). The goal is both to protect what's critical now and to identify early what might bestow advantage in the future. Scenarios bridge inside and out, immediate and future.

'My replacement is being recruited now,' Carter says. 'A platoon commander who joins at the age of twenty-four is commanding a battalion fifteen years later. But we don't know what they will be asked to do in fifteen years so we have to train now for a deeply adaptive mindset. It is exactly the opposite of the gig economy.' Carter can't know what challenges the army will face fifteen or twenty years from now. What he does know is that whoever leads the army then won't be able to rustle up the skills he needs the minute he knows he needs them. The lead time to develop that talent is too long. So he works from a variety of models of the future that help define a range of possibilities for which his men and women will be trained. He's learned that, while it's easy to talk about adaptive leadership, it's hard to produce. 'In my second tour in Afghanistan,' Carter tells me, 'it was interesting seeing how twenty-five battle group commanders behaved. Of the twenty-five, only two or three were generally tactically adaptive. Building an army where that is the norm cannot be done overnight.'

Carter received a lot of flak for ads specifically aimed at attracting as diverse a range of recruits as possible. Traditionalists scoffed at questions like 'Can I be gay in the army?' and 'What if I get emotional in the army?' But Carter insisted that he was trying to craft a fighting force that looked like the nation it would defend – a force for the future, not the past. Every five years, he develops multiple scenarios, wargaming them and drawing conclusions about the capacity the future army will need. He knows how easy it is to get this wrong. Over the past fifteen years, he says, Western armies have concentrated on stabilisation and counterinsurgency. But other areas – cybersecurity, underwater warfare, drones – got overlooked. He's using multiple scenarios to try to ensure that future strategies don't leave such gaping exposure.

Scenario planning began in the military, but it was at Shell Oil Corporation that it became most developed. In the early 1970s, all the oil companies ran a sophisticated, bureaucratic form of centralised planning (called the 'Unified Planning Machine' at Shell) that assumed business would continue into the future without significant change. But however big the Planning Machine was, it focused almost exclusively on financial information. Pierre Wack, an idiosyncratic French oil executive, regarded the forecasts that emerged from these systems as a dangerous substitute for real thinking – it was too easy to mistake financial models for reality. Instead, he argued that external volatility (what he called 'the rapids') would increase as countries began to nationalise their natural resources and the power of the oil cartel OPEC grew. To Wack, that meant that the companies themselves could lose control over price. How could they plan for this?

In what became one of the most famous scenario-planning exercises in history, Wack and his team designed a number of stories describing a changed world. One challenged the conventional wisdom that finite natural resources would always command rising prices. Instead, it asked the planners to consider what useful responses might be feasible if the oil price *fell*. This proposition appeared absurd, barely worthy of notice. But in 1973, when oil prices did fall and everyone else scrambled to understand what was happening, Shell was ready. The corporation had already decreased stockpiles, restructured to cut costs and decentralised, anticipating that the price shock would affect nations in different ways. The exercise enabled Shell to move from the weakest to one of the strongest of the 'Seven Sisters' companies of the global oil industry.[3]

The scenario planning Wack developed at Shell, and that the company still conducts today, follows certain rules. Multiple scenarios must be produced (usually two to four) based on the same rigorously researched and reliable datasets. Like the evidence presented to the Irish citizens' assembly, data cannot be ideological, nor can it be vague, opinionated fantasy, but must be derived from verifiable facts that are consistent and plausible. That means that the scenarios can be explained. Each has to be considered as seriously and fully as any other, as Shell's team has always rejected assigning probabilities to them. Soft data (cultural differences in different markets, for example) is as important as hard data. Scenarios should focus less on predicting outcomes and more on illuminating the forces at work across the organisation and the environments in which it operates. They must be relevant and challenging, pragmatic not ideological. And that means that they won't be tidy: like life, they are bound to be messy, patchy, full of paradox and contradictions. Using scenarios, Wack argued, 'is as different from relying on forecasts as judo is from boxing'.[4] If you understand outside forces, you might be able to make them work to your advantage.

Shell attributes to this planning process its capacity – not always, but often – to be ahead of the curve. It helped them adapt to a second oil crisis in 1979, to the collapse of oil markets in 1986 and the fall of the Soviet Union in 1989. They claim that it brought the company early to address the rise of China as an industrial force, in putting sustainable development on the corporate agenda and seeing natural gas as an intrinsic part of that. They do not claim that the technique has given them control or the ability to predict accurately. Rather its strengths lie in highlighting options and alternatives, in seeing possibilities otherwise obscure, and in building within the organisation the imaginative and creative capability that derives from asking 'what if . . .' and 'so what?'

In 2013, Shell published what it called its New Lens scenarios. These define three paradoxes at work in the world today: a Prosperity Paradox (economic development raises millions out of poverty but increases strain on resources and the environment, and increasing prosperity doesn't always increase wellbeing); a Connectivity Paradox (the digital world sparks creativity but also makes it harder to protect or derive livelihoods from creative products); and a Leadership Paradox (the greater the need for collective long-term solutions, the less the appetite for individual sacrifice). It argued that industries and nations typically find themselves in one of two places: either with room to manoeuvre, which makes them resilient, or trapped by institutional rigidity, which causes them to delay or prevaricate. For example, India, China and Brazil proved to be relatively resilient to the 2008 financial crisis because they had financial, political, natural and social resources that provided immediate options for quick response. By contrast, many European countries proved less resilient as they drifted, procrastinated and got stuck for years.

This concept, coupled with the three paradoxes, gives rise to questions from which the scenarios emerge: which paradoxes are most acute where and for whom? Which industries, nations and groups have room for manoeuvre and which are trapped? How will capital, collaboration and creativity develop? How will power and influence be distributed?

From these lenses and questions, two scenarios emerged, named 'Mountains' and 'Oceans'. In 'Mountains', power remains concentrated in elites; entrenched power hampers globalisation and economic development, making political reform difficult. Individualism remains a prevalent mindset, with a belief that people get what they deserve. The internet becomes balkanised, with elite access for the few. Oil loses ground, shale gas becomes a global success; clean coal and nuclear energy expand while renewables struggle to compete. Mass migration drives defence spending. 'Mountains' portrayed a world of volatile peaks and valleys.

'Oceans', by contrast, describes a world of greater cohesion, where power is more broadly shared. That makes reform slower but more effective in unleashing economic productivity and ambition for reform. Social justice emphasises solidarity over individualism: people believe that *systems* get what they deserve. The internet remains open, so political and business innovation are widespread. Rising prices make more expensive energy viable. Prosperity is more widely distributed and pervasive but resource stresses become acute. As climate change renders some parts of the world uninhabitable, populations migrate in search of food. Solar energy overtakes liquid fuels and coal, but weak policies strangle the growth of natural gas. The combination of biomass, carbon storage and solar power reduce greenhouse gases – but late.[5] 'Oceans' portrayed a world of swirling, dynamic growth.

Neither of these scenarios is either ideological or simple. Shell is an energy company, so its scenarios examine the world through the lenses of its concerns – consumption, transport, CO_2 emissions, water, weather, migration, food, political institutions – while ignoring social trends they don't expect to affect them, such as automation, genetic engineering or gender blending. But there is much about the underlying stability of institutions and the rule of law, both of which global companies need to thrive. The scenarios challenge organisations to consider: in this story, what can we do now and what should we prepare for? Do we have any capacity to influence the story and, if so, where and how? Just as General Sir Nick Carter used scenarios to address the need for adaptive leadership, scenarios can reveal the opportunity to examine today what could happen tomorrow.

A diaspora of executives who once worked in the Shell Scenario Unit has disseminated this approach across industries and institutions around the world. The process has evolved according to proponent and context and its most stalwart advocates readily acknowledge its challenges. The scenarios themselves aim to be morally neutral, but one Shell scenario planner 'found them too promiscuous in their willingness to envisage almost anything, even the most disagreeable events'.[6] There was some reluctance at Shell to publish the 2013 scenarios because they posit that the world will fail to limit the increase in global average temperature to $1.5°C$, as called for in the Paris Accord. Do scenarios run the risk of habituating people to prospects that are ethically repugnant? Might they provoke despair rather than creative thinking?

Today, some permutations of scenario planning have become technocratic, dependent on artificial intelligence and far less amenable to the soft data which, for all that it is hard to quantify, makes a measurable impact. Pierre Wack regarded computer modelling as the enemy of thought. Once quantified, he thought, models can become too rigid and their makers so wedded to them as to become blind to disconfirming data. Numbers acquire more authority than they deserve. One scenario planner, Angela Wilkinson, compared computer models in scenario planning to 'a heavy axe in the hand of a fireman – even if it hinders his escape from a fire, a fireman is reluctant to drop his axe. The axe is a help most of the time, but a dangerous burden in extreme events.' If you entrust scenario planning to data scientists, there is a real risk that strategy and data bifurcate so severely that the plastic, creative exercise of integrating them fails. And while it is clear that scenario planning demands a diverse range of people who are open-minded with deep intellectual curiosity, expertise and a capacity to think freely, those people can be hard to find.

As global head of intellectual property, Michael Koch used to run scenario-planning exercises within the global agrichemicals business Syngenta. He is evangelical about the process. On one occasion, he explained it to a group of senior British executives who were keen to understand how it worked. He outlined a scenario of abundance that he had developed at Syngenta. The falling cost of photovoltaic cells, coupled with improved energy storage, has made energy cheap and plentiful. Clean water is abundant and forests are regenerating. Food can be grown easily wherever it is needed with agritech providing cheap, renewable sources of nutrition. Robotics ensure everyone has ample time and big data systems underpin efficient, cheap, safe transportation systems. Pervasive connectivity makes all data available everywhere and virtual reality gives you any experience you want, anywhere, any time. There are downsides: with more data, decision-making gets harder because there's more bad data and it's harder to distinguish noise from signal. Anything can be copied, so fakes abound. More fundamentally, our economic systems derive value from scarcity, but in this scenario, there isn't any.

The gathering broke into small groups to discuss it. What would this world feel like? What would you stop doing and start doing? What would make you unhappy? Many enjoyed what was, for them, a playful process: free, creative, eye-opening. The scenario upended so many assumptions about modern economics and allowed them to explore questions they'd never considered before. What happens when laws of supply and demand *don't* influence price or consumption? In an age of abundance, scarcity itself would become scarce; could under-production become a new goal?

But one group was paralysed. Kock's scenario was too much for them. They could not imagine a world in which so many age-old, tested rules no longer functioned. Arguments about probabilities got nowhere. So much change was just too frightening to imagine. Kock says he has seen the phenomenon before. The most amenable to scenarios, he found, were young people who play a lot of computer games. Those are all forms of simulation where play is how to find out what happens next. Avid game players don't just get used to trying out different strategies, doing so is their idea of fun. It could even be the way to win. So they bring to the exercise a wholly different mindset, one that is open, fluid and optimistic that change isn't just possible but positive. The same is sometimes true in business school simulations, where teams less obsessed by winning find delight in trying out radical decisions that exert no real cost. This is, of course, how they learn. But executives in corporations, Kock concedes, 'need certainty like an addiction and they are so afraid of being wrong that they have lost the capacity to think freely'. A year later, Kock left Syngenta disappointed 'that they just couldn't let go of where they are today. So I think they are in a death spiral.'

Thinking imaginatively is harder than many people expect. We are all born with the cognitive capacity to reconfigure the knowledge we have, but how boldly we are prepared to do so may become a matter of habit. Sterility and paralysis might be blamed on corporate cultures, but I've encountered it when running scenario exercises for individuals who find it cognitively or emotionally impossible to leave their past behind. They can't imagine changing industries or jobs, learning a new skill or enjoying more freedom. They don't love where they are, but fear of change makes present misery more comfortable than future hope.

At Shell, one scenario planner said that team members needed to feel free enough 'to push within an inch of being fired'. But the planners hadn't started with the luxury of such an open, free-speaking culture. For decades, the company had been a byword for formality and hierarchy. But the ability to argue on the basis of context, data and imagination has become a hallmark of the way Shell works. At its most effective, this kind of thinking requires that everyone involved has to be able to ask anything, to make space for conflict and have the emotional and intellectual capacity to endure disagreement. Hierarchy and seniority lose some of their power. Where Kock found that the conservative, obedient culture of Syngenta couldn't accommodate this, Shell discovered that the process itself shifted the company's culture, making it more responsive and adaptable.[7] One of the great insights from scenario planning has been that the act of doing it can change the systems it strives to describe.

***

By 2015, the government of Slovenia was experiencing the paradox of prosperity that Shell had defined two years earlier: quality of life had improved steadily since the Second World War, with high levels of educational attainment and personal security, but Slovenians felt that their quality of life was worse than in the past. Despite being a relatively equal society, its citizens didn't feel they enjoyed equal opportunities when it came to schooling, jobs and housing. An ageing population absorbed a high proportion of resources and, while Slovenia was at the forefront of Europe's digital revolution, there was a widespread sense that the direction of technology was beyond their control. Perhaps most profound of all, citizens did not trust one another, having more trust in EU institutions than in their own. And that habit of distrust translated to weak democratic participation, with voter turnout among the lowest in Europe.

So the government promised to develop a new vision and strategy for their country. Most expected that, as usual, this would be the secretive gathering of elites holed up in a swanky hotel, drafting policies that would be dumped on the electorate. But instead, adopting the tools of scenario planning, the government tried to bridge the gap between daily party politics and wider, long-term social concerns. Fifty participants from government, regional communities, civil society and the business world – a balance of gender and age groups – used scenarios to galvanise discussions around the kind of society Slovenes wanted to create for themselves in the future.

One of the guides through the process, Betty Sue Flowers, was a veteran of scenario planning. A professor of English at the University of Texas, her literary finesse had drawn her into scenario planning with Shell in the 1970s. She is an excellent listener and a gifted editor – all qualities heavily in demand when trying to capture the complexity of a collective vision. Working on the Slovenia project, she noticed immediately that the problem of trust threatened to stall the entire exercise. Participants weren't open or willing to argue and debate together. If this obstacle weren't removed, she realised, the project would go nowhere.

'The problem dated back to the Second World War. Some families had backed the Germans because they were anti-communist and other families had backed the Russians because they were anti-fascist. That was all still in the room,' Flowers recalls. Scenario planning surfaces conflict and there is always a moment when everything seems to fall apart. But getting the conflict out in the open, constructively, is critical; it's how and when people start to acknowledge and consider alternative per-spectives. 'That's how the facts, and then the trust, emerge.'

Breaking through the barriers of distrust felt painful and slow. But when the facilitators unveiled a map they had drawn reflecting everything they had heard, the group erupted. 'When they saw their own thinking in front of them, they really hated it,' Flowers said. She had known such moments before, but none quite so intense and personal. 'They looked in the mirror and said: we don't want to be that!'

Flowers and her colleagues kept their nerve. Not liking what they saw in the mirror motivated the group to come up with an identity they could like better, and the project sprang into life. A new vision began to emerge that wasn't just a wishlist, or a bunch of campaign promises, but a map showing how trust, wellbeing and social innovation could build on each other. What emerged was a shared recognition that economic growth alone wasn't good enough. A more meaningful meas-ure of prosperity was social wellbeing. From this epiphany, the first draft of a Vision for Slovenia emerged.

The group didn't stop there. Through workshops and sur-veys, they spread the vision across the country, arguing that

'While the future cannot be predicted, societies can still make choices that shape their future. As such this is an antidote to the habit of distrust.'[8] Published on 9 February 2017, the vision provoked an explosion of cynicism. How could a few pieces of paper change the whole country? But one sentence captured the public imagination: 'In 2050, Slovenians are a happy people.'

Everywhere those words incited debate and discussion. What did they mean? What *should* they mean? What would make people happy – with their country, with each other, with themselves? Who was responsible for making it happen? Why wait until 2050? A national conversation drew in everyone and catalysed debates that drove the agenda of the next election. The new government's development strategy turned that agenda into action, identifying where, how and by whom action would be taken to move the country towards this goal of a better life for all. But the critical change, Flowers said, was when the scenario became more than a story: the government put a budget against it.[9]

Every scenario-planning exercise is different. At Shell, it's a well-oiled process, part of business as usual. In Slovenia, no one predicted that the vision would be so swiftly translated into policy. It wasn't just that scenario planning had elicited vivid, bold conversations where once stalemates had prevailed. The conversations had changed the way the country could think about itself.

That what started as a military framework and had morphed into a corporate tool could have such emotional and cultural power has been a discovery. Nowhere was this more profound than in South Africa, where Adam Kahane, a scenario planner working in Shell's London office, ran an exercise in 1991. With

Mandela out of prison and the ANC legalised, political transition was gaining momentum. But what direction would it take? What kind of transformation would it be? What would the future of the country look like? No one imagined it would be easy or susceptible to central control. Perhaps scenario planning would be a safe way to illuminate possibilities.[10]

Kahane recalls a popular joke at the time that defined two options: the practical option, in which everyone went down on their knees and prayed for angelic intervention, and the miraculous option, in which people learned to walk and work together. Asked what kind of team the project would need, Kahane specifically requested 'awkward sods', and got twenty-two current and potential leaders from across South Africa: black and white, left and right, from business, unions, academia, activism and politics. Kahane asked them not to bring predictions or advice but to explore only possibilities: what *could* happen.

Four scenarios emerged and, true to form, they were given descriptive titles: Ostrich, Lame Duck, Icarus and the Flight of the Flamingos. The connections between the scenarios illuminated key decisions the new government would face: whether to negotiate a settlement, how fast the transition needed to be and how sustainable the government's policies should be. Each scenario was written up at length, illustrated and distributed in all the national newspapers, reaching politicians, business people and NGOs around the country.

Did it make a difference? Kahane says that the discussions, between participants and then across the entire country, shifted what people thought was possible and what they believed was necessary. Complex and richly imagined, the scenarios discouraged binary thinking and forced people to face the real and immediate choices facing their new country.

Kahane and his firm, Reos Partners, have worked on over thirty national or regional strategic scenario projects, tackling issues such as education, healthcare, climate change and energy supply in Brazil, Canada, the US and Australia. Each exercise addressed problems that spanned multiple, complex organisations subject to external shocks beyond their control. All were ambiguous, riddled with internal contradictions. And so, as the epidemic of violence in Mexico raged, Kahane's process and experience looked like they might offer a way out of a seemingly intractable crisis.

'We had tried to do something like this before, in 2006, but our timing was wrong,' Rossanna Fuentes Berain recalls. By training, Berain is a journalist. She has the alertness of a bird, quickly turning to catch everything happening around her. Together with a business consultant, Julio Madrazo, they approached Kahane to see if his process could help Mexico. Without some methodology, they felt the current crisis would just continue. One of the first people Madrazo asked to join them was Alberto Fernández.

The working group (*grupo de travajo*) was spellbindingly diverse: an archbishop, police chiefs, members of the military and of organised crime groups, indigenous farmers, union leaders, politicians, household workers, bankers, doctors, academics, judges, civil and women's rights leaders, economists, state and national senators. The aim was not that the group be representative but that collectively members could see how different people experienced Mexico's problems from separate perspectives.

On 27 November 2015, fifty people gathered in Cuernavaca: close enough to Mexico City to be easy to reach, far enough away to avoid distraction. Emotions in the room ran high. Fear: at the coffee break, one participant thought he might have to leave because his family had received a death threat that he believed emanated from a group represented in the room. Curiosity: *I never in my wildest dreams imagined being in a room with these people, never mind having a meal with them, talking about our families!* Hope: *This is different, perhaps something different will come of it.* Relief: *My job is to oppose you in the media or the senate and I thought this would be a disaster but here we are talking to each other.*

Every participant got to know the entire group. Paired walks brought together those otherwise too wary of each other to talk: a gay person and an archbishop; a policeman and a criminal. But the hard work started with discussions of the present situation. Some believed that it was mediocre but manageable; others thought the country was heading for civil war. Coming to terms with the complex reality was painful as they all came to see was that there wasn't just one Mexico.

If you build a model of the world that excludes the people, ideas, forces you don't like or understand, of course your vision appears perfect to you. But nobody else inhabits that world or recognises it as true. Scenarios aim to capture ways of seeing the future that are recognisable to everyone. So they can't pay attention only to economics or only to politics; they can't exclude social cohesion or natural resources. Incorporating all of this tricky, unprogrammable soft data, of the kind so important to Pierre Wack, makes the work much richer – but harder. 'Making something binary seems simple but it is a way *not* to have a conversation,' the facilitator, Elizabeth Pinnington, explained. 'It's a form of bullying. Sure, you can say: "This person shouldn't be here, we have to annihilate drug traffickers", but that resolves nothing; it exacerbates the problem.'

By the end of the first weekend, the participants were tired. Almost everyone was glad they'd come and most experienced both disappointment and relief. The problems were harder than they'd thought – but they were developing a means of communicating. At the second meeting in February 2016, detailed work producing the scenarios began. The scenarios were entitled 'Mexico Posibles'. 'We started', Pinnington said, 'with the idea of possibilities: nobody is expert on what hasn't happened yet, so we aren't writing plans.' Once people got clear about the scenarios, Pinnington explained, there was always a very strong desire to improve them. Writing the scenarios, she and a team of editors worked hard, sometimes through the night, to incorporate all the ideas, caveats and refinements that participants insisted on. It looked like a gruelling process, working with so many who now felt themselves authors.

'The night of the initial edit,' Pinnington recalled, 'we started with fifteen scenarios and got it down to six drafts. When they saw the drafts, people were everywhere from interested to panicked: this isn't right, this isn't sharable! They were learning how to participate. Our editors would propose questions for the next draft: here are some options, what do you think is the most realistic? We did eight rounds of that. It's slow but it gives people the opportunity to say what they're thinking and to come to terms with what other people are thinking.'

By now, everyone knew each other quite well and a desire not to let each other down kept them going. But so too did Kahane's well-honed methodology. Everyone could speak, but no one for more than one minute. When the bell rang, they had to stop. An archbishop got the same amount of time as an indigenous woman; the labourer was as readily heard as a senator. It can be shocking, Kahane told me, when a household worker and a senator are treated equally, but it makes the process feel democratic and fair. Everyone is more willing to listen and the work doesn't get bogged down.

But as the scenarios were crafted, the world outside was changing and the organising group felt some innovation was required. 'After Brexit and Trump,' Julio Madrazo recalled, 'some of the scenarios were irrelevant because reality had already moved beyond them.' A fresh, second generation of participants joined the initial group. Where the first generation was composed largely of senior leaders working on a national level, the second were younger and had a more regional focus, working at city and state level.

On 24 February 2018, the two generations came together for the final session in Puebla, an ancient colourful city in the centre of Mexico. Meeting in a former convent, now a hotel, the atmosphere was one of a family reunion: warmth, excitement, anticipation. A playful check-in divided the large group – they numbered seventy now – into different configurations: by state, by favourite music groups, by numbers of siblings. Each sibling group had to describe the unique advantage of its family size. Those who were one of two siblings said it conferred balance; those with three said it prohibited exclusivity; five said it brought diversity; those with seven or more felt their families had taught them solidarity, democracy and self-defence. This was a fun exercise with a serious point: in any group, however diverse, people always have something in common.

The scenarios had been whittled down to three: 'A Hostile Mexico', 'A Paralyzed Mexico' and 'A Responsible Mexico'. But now the second generation wanted to introduce a new one, 'A Failed Mexico', that described the country fractured by guerrillas, gangs and paramilitaries. Huge, orderly debate ensued. Might organised crime and far-right or far-left extremists make common cause? Was inertia really the country's greatest enemy or did greater threats lurk outside the country? Nothing in this discussion felt theoretical; personal experiences in the group made each detail real. The fourth scenario was accepted and joined the rest for more editing, re-editing, polishing.

On 21March 2018, Mexico Posibles presented their four scenarios, on paper and as short videos, at the Palace of Mines in Mexico City. José Woldenberg, the first president of the country's Federal Electoral Institute, opened the event, saying: 'The future is built from today . . . there is no law of history that condemns us to be better or worse in 2030. These options are possible and their nuances and folds are infinite.'

A history of the project preceded a brief explanation of the process, defining a scenario as 'a history of what can happen'. Many participants strove to describe how the process had changed them. An indigenous woman, Tukarima Carrillo, told of her amazement at being listened to and taken seriously. 'Today I do not feel alone,' she said. 'You solve social problems with social processes.' Others spoke of their initial scepticism, losing their prejudices, the need for reconciliation. Many spoke about victims of violence, about migrants trying to make a future for their families. Everyone referenced a powerful network of trust. And Alberto Fernández spoke of his own initial ignorance: 'Businessmen do not know what the big problems in Mexico are. The vision of the problems that I had of this country was wrong. I learned that it is no use trying to implement solutions if you do not know with total depth and certainty the problems we have in this country . . . Only when we learn to break and create bonds, only when we pay attention to the differences between us, but realise that the same blood runs in the veins of all Mexicans, only when Mexico works the way that Mexico Posibles worked – to feel what others feel – can you start to understand what is happening in other parts of the country. And when we can work like that, no one can stop us finding the solutions to our beloved mother country.'

The speech was a startling confession of how little Fernández felt he had understood of the country he loved. Shocked by the limitations of his very curious mind, he emerged from the experience with a hugely enhanced sense of the complexity of the problems Mexico faced, but also with a deeper appreciation of the human talent that it contained. The weekends rife with conflict, with irreconcilable perspectives, had given Fernández new pictures of where he was and where he and the country might go. It was, he said, a life-changing experience.

Months later, when I talked to participants, everyone recalled one session when they'd gathered after dinner with a glass of wine in an old, round room, sitting in concentric circles, talking as night fell. Each was asked to tell a personal story. No arguments, no opinions or theories: only unvarnished personal experience for one minute. More than anything else, it was these raw testimonies that had changed people. 'These stories were so powerful and new to me,' Fernández remembers. 'I was sitting next to Rosina and she told a story about when she was twelve and living in Oaxaca and her father told her she had to get married. She said no, she wanted to study. Her dad said no, so she stopped eating. Her father said: if you are so strong, you can leave. So she left. She took the first bus in her life and went to the next village. Years later, she came back to run as mayor! They didn't elect her, because she was a woman, so she said, okay, I will change the laws. And now, 400 indigenous women are being elected in Mexican communities! And that created a feeling of admiration for the group and it broke all the walls of differences.'

Other participants understood for the first time why some had chosen organised crime as a direction, but they also appreciated how it felt to be a military commander totally outnumbered by organised criminals. A policeman struck up a tight relationship with a terrorist who'd thrown three bombs. He could see now, he said, that they each wanted a better Mexico. What emerged from the exercise were deeply adaptive minds.

The general election that followed in 2018 was one of the most violent in Mexico's history – over a hundred political figures were killed. The result was dramatic: all the established political parties were trounced by a left-wing populist, Andrés Manuel López Obrador, who won the first outright majority since 1988. 'At first, I was scared of the new government, but it was probably what we deserved,' Fernández reflected. 'But then we met with them and we realised: we are non-partisan, we are not self-interested, we don't have any party alignment and we are everybody in Mexico. And so we went to the government and said: How can we help? Where do you want us to work? It was really good. They told us one area where they needed our help was primary and secondary education. So it's great because we have another project! We are going to bring people from the best universities, from rural schools and all this diversity across the whole system so we can work together. Not just so the children have better Spanish and math but to transform the lives of kids and give empowerment to the communities themselves. We are not a political party – so we can be very open and work with everyone.'

***

Scenario planning originated with the recognition that much in the world is too complex to be predictable and that the future is too malleable to be revealed by hard data alone. Absolutely accurate forecasting is feasible, but only where everything is known and predetermined – and nowhere is that true. General Carter dismisses such forecasting, not on ideological grounds but on pragmatic ones: if he imagines the world is fully determined, he says he 'won't be successful'. Instead, scenarios illuminate the contingencies, contradictions and trade-offs of the real world, where no one interest or single perspective is in control. That's why they produce conflict but also epiphanies.

Scenario-planning exercises demand that we acknowledge that we all inhabit complex systems, only parts of which we can see or influence. They force individuals and organisations

out of their narcissism to confront how much of their success depends on others. This can illuminate opportunities or
trade-offs but it also engenders humility. Bringing together the
powerful and the powerless forces helps both to accept that,
while each may have hopes and visions for the future, neither
fully knows how to achieve them. These exercises also reveal
that every scenario incurs costs: the recognition that win/win
is usually a lie and that progress typically demands adaptation
and sacrifice. That's when they become uncomfortable again.

Scenario planning changes the people who do it. Seeing
ideas, people, trends and the immense non-linearity of life is
chastening. It's difficult, accepting the complexity of the world
and the ambiguity of personal experience. It's even harder to
learn how to participate. But one way to address social processes is *with* a social process, one that enhances alertness,
sensitivity and imagination. Most participants treasure the
experience – eventually. They do so when they come to see
how opposites can be reconciled and how positive change
emerges only when they are. No longer alone or intimidated
by the fear of conflict, making the future starts to feel viable,
practical and real.

But perhaps the most potent way in which scenario planning
changes people is by shifting their sense of time. In Cuernavaca
and in Puebla, the future – 2030 – seemed close and personal.
It was no longer an abstract idea, not someone else's problem.
It stared everyone in the face and it didn't feel a decade away;
it felt like tomorrow. The Mexico Posibles scenarios end: 'The
future is not . . . written. We have no time to waste.'

CHAPTER SIX

LIVING THE QUESTIONS

> The only true voyage would be not to visit strange lands, but
> to possess other eyes.
>
> — MARCEL PROUST, *The Captive*

A London theatre, packed. On stage, characters explore a
past that is murky, uncertain, infused with corruption. They
struggle with a present that is impoverished and dangerous,
where no one can imagine a future not mired in lies and fantasy. The central image of the play – a wild duck that has been
wounded but rescued – lives in the attic, alive but trapped.
Each character is full of contradictions, every sentence
bristles with ambiguity. And yet the play grabs attention.
When the trap in the plot is sprung, the audience gasps,
seeing for the first time how tortuous these relationships have
always been. When the play is over, they erupt in cheers.

After the performance, many stay behind for a discussion
with the cast. The questions are electric: how uncomfortable
is it to play these roles; how different is each performance; is
it about Trump or Brexit; how do you decide which version
of the truth to act? Most in the audience have come new

to the work; few know anything of its history or author. At the end of the evening, walking from the theatre to the Underground, a group of friends continue their fierce debate as one sighs: 'I need to go to sleep but my brain in whizzing.'

How is it that Ibsen's play *The Wild Duck*, written in Italy 135 years ago by a fussy, middle-aged Norwegian man, holds this cosmopolitan audience rapt? On publication, readers condemned it as nauseating, bizarre, archaic and empty, its characters as total idiots, morally dead, morose and tired; today it is considered a masterpiece, one of the many Ibsen plays performed every week around the world that cement his place as the creator of modern theatre.[1] Artists are frequently ahead – that's what avant-garde means – but what makes that possible? How does art stay relevant in times and circumstances well beyond any future its makers could have imagined? What is it about the way that artists live and work that puts them in touch with ideas and themes that last so long?

What lasts is, to some degree, random or accidental. We don't know whether ancient Greece had greater playwrights than Aeschylus, Sophocles, Aristophanes and Euripides, only that they are the ones whose work has been discovered. You need only look at ads for wildly hyped but now forgotten authors in the back of old books to see how ephemeral art can be. But all generations go back to art, discovering or redis-covering sources of meaning and insight that their makers could never have planned. There's no evidence that artists contemplate 'future proofing' – artists don't see the future as something to manipulate or guard against – yet we look to them for insight, perspective, ways to understand our own times that they themselves did not know. And, in work made

177

decades, centuries, millennia ago, we find what we're looking for. Unforeseen, unforeseeable: what do artists do that makes their work endure?

If artists have the capacity to make work that defies time, it is because instead of trying to force-fit a predetermined idea of the future, they have learned to live productively with ambiguity, to see it as a rich source of discovery and exploration. Instead of trying to reduce complexity, they mine it, undaunted by contradictions and paradoxes. Working in the interstices of uncertainty is how they forge their identity, making future works and worlds that they can't see before they get there – and which they may only dimly understand on arrival. They are propelled by a strong sense of agency, knowing that their work won't exist if they don't make it. As such, they are the opposite of the hapless executives too terrified by future scenarios to think for themselves. In this, they have much to teach us about how we can address the future with imagination and independence.

In the pursuit of industrial innovation, it's become fashionable to try to define recipes or algorithms for creative success, or to derive from neuroscience the cerebral patterns that generate imaginative work. This implies that we (or machines) can all be Bob Dylan, Picasso or Beethoven. That strikes me as both statistically implausible and crass, as one of the deep rewards of art lies in it *not* being formulaic. Generalisations about art always fail at some point because there are no rules that always work and no rules that are never broken. It is personal, human and unique. Nevertheless, artists do have routines, ways of sensing and making sense. But if experiments and scenarios offer ways of working into the unknown, artists illustrate ways of being that more tactical approaches to life miss. We may not all be artists, but we can learn from their habits.

NOTICE

Ibsen was a prodigious noticer: remembering guests who had shared his hotel years before, noting their reading habits, wondering whether a young man's light appetite might indicate disease, worrying about another guest's expensive habits. Nothing, it seems, was too small for his attention, not clothes, food, weather or syntax: he noted that the way people spoke changed as the day wore on, that men and women end sentences differently. His acute social awareness scanned the horizon for silent flares of anger or injury. He was an inveterate earwigger, overhearing and reporting other people's conversations. In the two decades he lived in Germany and Italy, his visitors always commented on how up to date he seemed. A tremendous gossip, he received Norwegian newspapers wherever he lived so that he could follow the ups and downs of friends and enemies. To write, Ibsen said, was to see.

In this, Ibsen is like most artists: febrile, alert, receptive, with a mind like a streetsweeper. The literary historian James Shapiro says this is true of Shakespeare: how acute his observation, how aware of the vast importance of trifles. Many artists are super-sensors, their humility manifest in their alertness to the small and unimportant. Colm Tóibín writes of Proust that he is always 'noticing, registering, sifting evidence and studying what lay on the surface, seeing what people wished to reveal of themselves when they appeared in the social world . . . He was intrigued by what was visible in a single moment in a room, at a gathering, how many generalisations he could make from a single glimpse or glance or change in the social air. He was concerned with manners as a painter might be interested in shade or contrast, as a composer might be interested in melody.' Noticing for artists is a habit of mind.

The visual artist Katie Paterson says that she is always tuning in to something – but without obvious intent. 'Nature, always. Telescopes. Observatories. Zen temples. Libraries. Swimming pools. Water. Universities. Iceland. Japan,' Paterson laughs, recognising that the list could go on. Much of what Paterson tunes into is sensual; physical texture, smell, light and sound are, for her, as full of meaning as data and news. *Hollow*, a sculpture completed in 2016, brings together over 10,000 tree species from the oldest tree in the world to the youngest – standing inside of it is to experience the feel and smell of time. Paterson's work starts with detail. 'It needs', she says, 'to be accurate to be imagined.' That requires intense attention – not being too busy to notice, not walking down the street staring at a phone.

Similarly, when he isn't in the midst of production, the filmmaker Mike Leigh needs to give his mind free range: 'Every time we finish a film, the gang always says: where's the next one? They want to do it! But it's so important to have time to do nothing. I don't mean nothing of course, that's just what it looks like. I read all the time. I look at pictures. I like being alone. You need time alone just to sense: what's going on, where are we right now? Nothing happening *is* something happening.'

Margaret Atwood describes a similar process behind the genesis of *The Handmaid's Tale*: a steady collecting of

clippings, each real, all gradually coalescing
of rigidly enforced misogyny that wasn't a fi
future but obvious to her around the world, once
to notice.[2]

These descriptions are strangely reminiscent of   anor
Maguire talking about the brains of her London cab drivers:
individuals stocking their minds and memories with rich,
random observations, the raw ingredients for later composi-
tions. But there is little didactic about this process; it seems
to be constant, diffused and undirected – scanning, noting,
collecting. Heads up, eyes, ears, minds open. This includes
reading that, at its deepest level, is experienced as life itself.
Virginia Woolf described reading as 'absorbing at every pore'
and her mind is saturated with it; it is, she writes, an addiction – but not an opiate. Almost the opposite, in fact. For
musicians, natural sounds seem to provide the same effect;
Messiaen in particular was a great collector of birdsong, but
natural and found sound has been a basis for music for as long
as it has been written.

This mind wandering is without intention or plan. But, con-
sciously or unconsciously, artists are incapable of not doing it.
It is why Dickens prowled city streets at night, Ibsen took long
daily walks and Virginia Woolf set out across London. They all
sought to absorb the minute details that others might ignore or
overlook but that artists collect. Where there is intention, it is
inchoate: there is, as yet, no plan. Instead, this way of being is
drawn to the unfamiliar, anomalous, ambiguous. This is not
a quest for confirmation or certainty. A form of imaginative
immersion, its purpose is undefined – and much that enters
this collection of raw material may never emerge. So it looks

inefficient, even wasteful, collecting observations that might never be used, which could simply trigger questions or provoke a train of thought.

At the age of ninety-three, the theatre director Peter Brook recalled an experience that has stayed with him since he was a young man, travelling in Afghanistan: 'I saw a man sitting in front of a prison. The situation he was in will never leave me. He was just sitting and looking at the prison. He offered to share some of his food with me but I didn't have the courage to take it so I said no. Now it seems a shame, not sharing. At the time I didn't know why he said that or who he was. I just had endless questions . . .'

The experience stayed with Brook, latent for over fifty years, available until needed. If needed. For anyone craving certainty or wedded to plans, this way of living is excruciating. There are no measurable goals, no reassuring benchmarks of progress. This way of life is not for the Pavlovian dog but for the independent cat: attentive and meandering.[3] Experienced artists learn over time to trust that something of value will emerge; their apprenticeship entails not just the acquisition of skills but of patience. It requires what the poet Patrick Kavanagh called 'the right kind of sensitive courage and the right kind of sensitive humility': the nerve to explore beyond predictable pattern recognition and to interrogate what isn't immediately obvious, important or inviting. To find anything original requires respecting the elusive. Where this occurs doesn't matter – as much richness might be found in a gas station as a grand museum.

Kavanagh also drew a telling distinction between two opposites: the provincial and the parochial artist. The provincial, he argued, 'Has no mind of his own; he does not trust what his eyes see until he has heard what the metropolis – towards which his eyes are turned – has to say on any subject.' So the provincial craves patterns, cares about fashion, longs to be on point. His mind is so full of preconceptions, editing and ranking as he goes that it is almost closed. He longs for predictions, signposts and pathways, not daring to explore alone. For Kavanagh, the provincial's is not the mind of an artist, because it is crammed with prescribed agendas.

The parochial mind, however, digs deep and keeps digging, confident that the parish is universal. It is here that timelessness might be found. Elena Ferrante's portrait of female friendship over a lifetime is a classic piece of parochial perspective, tracing in the dirty, poor streets of Naples the tensions of friendship and rivalry that transcend time and place. Richard Linklater's film *Boyhood*, twelve years in the making, knits together moments of growth and failure familiar to all families. James Baldwin's novels and plays speak as directly today to the excluded, overlooked and undervalued as they did to African Americans caught in the rage and heartbreak of the civil rights movement.

SIMMER

The great American documentary filmmaker Frederick Wiseman believes in daydreaming, which he described as paying 'as much attention to peripheral thoughts at the edge of my mind as to any formally logical approaches to the material. My associations are often as valuable as my attempts at deductive logic.'[4] Because explanation is not their game, ambiguity is productive for artists – though it takes courage and stamina to endure it. Unlike expedient work, imagination doesn't move directly from observation to action but from noticing to gestation. What do particular images, stories, observations mean? What are they saying? Mulling over the accumulated impressions and sensations internalises memories, turns them into source material, available for interpretation. A French contemporary described Ibsen as having two eyes – one reserved for observation, the other for reflection – and both his letters and play drafts reveal him toggling between the petty and the meaningful, the detail and the story. His daughter-in-law recalled how, when she brought him town gossip, 'One always had to tell him a story twice. First he listened, the second time he always asked very searchingly for details.'[5]

Of all these accumulated sensations, which ones matter? Artists must decide what to work on. The choice of subject comes with no guarantees but must override all other options. Many say that, while they accumulate a plethora of thoughts and impressions, only a few demand attention – but how and why isn't immediately obvious. After his encounter near the prison in Afghanistan, Peter Brook spent half a century doing other work; his productions of Shakespeare and Beckett and the revolutionary devising of *The Mahabharata* established his reputation as the most admired theatre maker in the world. The memory of the prisoner didn't leave him, he said, it just wouldn't come to the boil.

Artists use any number of words to describe the process between collection and making: gestation, filtering, perco- lating, simmering, mulling, distilling, digesting, waiting. No one I've ever talked to or worked with can explain how or why clarity emerges; they simply trust that it will. In practical terms, this means that artists wait for meaning to emerge. 'Be patient towards all that is unresolved in your heart,' Rilke wrote, advising a young poet, 'and try to love *the questions themselves* like locked rooms, like books written in a foreign tongue . . . *Live* the questions for now. Perhaps then you will gradually, without noticing it, live your way into the answer . . . this is what you must work on however you can and not waste too much time and too much energy on clarifying your attitude to other people.'[6]

There's an echo here of the CERN scientists who glean over time where physics might be going next. But where they collect and review data, artists use themselves and their lives as the colliders – the place where collisions occur, where signals can be traced and interpreted. What propels the work are questions that reverberate incessantly: what do these images, words, signals mean to me? Why won't this idea leave me alone? With no specific end in mind, the answers are undetermined and unpredictable. For most artists, the decision of what to work on remains unconscious and personal. 'I know the premise will come,' Mike Leigh told me. 'It'll come from my own preoccupations . . . eventually! I'm old enough to remember before 1967, the Abortion Act, when people had unwanted pregnancies, though I was never responsible for one myself. I just remember that. And for about forty years, I had this notion of making a film about that. And eventually I did, in *Vera Drake,* but not till 2004. But why then, not earlier, not later? I don't know. I don't really care!'

'It is always an interesting question, which to work on,' Katie Paterson said. 'I have a massive editing process going on, with all these ideas going on all these years. In a lot of my works now there is a practical element involved – I have to consider what is physically possible. But otherwise, it's just quite instinctive.'

Although his works hang in the Rijksmuseum, MOMA and the Tate, the artist Norman Ackroyd doesn't consider the ultimate destination of a work when he starts on it. Widely recognised as one of Britain's foremost landscape artists, his subjects emerged as he found himself drawn to the northern-most coast of Scotland. Patterns in an artist's work might be discernible looking back, but in the moment few claim any kind of foresight. Ackroyd explains: 'I've never had any grand plan, I just wanted to see those outliers – this little group of islands sitting off the edge of Europe that sits on the end of Asia and then you've got 3,000 miles of ocean before you come to America. So it really is the edge of everything. I want to try to squeeze the essence out of it.'

Observations, details, themes, experience coalesce into a starting point that uses, but is not, the artist's life. For the novelist and playwright Sebastian Barry, a few facts may be enough to triangulate a starting point. *The Secret Scriptures* started with an aunt who had been a piano player in an uncle's band and who was sectioned. His son's coming out and an uncle in the American Civil War initiated *Days Without End*. These are starting points, where the work begins to define itself inside and outside the artist. But at any moment the story could change. The crucial quality of a starting point is how much else it opens up. 'It's not like a diary, it's more like a system of thought,' Tracey Emin explained. 'How I work and how I think about life and how I think about things. I might be thinking: is sex to do with love? Is this a connection or is it not, is it completely separate? Is it lustful? Is it void of love? Is pure love nothing to do with sex? . . . I have to trust myself.'

Such questions may reverberate for years, with no guarantee that anything meaningful will emerge. Only the concatenation of other life experiences prompting further questions drove Peter Brook finally to create *The Prisoner*, his play in which a man is condemned to sit staring at a prison. This period of gestation defies planning and forecasting because its sole function is to sift through observation and experiences in search of new meaning. Waiting for that to emerge isn't for the faint-hearted. Looking and feeling unproductive, this period of time demands self-reliance, optimism and the courage to wait. That makes the working life of an artist unpredictable and precarious. But the capacity to tolerate uncertainty equips artists (and might equip us) better to function in a world that is unpredictable and precarious too, as to be an artist also requires finding the impetus to keep moving. The way to understand all those observations is to make something of them. For the work to take on a life of its own, the ideas and experiences that give rise to it have to move from the artist's mind to the canvas, the etching plate, the score, the workshop or the page.

STATE

Artists start without waiting to be asked. They have to begin. Where experimenters may carefully calculate need, passion and resources, artists supply all three themselves. The need and passion are internally generated. The resources are time and ideas, but time is not infinite. So choosing one subject means abandoning the rest, with no evidence to guarantee that the choice is right. The only way to find out is to start. Almost every artist describes their way of working as a curious combination of invention, which is conscious, and discovery, which is not.

This process of unfolding can be seen when the printmaker Norman Ackroyd produces the first state of a new aquatint. What is, for many artists, invisible work is made visible in the documentary series *What Do Artists Do All Day?*[7] For all that this is 'a big production day' and despite his decades of experience, to Ackroyd, the process remains uncertain and unpredictable. He isn't quite sure what will emerge.

Ackroyd's etching of Muckle Flugga, a small rocky island north of Uist, aims at something abstract. The great things of art, he says, 'are the human figure and the landscape it lives in. I am just trying to get a resonance of humanity.' But he can't see exactly what he is making. Because etching requires engraving with acid on copper in reverse, the plate shows a mirror image of what will become the final image. Years of experience and technical expertise mean he's not working in the dark – but neither can he be sure just what the image will look like: 'There's a huge desire to make the marks; that is the heart. I let the eye look at it and the hand do what the eye and heart wants and I just respond to it, because I feel I want to do it, so it's very instinctive.'

As he handles the copper plate, it's impossible for the amateur eye to discern a defined image. To give the picture tone, Ackroyd grinds pine resin to a fine powder that falls onto the copper plate, randomly like snow. He then heats the plate so that the resin melts into it. At any moment, the image could still change. He takes breaks, careful not to overwork the image. Etching with acid is, he says, a high-wire act, because he can't go back. In common with many artists, Ackroyd doesn't quite know when the work is finished. Every step along the way is a choice: does the piece still earn attention, or would he do better to move on to another print?

By the time he puts the plate into the press, Ackroyd has a feel for the piece, but he still can't be confident of the result. Every stroke, every drop of acid, each fleck of resin is a decision, but what all of those choices add up to remains to be seen. When the print emerges, it is a strong image, simple and pure. Ackroyd appraises the work so far: 'That's a good start, a few little things need adjusting. As a first state, that'll do.'

It has taken days to make this first state of the print and months more to think about it. But Ackroyd's routine – doing, thinking, reflecting, doing some more, assessing – is much like a musician composing, an author or poet writing: moving in and out of focus, trying to get a feel for something that doesn't exist yet. Sebastian Barry once described how he spent nine months writing a long, dark opening for *Days Without End* only to wake up one morning and throw out all but a page and a half, at which point he didn't know if he had a book or not. Only when he found a new first sentence – 'The method of laying out a corpse in Missouri sure took the proverbial cake' – did he begin to discover what would be a new style. Afterwards, he could not remember writing the sentence and, to this day, still now faces the fear in his writing that the next word won't come.

Getting started doesn't determine the ending; much still remains open and contingent, a matter of both invention and discovery. That means the work can continue to evolve and adapt over time – but it also means that at no point is the work without worry. So it takes stamina. America's great documentary maker Frederick Wiseman acknowledges that there is always anxiety 'that it's not going to work, a fear of failure. But that anxiety is a motor to get it done.' Tracey Emin talks about being intimidated by canvases, her need sometimes to draw as a kind of warm-up to overcoming her trepidation. Some of Emin's paintings sit for years, she says, waiting to be finished or developed – or changed completely: 'Hurt Heart was a great painting, with two small figures holding each other and it was really really sweet. And I thought: I can't live with that. And then I painted over it. And I was going to write Heart over the top, but I spelt it wrong and put the U and then I just wrote "Hurt" and I crossed it out and then I put "Heart". I didn't expect to be making that painting . . .'[8]

'With every single project,' Katie Paterson told me, 'there is always a point where I think: what's going on? It is never going to work. It's usually a bad sign if I *don't* have that moment.' Lack of certainty is uncomfortable, but it doesn't paralyse her. 'If it seems possible here on earth, I will go for it, keep going for it. I've never been daunted by ideas not being possible. So far, I've never had to totally give up . . .'

Paterson's latest project, *Future Library*, is defined by uncertainty over time. In 2014, in the Nordmarka forest outside Oslo, she planted a thousand trees that will produce paper to print a book in 2114. Once a year, for a hundred years, authors will submit manuscripts commissioned for the book. These can be stories, poems, a novel, a sentence, but no one but the author can read them until, nearly a hundred years from now, the complete book is published. Even Paterson does not read them. The first author to take part was Margaret Atwood, in 2015 novelist David Mitchell, in 2016 the Icelandic poet Sjón, in 2017 the Turkish novelist Elif Shafak, in 2018 the South Korean novelist Han Kang.[9] The idea came to Paterson, she said, when she found herself drawing tree rings that she associated with chapters in a book. She felt certain that this was one of her many ideas that would never come to fruition – but she was wrong. 'The project is very much about ideas and imagination,' she said, 'but they're physically expressed: in the room where the manuscripts wait, in the manuscripts themselves, in the trees which will make the paper. When I started, I didn't even know if writers would be up for it. It is so meaningful for me because it just keeps evolving, as a continuation of our lives into other people's lives . . .'

Paterson doesn't allow herself to read any of the manuscripts; the only people to know the contents is the author. Just as in Ackroyd's printmaking, there is much in this work that remains deliberately unknown, to be discovered not determined. Paterson can't be sure the work will be kept going for the full hundred years. In setting a timetable for the project that goes beyond her own lifetime, she embraces uncertainty on every front, never knowing whether its sponsors will abandon it, or if authors will continue to be entranced by the invitation. She cannot know who the people are who will read the final book or what they will make of it. But it is the unknowability of the whole project that makes people love it. Such work cannot derive from second-guessing, by trying to resolve ambiguities or nail down the future. It can only be imaginative, provisional and fragmentary, on the part of Paterson, her authors and all those who flock, once a year, to watch a new, mysterious ritual as the manuscripts are handed over.

A good project, Paterson says, is one that keeps evolving. The more you explore, the more you find, so you have to keep alert to what you might not expect. The reason that artists so prize openness and are attracted by ambiguity is that not solving problems ahead of time keeps the work alive, capable of adaptation and variation – and it makes the work itself live. For Mike Leigh, the starting point for *Vera Drake* was the forty-year-old memory of the Abortion Act. That made him consider the kinds of people who performed illegal abortions, which led to the creation of the character Vera Drake by the actor Imelda Staunton.

Famously, Mike Leigh begins filming without a script. 'We never rehearse the details, just the premise,' Leigh explained. 'We improvise on location.' Leigh's shooting 'script' is a list of scenes that identifies only the practical details that the crew needs. No one knows how each scene ends. When Vera Drake is arrested, the actors playing her family members did not expect this would happen and they didn't know what she was being arrested for. This is Kavanagh's 'sensitive humility' at work: daring not to assume knowledge but letting implications play out. Not rehearsing a scripted scene, Leigh believes, gains in raw truthfulness what it might lose in perfectibility. 'We discovered what happened next by being there and watching what happened. You arrive and the end presents itself. All sorts of forces, practical and spiritual and thematic and psychological and emotional, objective and subjective, bear on events, but how – well, you have to be there to find out.'

Working this way isn't easy, particularly for actors. Not knowing for long periods of time what will happen to their character, how important (or not) they will be to the final film, is precarious for those who are already pursuing an insecure career. What's rewarding, for them and for us, is that what happens feels so real because it grows out of detailed knowledge of the characters they have created. It's through the detail, Leigh says, that you hit bedrock: 'The stuff that's real and that is always there, if you keep looking. That is the stuff that lasts.'

Of course, not all filmmakers or directors work this way. But most hope for something unforeseen and often unexpected in the moment – in rehearsal or when shooting – that brings the work to life. Instead of denying ambiguity, artists illuminate and explore it. When they are successful, the work creates a context in which we dare to experience some of the complexity and ambiguity of our own lives.

When Ibsen wrote, he used what his biographer, Michael Meyer, calls 'double-density dialogue': a language at once ordinary but oozing ambivalence and subtext that gets under the skin of his audience. At the time, this language was entirely new: the idea that what characters said might not be true was revolutionary. It infuriated his critics, who insisted life wasn't like that, but his plays endured because it is. Ibsen understood that there is no freedom – not for him, not for us – without uncertainty. So he created stories and a language that threw his audience off-balance, unsure how far they're responding to the play and how far they are discovering something in themselves. Investing his characters with our own beliefs and fears, private associations and public parallels, he made us a living part of the action.

Similarly, in his editing of T. S. Eliot's *The Waste Land*, Ezra Pound insisted that much of the bridging, explanatory material be removed. (It became so short, in fact, that Eliot added notes to fill out the book.)[10] On one level, this made the poem hard to understand because readers had to work to create the connective tissue themselves. But across the decades, it meant that the poem became theirs, enhanced and evoked by the associations readers bring to it. Explain less, mean more. That way, the makers and recipients of art become what Toni Morrison called 'co-conspirators'.[11] Being true to a single moment is how to stay true to all moments. It keeps the work alive.

Even the most solitary of artists, therefore, work with others: their readers, viewers, listeners. Most accept that they can't control the response provoked by their work; that's where humility comes in – again. Much is a matter of trial and error – or, you could say, experiments. Because trial and error is how children learn, and because it often looks like play, this way of working and being is also frequently misinterpreted as infantile. No rules (unless self-generated), no hard targets, no concrete goals: it doesn't look like work as it's commonly understood. But artists are among the toughest, and most tough-minded people I've ever worked with. Katie Paterson, negotiating the colour gradients in the 4,400 pieces of wood that make up her architectural sculpture *Hollow*, said she tried *not* to become an artist, because she knew how hard the work and the life would be. There is a paradox here: that wildly imaginative work requires tough mastery of discipline and detail.

'Once we got going,' Peter Brook explained, '*The Prisoner* took a year and a half to develop. We started simply by just enjoying every sort of idea. Try. Try . . . At the end of the day, you think: *We've really got somewhere now.* Then the next morning, you go through it and think: *What a lot of shit.* And start again. The only process is trial and error. If you can't recognise the error, you're in trouble. All the time, you're in doubt. If you go home thinking it's in the bag, you're in trouble.'

After a performance of the play, when Brook was asked at what point the script had been nailed down, cast member Donald Sumpter jumped in with the answer: 'Yesterday.'

FAIL

On completing *Days Without End*, the novelist Sebastian Barry concluded that the book would sell so poorly that he would need to write another one fast. In fact, it made him the first author ever to win the Costa prize twice. Artists are often poor judges of their own work, if only because what might be said to succeed in art depends not on the work alone, but how it lives and breathes in the world.

In our data-obsessed age, pseudo-scientific attempts have been made to measure the success of art, largely according to how often works are read, viewed, performed or sold. This is nonsense, of course. Shakespeare was not the most popular of his contemporaries,[12] and, judged by this heuristic, for 200 years *King Lear* would have been pronounced an abject failure, because it was regarded as too dark and difficult to perform; today it seems the most modern of Shakespeare's work. For nearly a hundred years, little serious attention was paid to the nineteenth-century poet John Clare; his working-class origins and prolonged periods of mental illness accorded poorly with

Victorian ideals of poetry. Yet in the middle of the twentieth century, his voice, his story, even his lack of punctuation suddenly appeared modern. The times had risen to meet Clare. His work, as W. H. Auden wrote, had been 'modified in the guts of the living', just as today a whole new generation of readers and artists is rediscovering James Baldwin, an artist who, by the 1980s, felt himself to be overlooked and under-rated. This gave him no pleasure, but neither did he accept it as the final judgement. He knew that the times rise, and fall, to meet or leave artists.[13]

Appreciating the complexity of the environment in which their art operates means that artists know that they can't hope to control the reception to their work, that they can neither predict nor force the future. The recognition that so much work fails is painful, but accepting it gives them freedom. For many, the disappointment of a finished work merely points the way to how it should be done next time.

Only after finishing his first film, *It's Impossible to Learn to Plow by Reading Books*, did Richard Linklater say he knew how to make the next one. The playwright Peter Barnes told me that when two huge plays – *The Bewitched* and *Laughter!* – were greeted with damning rejection, he knew he had to start again, to reconstruct his craft from scratch. He started with monologues, then dialogues, then trios: a conscious act of renaissance. Like so many, he recognised that the best he could hope for was better, not best, never perfect. 'A perfect poem is impossible,' Robert Graves wrote. 'Once it had been written, the world would end.'

Better is the chance to change. The future isn't something to be nailed down, defined and programmed. The only way to influence it is to keep noticing. While an efficient mindset prizes predictability and continuity, an artist's passion for exploration develops the capacity for change.

For years now, we've been encouraged to develop 'brand you', to adopt, as businesses or individuals, an unwavering, fixed positioning that everyone can recognise and rely on. For artists, brands are toxic, suppressing the lively evolution that keeps them, and their work, growing. Peter Brook says that, just a few weeks into rehearsal, a director isn't the same person; the work reveals and develops them. That is what the work is for.

Artists often change before they have to. Fans and followers frequently deplore these moments of evolution, when musicians adopt or abjure new technology, when painters change media, when writers shift style or genre. Ibsen was forever frustrating his champions by his furious refusal to be tied down by their definition of him. Picasso's shifts in style baffled critics. Fans of Schoenberg's gorgeous classicism were dismayed and disgusted by his adoption of the twelve-tone scale. Even James Joyce's staunchest supporters balked before diving into *Finnegans Wake*. Many Miles Davis fans never forgave his electric years. It took decades before Bob Dylan's fans got used to the idea that change was the point, that the developing self was Dylan's subject.

'Ninety per cent of me has changed,' Tracey Emin says. 'I want to see new things. There's no point looking over your shoulder to see who's coming up behind you; you should just enjoy the run, be with it and do it in your own way.'

Minds digging deep can't predict or promise where they need to go next. They pursue no agenda, except perhaps the need to be free. 'If you stand outside any position,' Patrick Kavanagh wrote, 'you aren't at its mercy.' That is the benefit of doubt. It is why authoritarian regimes fear artists and why their citizens look to artists to be truthtellers: because they don't simplify but clarify. Search Shakespeare as closely as you like, you will find no ideology, no programme. Artists with staying power know that art isn't about finding answers, defining solutions; it's about better questions.

Beckett, often asked to explain what had happened in his plays, said he didn't know. No Ibsen play ever really ends; it leaves the theatre in the heads of the audience. Writing of Joyce and Chekhov, Virginia Woolf observed that their work leaves questions 'to sound on and on after the story is ended', flooding us 'with a view of infinite possibilities'. Drawing conclusions, Chekhov wrote, is up to the jury, not the artist. Art lasts not because it nails down human experience, but because it refuses to do so.

**

Mind wandering. Diffuse but intense attention. Travel without an agenda. Non-linear. Undetermined. Unplanned. Open to reflection, accident and discovery. Inefficient. Inconsistent. In all of this, artists live and think in ways that are opposite to the linear, cause-and-effect, rational assumptions and efficient goals that underpin much of modern life and institutions. Instead, artists respond to the complex system that is life with the complex system that is the human mind.

The capacity to pay attention, make sense, act and change ahead of the curve is today the holy grail of most organisations and nations. When the investor Warren Buffett and the economist Ian Goldin describe themselves as artists, they imply that following the rules alone can't give individuals, companies or countries the alertness they need to evolve and adapt. In an age of uncertainty and change, being able to sense what to do in advance of reliable prediction could make businesses or non-profits smarter, more inventive and more relevant. Sense-making, the intuition for change and capacity to pursue it energetically is what markets applauded in Steve Jobs, a man who wasn't an artist but thought like one. That is what many organisational strategists yearn to emulate. The billions of dollars spent on digital transformation programmes start with the dream of turning hierarchical, bureaucratic, data-driven organisations into visionary insight machines. If only everyone could think and act like an artist . . .

It's a tall order and not without its challenges. Few leaders are prepared to give their workforce the kind of freedom that artists seize for themselves. The prevailing efficiency ethos and an addiction to planning and measurement are too embedded, and the risk feels too great to do what Jos de Blok did with Dutch homecare nurses: let people think for themselves. Each time I talk to chief executives or boards or senior leadership about less management and more freedom, they understand the opportunity but cling to the ancient reassurance of scientific management. Standardising and measuring work is what they are good at, and most are more comfortable reading surveys about employee engagement than talking to people about what it feels like to work in their company. They're up to their necks in a status-quo trap, believing that a well-measured if scary present is less risky than an ambiguous future.

But not everybody's quite so stuck. Investors look to start-ups to find in them the benefits that thinking like an artist bestows: a greater sense of zeitgeist, a willingness to probe, the freedom to change and to experiment. When less enslaved by competition and over-heated markets, the entrepreneurial ecosystem could be seen as a vast network of sense-makers, all aspiring to the creativity that forges a future instead of incrementally improving the past. Huge corporations appreciate that learning how to sense what's possible is an urgent strategic demand requiring the freedom to explore. So corporate 'hackathons' – such as Microsoft's One Week, when the entire company comes together to 'dream big' and work together on thousands of different, speculative projects – are an attempt to emulate the freedom big companies envy in small ones. A week may not be much, but the fact that it is an event signals how profoundly this way of thinking is not business as usual for most organisations.

Companies famous for their ethos of self-management – W.L. Gore, Morning Star, Arup, Patagonia – have found that letting people choose what to work on energises the imagination and intelligence of each employee, not just the few at the top. They flourish in large part because, where people grow and change, organisations do too. But in more traditional businesses, the conflict between freedom (which allows creativity) and bureaucracy (which attempts to constrain the risk inherent in creativity) is more often resolved in favour of the certainty that comes from hierarchy, defined goals and targets. Innovation is appealing, even essential, but the conditions required to support it are too ambiguous and uncertain for corporate comfort. There is huge appetite for structural determinism – a blueprint that can guarantee creativity, despite the obvious paradox implicit in that desire.

When it comes to the future, what matters is to invigorate the search, not to determine the outcome. Many artists, and people who think like artists, are inimical to formal organisations and the feeling is frequently mutual, with managers fearing or scorning whatever can't be easily predicted, planned or managed. Allowing people at work to think like artists takes far more than colourful walls, toys, murals, beanbags and open offices. It requires quiet places where it's easy to think. Free time – away from the office, from meetings, from rules and standard operating procedures – is essential for mind wandering. Few great ideas are born at a desk. To have insights that are relevant to life requires having a life, one rich in experiences and the time to internalise them. That requires trust: that the difficulty, the not-knowing, the periods of confusion and frustration, will amount to something worth the effort and the risk.

Providing a productive environment for creative thinking is not the same as learning to think like an artist oneself. That's an individual choice: to make the effort to notice where we are, what's around us, what's missing, to take the time to reflect on what it could mean. The paradox implicit in autonomous vehicles or GPS pertains to us too: if we don't use our human capacity for creativity, mind wandering, discovery and invention, we lose it. We could be more adventurous – exploring what we don't know, investigating what makes us uncomfortable, thinking without bannisters. To be where we are sounds simple and it feels like an easy habit of mind to instil. But creating and retaining memories and developing the capacity

them – the foundational activities of imaginative
iminished when we let technology take the strain.
graphs results in poorer memory of what we've
seen. Online research gives us information faster but it doesn't
last as long. The more we multi-task, switching as frequently
as every nineteen seconds between diverse sources of information and entertainment, the less capacity we develop to
pay and hold attention.[14] As scans reveal the physical changes
this kind of activity imposes on our brains, the downside of
neuroplasticity becomes visible as all the gestational work of
artists slips from our grasp.

What we lose when we surrender so much of our time and
attention to generic technology is not just the opportunity
for personal experience, but the chance to create from it our
own sense of the world, our place in it and what the future for
both might be. The more time we spend visiting places that
others have described, the more we follow the paths others
have made, reading what we're told, seeing what the algorithm
recommends, listening to what crowd-sources admire and
eating what's already been photographed, tasted, marketed
and measured, the less capacity we have to see what we didn't
expect, to hear what we weren't told about or to ask questions
that haven't already been answered. We lose our own perspective and imagination and in this everyone is impoverished:
ourselves and anyone who looks to us in vain for fresh insight
or understanding. Artists try to make the most of their minds.
In the quest for predictability, we risk making the least of ours.

Artists think for themselves. In doing so, they claim the
influence the future of their own lives, of their
of anyone who witnesses it. These aren't the stale,

frightened minds of executives who can't imagine even par-
ticipating in a different scenario but the highly adaptive minds
that seize, in uncertainty and ambiguity, the freedom required
for adaptation, variation and change. That's what they can
teach us, too.

CHAPTER SEVEN

BUILDING CATHEDRALS

Standing in the middle of a golden cube, three stories high, it's easy for the three of us to feel small. Walls pleated like ice cube trays await 800 metric tons of liquid argon whose brutal cold (-186°C) will make the walls shrink on impact. Outside the cube hang two huge steel frames each covered with 4,000 invisibly fine cables designed to capture signals from neutrinos, sub-atomic particles similar to electrons but with no electrical charge, whose mass may be zero.

We are standing inside protoDUNE, a neutrino detector that represents the next generation of machines at CERN, the European Organization for Nuclear Research. DUNE stands for Deep Underground Neutrino Experiment, and when the prototype phase is finished, the full project will consist of two detectors like this one – but each twice as high, twice as wide and seven times as long as the model. A tunnel running 800 miles from the Fermilab in Chicago to the Sanford Underground Research Facility in South Dakota will connect them. In particle physics, the smaller the particle you're trying to catch, the larger the machine needed to catch it – and neutrinos are very, very small. DUNE is just one of the twenty-five projects underway at CERN today. Each involves scientists and engineers all over the world tackling potentially insoluble questions. What they will find (if anything), how long that will take, how much it will cost and how much value will be produced – all of this is uncertain, can't be planned, predicted or forecast.

CERN is a cathedral project. The phrase is Stephen Hawking's and he used it to describe 'humanity's attempt to bridge heaven and earth'.[1] Like the great medieval cathedrals of Europe, they are destined to last longer than a human lifetime, to adapt to changing tastes and technologies, to endure long into the future as symbols of faith and human imagination. Cathedral projects are distinct from megaprojects such as dams, bridges, spacecraft and power plants because they have no end date. So the longevity and scale of their ambition makes them intrinsically ambiguous, uncertain and full of risk. Who could write a 1,000-year plan? What new technologies might render any plan too long, too short, too expensive – or irrelevant? What kinds of people and skills are needed? Cathedral projects challenge to the utmost our capacity to imagine and adapt a future we can't see or predict. And their success illuminates just how far we can expand our capacity to deal creatively with what is uncertain, complex, ambiguous, invisible. *Not* knowing the future can unleash a freedom to invent and to improvise. But they also demonstrate just how far robustness depends on legitimacy: the public understanding and support that allows them to endure.

Cathedral projects don't start with a business case; their primary aim isn't to be drivers of economic growth or to solve practical problems. At the end of the Second World War, when most nuclear physicists in the US and USSR found themselves locked into developing nuclear weapons, CERN was founded on the principle that the search for human knowledge was valuable in its own right and to all people. It was deeply informed by the faith that working together was one way to prevent the world from falling apart again. Many great pioneering researchers had remained in Europe – Niels Bohr, Erwin Schrödinger, Raoul Dautry, Edoardo Amaldi – but they lacked facilities and resources. So, in 1953, twelve founding nations came together to create a new European Organization for Nuclear Research, with each country providing both funding and scientists. Its mandate was specifically pacific and collaborative and its guiding principle was the pursuit of particle physics knowledge on a global scale. Beyond that, everything was born in ambiguity. How it would operate, with whom, on what timelines, to what end, at what pace: all of this had to emerge.

Two of the first scientists to join the nascent organisation still work there. Giuseppe and Maria Fidecaro started their work in a barracks near Geneva Airport, a site full of people, as Giuseppe says, 'sometimes lubricating, sometimes friction'. Now ninety-one, with a shock of white hair and stooped with age, he looks like Mr Burns in *The Simpsons* – except that the gleam in his eyes isn't malice or greed; it's just abiding excitement about physics. Maria points out that the uncertainty of the work then was nothing compared to the war she'd just survived. From the day they started at CERN, change was their norm. Maria had expected to work on a new particle accelerator – but when new technologies made it possible to generate ten times more energy, the original design was thrown out. Maria shrugged off the change of plan with nonchalance. It's all very well to plan, she says, as long as you accept that the future will not be what you expected and you stay open to happy accidents. 'Adventure is a fact of life!' Giuseppe adds, laughing. 'You schematise it in a way and try to interpret it, but this is a fact of life.'

Straddling the Swiss/French border, the CERN campus is littered with huge pieces of discarded accelerators; you'd need a very open mind to view them as sculpture. They are testament to a core capacity at CERN not to get too wedded to specific designs, plans or theories. The mindset at CERN is both tight and loose: rigorously committed to doing physics that matters at a level of acknowledged excellence, but loose in its responsiveness to new ideas and technologies. Plans aren't sacrosanct, but accuracy is. This paradoxical combination of super-human scientific detail with human improvisation requires a mindset that is both open to change, to disconfirmation and correction, but which can function in a discipline that demands absolute precision. Such punctilious flexibility is a CERN hallmark, as critical to the institution's management as its science.

As director general between 1994 and 1998, Christopher Llewellyn-Smith led one of the most ambitious phases of CERN's existence: the funding of the Large Hadron Collider. In 1983, the W and Z bosons had been discovered at CERN – a discovery for which Carlo Rubbia and his colleague Simon van der Meer were awarded the Nobel Prize. This proved the existence of bosons (a particle, named after scientists Bose and Einstein) and spurred the hunt for the Higgs boson, as first proposed by Peter Higgs in 1964. But the collider that had found W and Z wasn't up to the next task and a new collider – bigger, of course, and far more complex – was expected to cost $3 billion, more than had ever been spent on a single machine at CERN. In leading what he expected to be a huge battle, Llewellyn-Smith dispensed with the large bureaucracy he had inherited and instead created a small team to help him master the intricacy of raising such vast funds. Being an outstanding physicist wouldn't be enough; now he needed to adapt, becoming a politician and a diplomat.

'This was the greatest financial risk CERN had ever undertaken,' Llewellyn-Smith recalls. 'The British were very anti. The Germans were struggling under the cost of reunification. There was no public support. We were prohibited from taking out loans. To reduce the budget, we agreed to do it in two stages and, because they were so costly, to leave out every third magnet. (We had no idea whether that was even technically possible.) The idea was: build it like that, then add the rest. In the long run, it would have made it more expensive, so it's stupid. But it was a way to get it built. So I agreed – on the basis that any outside money I raised would accelerate the project, it wouldn't mean that existing members contributed less.'

Llewellyn-Smith was forever being asked to predict the financial return on the project. But he insisted that nobody could guarantee the value of work that had never been done before. If the experiments were too tightly constrained by financial promises then there would be no discoveries and the work would be worth nothing. On a voyage of exploration, how can you price what you'll find before you even set sail?

In the United States, when the discovery of the W and Z bosons had been announced, a *New York Times* editorial summed up national ignominy with the headline: 'Europe W, US not even Zero'. Mammoth cost overruns and poor management caused the Americans' own super-collider project, the SSC, to be cancelled in 1993, and it became obvious that, for US scientists to stay in the forefront of particle physics, they would have to join CERN. For Llewellyn-Smith, that was a piece of unforeseen luck. But he would need to persuade the United States and Japan – wartime foes and scientific competitors – to work side by side at CERN.

He convinced the Germans to relax their opposition to loans and persuaded other member states to adopt a more realistic approach to the $9 billion budget. But his primary, unwavering argument focused on the value of pure research. Transistors had come about not from searching for them but from the study of wave mechanics and the quantum theory of solids. Computers weren't invented by people wanting to build computers, but by physicists who needed to count nuclear particles. Induction coils in motor cars weren't made by people wanting to facilitate motor transport but by Faraday centuries earlier.

Margaret Thatcher's assertion that 'The value of Faraday's work today must be higher than the capitalisation of all the shares on the stock exchange' might be true – Faraday's discovery of electricity did inaugurate the modern world, a contribution too vast to quantify. But it didn't explain the foundational belief at CERN: that great, valuable discoveries derive not from planning but from adhering to a total commitment to the pursuit of new knowledge. Cleaving to that guiding principle while refusing to constrain the work with guarantees made the gigantic cost of what became the Large Hadron Collider a tough sell for Llewellyn-Smith. Billions of dollars – and *no* forecast return?

That CERN has generated valuable spin-offs, however, is unarguable. Today, smaller accelerators of the kind pioneered at CERN are used in the semiconductor industry, for sterilisation of food, sewage and in hospitals, for non-destructive testing of materials and in cancer therapies. The superconducting cables developed for particle accelerators are now fundamental components in MRI and PET scanners and are also used in control systems, cryogenics, high-vacuum systems and electrical engineering. Solar energy collectors use thin film technology, also developed at CERN. But the most famous CERN spin-off of all is the World Wide Web.

Because CERN grew into an international organisation committed to the open sharing of its data, it attracted pioneering computer scientists who built the information systems to do this work. As the amount of data expanded, so did the complex requirements of the network designed to support it. By the 1980s, CERN had email and scientists were able to send files – they just needed a PhD in computing to understand how to do so. By 1989, CERN was the largest internet node in Europe. Tim Berners-Lee, then a fellow at CERN, identified the need for a standard language and protocols, but at first his ideas attracted little interest.

Berners-Lee and his collaborator, Robert Cailliau, realised that they needed a catchy title to capture the scale of the project's potential. He'd wanted to call it 'Mine of Information', but in French the acronym 'MOI' sounded rather self-centred. 'The Information Mine' ('TIM') was no better. While 'World Wide Web' sounded bigger, the little abbreviation – www – more accurately reflected the fact that CERN, at the time, possessed just two primitive servers. Eventually, on the third attempt, a supervisor's comment – 'vague but interesting' – gave Berners-Lee the backing he sought. Many insiders questioned the investment – was it really core to the mission of CERN? Not a single commercial company expressed any interest. By the time he was done, CERN had invested twenty-eight man-years in the project and, in accordance with all its work, CERN released it free to the world.

None of these spin-offs had ever been part of any plan or forecast; they have emerged from the way that work at CERN is done. Huge projects, like the LHC, are undertaken without certainty that they will find what they're looking for – or find anything at all. They require technology that hasn't been invented yet, materials stretched beyond their known limits and collaborations with institutions and commercial corporations that may not have been identified. What gives the twenty-two national members and the directors general of CERN confidence is the way people work there.

The colliders and the experiments are designed by young scientists, because that's where the newest expertise lies. Parts of the enormous machines are built in eighty or ninety institutions all over the world, each taking responsibility for their part of the project. It has to work that way, Llewellyn-Smith argues, because it's too complex to centralise. Shared belief in the guiding principle – new knowledge for peaceful purposes – compels the creation of complex networks of trust and expertise, inside and beyond CERN itself, all enlisting on the same voyage of discovery. It's a simple but forceful way to address complexity.

For young scientists working on the CERN campus, the work can be confusing at first. They don't strictly have bosses but join a group that interests them and then that group decides where to start. Many, but not all, groups combine hardware and software people whose expertise is phased. At one stage, welding may be the central issue, then the focus may move on to electronics. Once a piece of equipment is built, physicists take over. The ebb and flow – between theory and experiment, between science and engineering – has to be loose to facilitate the emergence of the best idea that will move a project forward. Bearing in mind that everything done at CERN will never have been done before, there can't be any rules about how to do it: where would they come from?

Engineers demand detail and specificity; physicists have to ensure that the theoretical aspiration of the experiment isn't compromised. Both must succeed but neither can take precedence. Shared ambition drives avid collaboration: not to fall short, not to let each other down, to bring your best with a passion to do together something that could never be done alone. Everyone has expertise but everyone also needs help for the project to yield results.

So much of the talk at CERN is so abstract – invisible particles, complex theories, unproven hypotheses, amorphous organisational structures – that it is a surprise to see, at the entrance to the Large Hadron Collider, a wall of giant spanners. The test of pure theory turns out to be mightily mechanical and, until DUNE is up and running, the LHC is the biggest single piece of machinery in the world. Inside it, proton beams (and sometimes heavy ion beams) are aimed at each other to produce collisions. These can't be seen but pass through detectors that send signals to one thousand computers at the rate of millions of gigabytes per second.

The LHC control rooms receiving the data operate 24/7 and everyone, from professors to students, has to do time here. (When one famous British scientist made it clear that he regarded such work as beneath him, he was sent home.) The LHC was built for the community, by the community and must be maintained by everyone whose work it supports and develops. That will remain true for as long as the machine runs, which (for now) is estimated to be until at least 2030. Since every collider ever built at CERN has outlasted its plan, even the LHC shutdown date is uncertain.

Marzio Nessi, the technical director of the LHC, oversaw its construction from the first drawings to its first operations. In his hard hat and overalls, he looks and sounds like any site foreman. Italian by birth, he shows off the site with an eloquent mixture of pride and humility: 'I thought it was impossible! So many problems: how to develop electronics in such a hostile environment, how to handle the radioactivity produced by so much energy and so many secondary particles, how to build something so big. But there is an incredible network of knowledge here at CERN and you have to believe that somewhere there is the right idea. When you manage a project like this, you are managing the network of 200 institutions, forty nations, thousands of scientists. Nobody has done something like this so you can't have a hierarchy, you can't have prima donnas. You have to respect everyone and ask for help, share the problems and believe that between all those minds, the answer will come.'

Nessi's professional pride isn't in the LHC's physical grandeur but in the spirit with which it was achieved. His eyes light up as he recalls years of tension and debate. Pointing out where, in the giant complex, teams from China, Pakistan and Israel worked side by side, he recalls how, at first, Pakistani scientists were reluctant to work alongside Israelis – but after a few months nobody cared where anyone came from. All that mattered was the quality of the thinking and the credibility of ideas. Professional respect develops tolerance; people are judged by their work, that's all.

Over 10,000 people contributed to the design and construction of the LHC, but most weren't on the Geneva campus. Thousands of commercial companies helped CERN answer its questions and most say that their collaborations have forced the companies to be more ambitious, working to higher technical specifications than they thought possible, generating new products they might not have considered or saw themselves as capable of making, thinking beyond planning, acquiring expertise and lustre through their association. The scientists onsite and the thousands offsite are testimony to the human capacity to rise to challenges previously thought beyond reach. The difficulty of the work isn't an obstacle: it is the draw. Of this experience, Nessi says: 'We hope the companies take with them our way of working. The understanding that you can't have prima donnas, you need team players who aren't trying to prove, they're trying to understand. People who are open and share and like searching for surprises. That aren't always worrying about the outcome, aren't always thinking about themselves. People have to share knowledge or the cathedral can never be built.'

Pulling in all the expertise and thinking he could find, Nessi made no distinction between age or background, public or private sector, nationality or status. Ideas respect neither hierarchy nor bureaucracy; his job was to hand great problems to people with the energy, courage and commitment to figure them out. In the creation of something so new, everyone was a novice.

Not everybody feels comfortable with the radical democracy and freedom that such experiments demand. But those who do best accept that nobody knows all the answers. And this, Nessi argues, is the only way to address complexity: not by trying to simplify it or pretending the work is easy, but by presenting problems of mammoth difficulties as opportunities to experiment with one's own intellectual, imaginative capacity. Nessi's fundamental task was to make this way of working normal.

Much of the work takes place in the vast lunchroom: big long tables, huge windows. Everyone is there: the Fidecaros, Nessi, Llewellyn-Smith when he was DG and Fabiola Gianotti, who is director general now. You can't tell the difference between the world's leading theoreticians, visiting laureates, artists-in-residence and the newest arrivals. All day long, the space is full of clusters of scientists gathered in informal seminars and working groups. In this easy atmosphere, it can be hard to remember how much is at stake. It isn't just that the cost of CERN is comparable to the entire budget for Oxford University or that the LHC was the costliest project ever undertaken at CERN.

For years, CERN's theoreticians and mathematicians explored and designed experiments to prove string theory. They failed. Llewellyn-Smith isn't sure that those who worked on it wasted their lives – they made some contribution to mathematics – but there's little to show for it. In one office, a skeleton (ostensibly a dead physicist) hangs with a sign around its neck that reads: *SUSY: You'll be in my class when we discover the first SUSY particle.* It's supposed to be a joke. SUSY stands for SUperSYmmetry, a theory that might explain some peculiarities of particle physics' standard model, which describes our current understanding of the universe. Researchers tell me it's a nice theory; it should be true. But eighty years of work have failed to find any evidence that it is, and the scientists working at CERN know they could be dead before anyone finds out for sure. There was some hope that finding the Higgs boson would rule SUSY in or out; it did neither. The scientists who devoted their lives to this work can't go back now and start on something different.

But the longevity of the work is central to the motivation of those who take part in it. The work has meaning, because it's audacious and because it connects this generation with all the generations of scientists on whom their research builds. Everyone I met working on the protoDUNE was eager to tell me that the idea to use liquid argon had come from the Nobel Prize winner Carlo Rubbia, who discovered the W and Z bosons in 1983. However small, however short-lived, their work sits on his shoulders and gives these young researchers the opportunity to be part of something that goes back generations. That continuity outweighs uncertainty, infusing the work with a sense of grandeur and importance that touches everybody. Scientists working there today hope to be the shoulders on which future young scientists can stand tomorrow. The future casts a very long shadow over CERN.

'The cathedral is the people,' Marzio Nessi insisted, then corrected himself. 'Not even the people but the way the people work together. Being able to work in this way, to share what you know, what you learn, on the way to knowing more and understanding more: this is what is CERN. Bigger than the colliders, bigger even than the questions and the knowledge: the ability to find out knowledge together, no matter how big or small or difficult, that we can do this all together, that is truly what is CERN.'

Unwittingly, Llewellyn-Smith and Nessi and their thousands of collaborators have evolved a way of working which is the inverse of most industrial organisations. Since the nineteenth century, those have typically started small. Success causes them to scale up and, along the way, the division of labour requires increasing specialisation. As organisations grow, hierarchies and bureaucracy develop, measurement and rules drive standardisation and efficiency. As the work becomes atomised, it loses meaning and motivation is supplied by targets and rewards to keep the work on track. Such institutions have succeeded when uncertainty has been largely absent. But as they grow and complexity increases, their own hierarchies and bureaucracies overwhelm them. Eventually, the only way to function is by adopting shorter and shorter timeframes: quarterly returns or just-in-time production processes limit uncertainty. But the shorter the time frame, the smaller the aspiration, the more ephemeral the human rewards. Obsessive managerialism, with its measurable, predicted targets, overwhelms them, narrowing perspective and obscuring context and meaning.

CERN is exactly the opposite: it didn't start small and get big. It was born in huge ambition with just one guiding principle that has remained constant: the pursuit of particle physics knowledge on a global scale. This is its lodestar, shining light on knowledge ripe for discovery, which in turn defines what the work could be and how it is to be done. With everyone's eyes on uncovering new knowledge, coherence is achieved but flexibility and adaptability aren't lost. Just as important: motivation isn't dissipated when everyone identifies so closely with the work. It's an elegant way to address complexity, because it can contain change while compelling commitment and imagination over long periods of time without becoming rigid or sclerotic. This is another of CERN's unplanned discoveries.

CERN demonstrates that uncertainty, complexity and an inability to predict need not constrain aspiration. We aren't condemned to short-term, atomised work just because we can't see far into the future, but become more expansive and imaginative when looking far ahead. CERN has succeeded not because it denies the uncertainty in which it functions – but because it embraces it as a motivator. The very scale of the place drives its scientists to explore and test new ways of working that they could not predict. Where more traditional management structures depend on clear forecasts, measurable goals and promised rewards to incentivise their workforce, the work at CERN suggests that ambition is more motivating. If all uncertainty were eliminated, so too would be excitement and meaning.

**

CERN isn't unique. All cathedral projects start with a galvanising, guiding principle that releases and energises the capacity to adapt and evolve and allows the future to emerge. The Human Genome Project – also an open, international collaboration at ease with uncertainty – shares many of CERN's characteristics.

Begun at the Sanger Centre in Hinxton, Cambridgeshire, in 1990, at a time when the emergence of new technologies suddenly made gene sequencing feasible at scale, its initial phase was riddled with controversy and backstabbing. What had started with global co-operation rapidly turned into a fistfight between academic scientists who wished to make all of their findings public and Craig Venter, who claimed that his venture-backed company Celera could do the work better, faster and cheaper – but who wanted to make gigantic profits by controlling the data. The public fight made Venter look big and bold, but commercialising the genome was an old-fashioned, petty aim compared to the vast potential of releasing it to the world.

The Sanger's first director, John Sulston, another scientist/diplomat, inaugurated and led the project with American colleagues. He had already won a Nobel Prize for his work in genetics, but his colleagues later thought he deserved the Peace Prize for the way in which he fought for and won open access to the data. But when the first sequencing of the human genome was published to great fanfare in 2003, the work wasn't over. Many predictions about genomes had turned out to be wrong and new features of genes had emerged that nobody had anticipated. It turned out that we didn't need one human genome – we needed thousands of them to understand and interpret all of the associations within genetics.

The next phase of the work has been institutionalised as the Wellcome Sanger Institute, still in Hinxton, but now a sprawling bucolic campus that is, like CERN, a magnet for scientists from all over the world. Those who wish to work as superstar soloists aren't welcome; the work favours team players who appreciate that the only currency that matters is a good idea. And these scientists, too, approach discovery with enthusiasm.

'We don't know what we're going to find,' Julia Wilson, associate director of the institute, told me. 'We aren't trying to prove something one way or another; we don't start with a hypothesis. We're tackling big, unanswerable questions with infrastructure and the political, financial, intellectual freedom to address them. So the scientists that we bring into the Sanger have to have big ideas; the only limit is their imagination.'

The Sanger's guiding principle is the improvement of human health. Like CERN, the work is conceived in five-year cycles. It is divided among thematic programmes – cancer, ageing, cellular genetics, human genetics, parasites and microbes – and researchers are expected to contribute across these. Yet the organisational structure is designed to accommodate change.

In 2018, work started on creating a map of the genes in DNA sequences of every cell type in the human body. The hope is, ultimately, to be able to zoom into a kidney cell to understand its genetic design and what it does. It was a huge undertaking that was nowhere in the 2015 plan. But because the idea came along and was feasible, because the technology is available, because it can contribute to human health, because it follows the Sanger's guiding principles of uncovering new genetic knowledge, free to the world, the map was approved.

The data is tight, the structure is loose. At the Sanger, there are no targets, no KPIs (Key Performance Indicators) and no benchmarks. The only standard that matters, Wilson says, is excellence. How could you measure what you don't yet understand? But work so open-ended, without guaranteed, predictable outcomes, requires enduring public support.

The emergence of gene editing, controversies around genetics and the synthetic creation of new organisms have made the Sanger's mission more urgent than ever, and Wilson was distinctly uneasy when I raised the issue with her. But were the public to lose trust in the science or the scientists, the organisation could lose the freedom to determine its own path. For that reason, the Sanger invests significant resources into the public understanding of its work. It is considered essential that the public appreciate what genes, genomes and genetics are, what they can and can't do, what scientists should and should not do with them. But everyone I spoke to recognised that the Sanger, and the scientific community at large, is falling behind on these issues.

Having retired from her career in intelligence at MI5, Eliza Manningham-Buller now chairs the Wellcome Trust that provides the bulk of the Sanger's funding. She understands better than most the fundamental requirement for public trust and understanding – and the speed at which that can be lost. 'On ethics, we are behind the curve,' she concedes. 'If you are creating organoids, synapses in petri dishes, the science will be moving so fast that we won't have adequate ethical work being done to support it. We are still fixated on issues of consent: who has consented to our using their DNA? We haven't got that right yet – but meanwhile, other, bigger issues are emerging and will keep emerging.'

This isn't just an issue of who owns what data, or how to reassure the public that their contribution will be anonymous. Poor public understanding of genetics threatens to make people reluctant to contribute their DNA, suspicious of the therapies that emerge and resistant to new discoveries.

Legitimacy – that comes from the public's trust that the work is valuable and relevant – secures the longevity of cathedral projects. Guiding principles produce coherence internally, but that's inadequate if it isn't shared externally by a wider, broader audience. Only as long as the public believes in them can scientific communities preserve their freedom to pursue difficult work that takes time and is hard to predict and articulate. That legitimacy isn't guaranteed. A failure to explain, or to manifest public accountability, is their biggest threat.

In the 1978, the birth of Louise Brown, the first so-called test-tube baby, prompted such a challenge to the scientific community. Was science moving too fast? Were the new techniques of artificial insemination and *in vitro* fertilisation morally justified or socially acceptable? Fearful that public ignorance and misunderstanding would prevent the development and availability of these new technologies, the British government convened the Warnock Commission in 1982, giving it two years to produce guidelines that might enable the new science to develop public support and understanding.

By training, Mary Warnock was a philosopher: a helpful background, she told me, and not just because 'philosophers really have no subject of their own'. Unlike scientists or lawyers, they have no vested interest in anything except thinking. Her commission, made up of doctors, lawyers, healthcare executives and social workers, was essential, she believed, if scientists weren't to run away with the new technologies, having never forged any public support. A leader in the field of fertilisation, the UK government didn't want to lose economic advantage, but that alone wouldn't be enough to secure social acceptance. Banning their innovations couldn't be the answer either; everyone on the commission agreed that the 'sheer awfulness of infertility' meant that some accommodation had to be made. The most divisive issue was the destruction of human embryos that research and *in vitro* fertilisation necessitated: could this ever be sanctioned?

'We wanted to look into the future,' Mary Warnock told me, 'but not in a sci-fi way – in a pragmatic way. We had excellent briefings so that everyone was in full possession of the same information. And we were able to craft an answerable question: not when does life start (which is philosophically unanswerable), but at what point do we attach *value* to human life?'

At the age of ninety-four, Warnock recalled how deep divisions ran. One member of the commission even organised secret meetings behind her back. But all agreed to reach a conclusion based on 'argument rather than sentiment'. At the end of two years, Warnock submitted her report, endorsed by the full commission. There were two dissenting opinions – a virtue, she wrote in the foreword, because it showed how broad the discussion had been. The report explicitly rejected any kind of cost/benefit analysis, arguing that the moral nature of the subject demanded asking whether such technologies were ever right. No calculation of aggregate economic gain could answer such a question. Its conclusion recommended a rule banning research on any foetus more than fourteen days old. The rule became law and remains to this day and the Warnock Commission was celebrated for creating a consensus that most could accept and everyone could understand.

Cathedral projects rest on a foundation of such public appreciation and support. Without it, they are exposed to vicissitudes in taste, social mores and political volatility. For the Wellcome Sanger Institute, that need lends an urgency to securing a better understanding of genomics. With it, their work could continue for generations to come. Without it, longevity may be in jeopardy. That cathedral projects endure is because people continue to believe in them. Nowhere was this more extravagantly tested than in the long, tortuous history of the Sagrada Familia in Barcelona.

***

The idea for the church was rooted in sacrifice and suffering. As the modern city of Barcelona expanded, the Spiritual Association of the Devotees of Saint Joseph acquired the land for a huge cathedral, funded only by alms and private donations given to atone for personal and societal sins. In 1883, within a year of laying the foundation stone, the original architect, Francisco de Paula del Villar y Lozano, resigned, ceding the work to the 31-year-old Antoni Gaudí. The young architect had never attempted anything on the scale of a cathedral and he was expected merely to oversee the completion of Villar's neo-Gothic design. But Gaudí was too original, too zealous and too devout to create a religious building according to generic traditional principles. Over time, he reconceived the church in an extravagant and idiosyncratic direction: a vast ornate statement of fervent religious devotion. His vision required extreme innovation in craftsmanship, engineering and artistry. It would also demand money on a scale that no one foresaw when he started and no one fully appreciated even at the time of his death, forty-three years later, when just a quarter of the building was complete.

Gaudí's vision for one of the last cathedrals being built in Europe overflowed with radical architectural and iconographic invention. Leaving behind detailed drawings and plaster models, Gaudí hoped that his vision would be completed by his assistants. His plan didn't take politics into account.

Even before Gaudí's death in 1926, churches had become targets for violence and revenge, but for much of this time local love for the Sagrada Família left it unscathed. That support fractured in the Civil War. In 1936, the Iberian Anarchist Federation (FAI) attacked the church, burnt down Gaudí's office, smashed plaster models and sculptures and destroyed notebooks full of calculations. Correspondence and writing that detailed Gaudí's intentions were trashed. Twelve people associated with the Sagrada Família were killed. Two years later, Domènec Sugrañes, Gaudí's assistant who had loyally continued the work, also died. By 1939, the crypt had been turned into toilets.

Peace, of a kind, came with Franco's rule, but his hatred of Catalonian republicanism ensured no state funds or support for the Sagrada Família. In the 1940s, when starvation was used as a weapon against dissidence, a vast, expensive, unfinished building garnered little support, and work on the cathedral slowed to an almost invisible pace. Black-and-white photographs from the period show tiny old women on the street selling cakes and raffle tickets as they try to raise meagre funds for the extravagant fragments of a church that dwarfs them. Supported by nothing but the will of Barcelona's citizens, the building had become the city's icon of persistence, devotion and endurance.

That the Sagrada Família was under construction at a time not just of political volatility but also of artistic turmoil rendered Gaudí's project even more precarious. Not everyone liked – or likes – the exuberant complexity of his colour, glass, stone and steel, the exotic mash-up of abstract and figurative styles. Whatever Gaudí's mixture of Gothic and art nouveau was called, by the time of his death it had fallen out of favour. *Noucentisme*, a specifically Catalan form of modernism, rejected Gaudí's ornate figurative style. Picasso detested Gaudí's work while Orwell described the Sagrada Família as 'one of the most hideous buildings in the world'. Gerald Brenan, a great writer on Spanish culture, observed that 'Not even in the European architecture of the period can one discover anything quite so vulgar and pretentious.'[2] Postwar buildings like Mies van der Rohe's Seagram Building, the Matisse chapel in Vence, Basil Spence's Coventry Cathedral and the Post Office Tower in London articulated a confident, technological future – the remnants of an unfinished nineteenth-century church designed before cars and electric light did not.

Only Gaudí's disciples and supporters kept the work alive. By the 1950s, fundraising and sculptural work started to gain some momentum. An archive and small museum brought together what remained of notes and plans. By the 1960s, the site began to attract curious visitors. But in 1965, such persistence drew more ire from young intellectuals and architects, including Joan Miró, Alvar Aalto and Le Corbusier. If the cathedral was Gaudí's great work of art, how could it be completed by other artists whose interpretation of his intentions was so subjective?

Little money. No critical support. Gaudí was dead, his style was dead. The building had no future. Only the city's deep identification with the Sagrada Família eked out resources sufficient to keeping the construction alive. The chief architect, Francesc de Paula Quintana i Vidal, continued his work until he died in 1966, aged seventy-four. But then slowly the outlook changed.

After the death of Franco, Spain began to open up to tourism. Gaudí's unexpected motifs of trees, flowers, foliage and fruits, turtles, birds and signs of the zodiac thrilled visitors. When the Olympics came to Barcelona in 1992, over a hundred nationalities visited the basilica and went home exclaiming over the crazed, hallucinogenic use of colour and geometry. Charging for admission meant that, for the first time, it wasn't just the citizens of Barcelona who would pay for the church to be built. Now the whole world did. The original guiding principle of the project had expanded. What had once been a local expression of devotion to the Holy Family as a symbol of shared humanity was now seen around the world as a potent articulation of the universal capacity to endure and adapt.

Gaudí's designs were not just visually startling. They depended on extreme manipulations of geometry: paraboloids, hyperboloids and helicoids, often combined at a level of complexity that can't be seen by the naked eye. It's hard to imagine how, in the nineteenth century, the building could ever have been finished. But by 1980, a miracle arrived in the shape of computer-aided design. This new technology – of a kind Gaudí could never have foreseen – made the 3D mapping of each part of the building easier and faster. Laser cutting, computing and automation all accelerated the work of growing teams of engineers and builders. Money, resources, technology: for the first time in its history, the Sagrada Família started to make the transition from chimera to reality and, in 2010, the basilica was finally consecrated.

At the beginning of the twenty-first century, over 2 million people visited the cathedral, attracted in part by the unique opportunity to see a cathedral taking shape before their eyes. With income of €50 million a year, the project also became a company with a staff of a thousand people led by Chief Executive Xavier Martínez. But still new, unimagined problems arose. While annual tourist revenue provided the project with ample funding, the 16,000 visitors a day meant that construction couldn't continue safely. Stop the tourists – no money for the construction. Stop the building work – the tourists dry up and the building is never finished. Stopping the weekly mass wasn't an option, worship was what the building was for. Once again, the Sagrada Familia seemed impossible.

But Martinez, like CERN's Marzio Nessi, takes impossibility in his stride. Driven by his passionate commitment to the power of this church, he scoured the world looking for answers and identified one firm capable of solving his problem. In the City of London, a site for a new skyscraper nicknamed 'the Cheesegrater' had been so tightly hemmed in by existing buildings that it had to be constructed off site, then disassembled, trucked in piece by piece overnight and re-assembled. The engineers who had pioneered this form of construction worked for Arup, a company famous for its stated principle of only working on projects that matter. After a hundred years of dogged devotion, there was no doubt in anyone's mind that the Sagrada Família mattered.

The business operation that manages the project is housed in a conventional office that is far from Gaudíesque: stark white walls, modern steel furniture, rows of desks and computers. Martínez's office is ordinary too except, perhaps, for the crucifix on his wall. To him has fallen the challenge and, in his eyes, the rare gift of finally being able to promise a completion date for the church: 2026, one hundred years after Gaudí's death. After all the vicissitudes of its constructions, I ask, is he confident that now it can finally be finished?

'Oh, sure,' he says, putting quote marks around his words and laughing. 'Sure' is not a word readily associated with this project. Completing the building by 2026 will require a few more miracles. The foundations of Villar's original church were designed for a building 70 metres high – but Gaudí's design called for a height of 172.5 metres. Reinforcing the foundations will help but won't solve the problem entirely. Instead, the towers have to be much lighter, their thickness reduced from 2 metres to just 300 millimetres, using materials that didn't exist when Gaudí was alive.

Out of town, the construction site, where the new pieces of the cathedral are made, looks more like a car production line than a church. It is here that workmen rehearse assembling the additions so that, when the parts are trucked into the city, adding them to the cathedral is quick and safe. Mixing modern materials with traditional craftsmanship has demanded huge flexibility in everyone's thinking. For the most part, the crew is optimistic that the building will be completed by 2026. But one sandy-haired engineer, Esteve Umbert, acknowledged that after such a long and troubled past, nothing is guaranteed. 'It is really a challenge but you never know,' he says, smiling.

'The story can always change. But you fall in love with the challenge. There's meaning in the work. My work will be there for hundreds of years . . .'

As 2026 approaches, uncertainty recedes. What happens after that? The cathedral lives on and CEO Martínez will be fifty-seven. But most of his workforce won't be needed any more and Martínez will have to manage the winding down of the organisation he created. Having been able to make a contribution is, for Martínez, satisfaction enough. 'To do well the things that matter, that is my job. That is enough,' Martínez said. 'You know, our local business school, IESE, ran an executive programme, spending a week in the US, visiting Amazon, Google, Microsoft. And then they visited this. There was a lot more to explain here! Values. Sticking to Gaudí's values. At Microsoft, it is the bottom line that pushes things. If I were a manager at MS or Google, my main preoccupation would be my salary. At Sagrada Família, that isn't important. What is important for us is a higher idea. We need self-discipline. We need self-criticism. We need to do whatever we do better always. That's what we worry about.'

Cathedral projects start big and grow in the face of uncertainty and complexity. Their huge ambition inspires people to stay humble and to measure up to the guiding principles that inspire them. For everyone building the Sagrada Família, that humility includes accepting that, eventually, they won't be needed. After 2026, Martínez will no longer decide how the cathedral's funds are spent; that job will transfer to the bishop. Restoration will always absorb a lot – but where will the rest go? The people of Barcelona and the people of the world feel that they own this church, they have sustained it all

this time. This will be [...]
can maintain its legitimacy [...]
the work of the people. Ther[...]

Nobody I met who runs [...]
takes their longevity for granted. [...]
attempted to 'future-proof' them a[...]
absurd. Instead, they have the courage t[...]
or when their project might die.

When CERN announced that the new co[...]
$22 billion, many asked whether that money wou[...]
spent on the more immediate threat of climate[...]
Christopher Llewellyn-Smith, who even in retiremen[...]
loves CERN, doesn't believe it has an indefinite right to ex[...]
It should last, he thinks, only as long as there are big questions it could answer. He'd often debated with his colleagues
when they would know if high-energy physics was finished
as a worthwhile field to work in. He believed that would be
only when it ceased to attract first-class minds. His colleague,
Murray Gell-Mann, thought it would be when the science
became predictable. The two were really agreeing with each
other: that the field will no longer matter when it isn't complex, ambiguous, uncertain or difficult enough.

At the Wellcome Sanger Institute, Julia Wilson and her
colleagues contemplate sequencing the genome of every living
thing on the planet, a scientific odyssey that may hold the key
to life on earth. But that will only be feasible if man's life on
the planet becomes sustainable and if the public retains its faith
in the institute's research as a public good. If the public grows
cynical or angry about the uses to which the research is put,
the institute could die.

hitectural
round the
arners as
n unfin-

charted
em and
. They
uture:
CERN
s that
eeps
uid-
erge

another test for the project: whether it
into the future when it is no longer
are no guarantees.
modern cathedral project
Nobody has, at any point,
nd most find the idea
contemplate how, if

llider will cost
ld be better
change.
t still
ist.

starting with
outcomes only as landmarks showing
where they are. They map the future not by trying to pre-empt
or co-opt it, but by believing in it, being ready to explore and
map whatever awaits finding. With aspirations too great for
an end date, they sustain people by making them feel big,
important and giving them the opportunity to do work that
lasts. In all of this, they stand in startling contrast to many
conventional institutions.

It has been fashionable in recent years to talk of the need
to adopt a purpose: something akin to a guiding principle,
which defines what an organisation stands for. The speed
with which the word 'purpose' has been adopted speaks
volumes about just how purpose-less much work feels now.
When, in August 2019, 181 business leaders, representing 30
per cent of the US market's capitalisation, signed a statement

asserting that the purpose of all companies was to 'promote an economy that serves all Americans', many applauded a broader and longer term vision for business.[3] A deliberate departure from Milton Friedman's belief that companies serve shareholders alone, the statement challenged business leaders to articulate their purpose and their means of fulfilling it.

Harvard business academics rushed to demonstrate that serving a broader purpose was great for growth and profits too; shareholders could have their cake and eat it. But even the proponents of the statement were wary, wondering whether, a year hence, any company would have made meaningful changes. In the same week that the chairman and CEO of Johnson & Johnson, Alex Gorsky, signed the statement, his company was ordered to pay a $572 million fine for the company's role in opiate addiction in Oklahoma, suggesting that serving all Americans remained a distant goal, rather than an active guiding principle. And, in an era of climate change, that stated purpose to serve 'Americans' only seemed out of sync with globalisation.

So will purpose statements turn into another vague management fad? Most are meaningless, lathered on top of old value statements and mission statements without any substantive change in power structures or decision-making. Lloyds Banking Group defines its purpose as 'helping Britain prosper', which didn't prevent mis-selling but apparently does encompass everything from digital skills training for charities to tackling domestic abuse.[4] What the debate around corporate purpose most clearly voices is how far organisations struggle to understand and articulate their role in the larger world that they inhabit, and on which they depend.

Cathedral projects, meanwhile, have to inhabit and sustain an ecosystem, because they are too ambitious to survive on their own. Their guiding principles must be tight enough to define direction and loose enough to let work evolve and adapt as the whole system changes. Defending and holding that tension, refusing to simplify what is complex or to reduce what is ambiguous, is the critical job of the men and women who lead them. Guiding principles, lodestars, illuminate what matters but also, crucially, steer away from anything that does not. (It's an interesting thought experiment to contemplate what Google might have done differently had it cleaved to its original principle of doing no evil.)

Where they are meaningful, effective and well understood, an organisation's guiding principles confirm legitimacy because the public trusts them. Recently, many technology companies (in private) have conceded the need for a Warnock-like commission to define the boundaries of their operations, to protect them from competitive overreach. It's a revealing but sad confession of how few principles govern their everyday activities, and a bracing reminder of how important it is for any organisation to understand the role it plays in the wider world.

True cathedral projects aren't just long, they're broad: in their base of support, in the number and diversity of people and ideas that they bring together. In doing that, they create and sustain the legitimacy that allows them to endure. Lose that and they're finished: anachronisms or pariahs that will dwindle and die. They remain public goods only as long as the public says so. In this, they are profoundly democratic. Big as they are, they depend fundamentally on individuals with the courage and energy to invent what no one has even begun to imagine.

PART THREE

LIFE HAPPENS

CHAPTER EIGHT

SIMPLE, NOT EASY

Suddenly the future is here. We experiment, explore and aim high, but life can prove more inventive than we are and, in an instant, we are shocked into a crisis: of identity or endurance or survival. However much we are prepared to make the future, it sometimes arrives too soon, too fast and threatens to make or break us.

Such moments are, by definition, unpredictable, but what does it take to survive them? Luck and endurance of course. But, going into a crisis, what assets could provide robustness, the better chance of survival? Existential crises occur every day – in private agonies of choice, in the volatility of large corporations, in the tragedy of global emergencies. If we're lucky, we watch from the sidelines, hoping that these won't be our future. But when they arrive, what will we need?

Three stories.

1

Most funerals double as family reunions. This one was no different: three generations in London to pay respects to Aunt Nonie, who'd always been a little difficult. Afterwards, we gathered in her home to eat, drink and gossip. As usual,

Father John was the centre of attention: such a privilege having a handsome young priest in the family, providing a personal send-off.

As the attention died down, John sought me out. 'Have you got a minute? Let's step outside, it's stuffy in here.' We went out onto the street, a mild day. The same generation, he had officiated at my wedding when I married his cousin. He conducted Michael's funeral too. Though we are fond of each other, it seemed that John and I met only at life-changing events.

'When are you heading back to Waterford?' I asked.

But John hadn't travelled, as I'd thought, from Ireland. He had come from Stroud, a Catholic retreat house in the Cotswolds, mostly used to patch up alcoholics and paedophiles. Ostensibly he was there to rest and recuperate from stress and overwork. In fact, he'd been sent to Stroud because he had fallen in love and now had to choose: the church or Mary.

In theory, John was already married to the church. When he had been ordained, his mother had cut the cake with him. For a poor Tipperary family to produce a graduate from the leading seminary in Ireland was a triumph. It wasn't just his doting mother who thought so. We all recognised John's talents: capable of organising anything, good with finances, wonderful with people. The Catholic Church was always on the lookout for men with such finesse and authority. He was sure to make bishop. 'I don't even remember it being a choice,' he told me later. 'It just seemed my life was sorted. I was idealistic, it felt like I could contribute to society, but what really drew me in was the certainty. My teachers were overjoyed, the local priest was thrilled, the bishop was delighted.'

Celibacy hadn't seemed like a big deal at the time, not compared to the opportunities that would open up for him. In seminary at Maynooth, it had felt like the church was changing, losing its old rigidity, flattening the hierarchy, embracing community and the poor. Liberation theology, a new church for the poor, gave the church a fresh dynamism. As a student, John had been sent to live in a rural village, with instructions to learn everything about the hopes and needs of the people he would serve. Education, homelessness, marriage: as social servant, the church was central to all the issues of the day and John was inspired at Maynooth by the intellectual, social and spiritual challenges he would face.

By the age of twenty-five, he was running a parish and life was heady. Living in a freezing old rambling house, serving mass, teaching science and religion, he had two full-time jobs but more than enough energy for both. Working with groups of young people, or with isolated rural families, John developed a passion for conversation, exploration, the bonding needed to be helpful. He had no real interest in power or status; the daily pomp of ritual wasn't what excited him. Where his more conservative colleagues defined their job as the dispensation of sacraments, John was fired up by helping his community find in their lives something that deserved celebration.

By 1982, John was in another big, old, cold house, this time in the centre of Waterford. As youth director for the diocese, he was seen as a radical: meeting young people in coffee shops, talking to them about what they wanted from the world and from their church. He was popular, unstuffy, accessible. If asked, he'd talk about birth control, about inevitable stresses in married life. Local radio and newspapers adored the charismatic priest while young people found him easy to talk to because, well, he was young too. He was changing, but the church was not.

Over the next few years, advising couples preparing for marriage, he started to wonder: what did he know about relationships, having never had one? Talking about contraception, he started to feel a fraud: what did he know about sex? It was grand hanging out with his contemporaries, going to parties and blending in at dances, but the job inserted distance between them: he was expected to have authority in areas where he felt he had none.

He took to going around town in mufti, uncomfortable in the clerical dress that seemed to flaunt power. One of his colleagues told him he was a disgrace and he was stopped from doing youth work. He made it his business to visit the rougher parts of town, to get to know who lived there and how. When a girl was raped and he went straight over, eyebrows were raised – eyebrows, John felt, that would have remained unperturbed had she been a middle-class girl. 'I had nothing to offer apart from human kindness,' John later recalled. 'But just my being there, people were amazed: the church would do that for us? *That* was our job: to challenge the comfortable, to comfort the challenged. They had everything to say to the church but the church had absolutely nothing to say to them. They made me feel I didn't want to represent an old, oppressive institution.'

People came from miles around to hear his sermons and he wanted to bring his struggles to walk alongside them. But that wasn't what the church mandated. With no institutional support, and no personal allies, the work became exhausting, lonely and confusing. He was getting burned out.

What support John got didn't come from the church but from the people he had supposed himself to be helping. He was learning more from his contemporaries than from his colleagues, from doctrine or liturgy. As the group of young friends started to divide into pairs, John spent more and more time with Mary. She'd heard about John – 'the cool priest in the next parish' – and, together with friends, they went to dances, parties, out on walks together. Mary worked 30 miles away, in a jewellers' store in Dungarvan. She hated her job and despised her bully boss, but the economy was rotten and there was nowhere else to go. Today, Mary says that she had a reputation for being so sensible and down-to-earth that nobody imagined anything could be going on – although soon something was.

In a village where everyone knew everything about John, including what he ate for breakfast, privacy was impossible. He and Mary could be seen in the company of friends, but never alone. Living 30 miles apart in an age before mobile phones, every meeting was difficult and risky. They had to be, John said, 'unbelievably covert'.

'We had a few holidays together,' Mary recalled. 'The Isle of Man for two weeks – *nobody* goes there for that long!' It sounds funny but it was agonising: the sense that everyone was watching, ready to judge. The strain was so great on Mary that she quit her job and became unemployed. Neither had any support because no one knew. John had given his life, his faith, his identity to the church. If he wasn't a priest, who was he?

'So much of my person was connected with my role but that just showed me how ill-equipped I was,' John recalled. 'Towards the end, I couldn't preach. I couldn't stand physically at the altar. I just rattled off a few words and collapsed. I couldn't do the job any more.'

After John told his bishop about Mary, he was dispatched to Stroud. The time was supposed to be for healing but, for six months, surrounded by alcoholics and paedophiles, never allowed out alone and forbidden any communication, it was clear that the church hoped to brainwash him into returning. Before going, he and Mary had made no promises to one another. Both were adamant that whatever choices each made had to be freely on his or her own terms, not burdening the other with baggage. So, at this point in their young lives, John and Mary had nothing. They didn't have each other, they had no jobs, little money, no home of their own.

Mary says she did a lot of what she describes as 'angst walking' in the Irish countryside – thinking, alone, in silence. She had faith in John but did not know what he would decide. All she could do was wait. No one to talk to, no comfort, full of doubt and questions, nothing about Mary's life felt romantic. John knew something had to give – but what? For both, pain, exhaustion and loneliness converged on a single question: what would you do if you were free?

Staying in the church offered John certainty and security. But the price would be high. He would have to move far from Mary; it would be unbearable to live in the same town, seeing her every day. He had seen such priests: adrift, their surrender looked like a kind of death. On the other hand, if he left the church, he would lose everything: career, financial security, public respect, the love of his own family, his identity.

'At Stroud, they asked me when I would stop celebrating mass,' John said. 'The question startled me; I had been thinking about moving away from the church but I hadn't begun to think about becoming a lay person. I had no idea who I was without the church. I hated all the old trappings but without them . . . who was I?'

When news of Nonie's death came through, the church refused John permission to attend her funeral. He replied: either you let me go or I'm out altogether. By the time they conceded, his mind was made up. The mass I witnessed was the last John would ever celebrate.

Standing in the London street, leaning against a parked car as he told me the story, John became self-conscious, aware that we had been talking for a long time. Would people inside start to notice? Hyper-alert to gossip, his new self was so new, so raw, he didn't know how to wear it. What was he going to do now? He'd need somewhere to stay, somewhere he and Mary could be together. I told him they could come and stay with me for as long as they liked. Recently widowed, I had a big empty house and more than a little sympathy for people trying to forge a new life.

In the end, John said, it all became clear: if he looked for guarantees, he'd be lost. With Mary he had the chance of life; with the church he had none. If the church wouldn't let go of the past, he had to, to act for himself, not as the agent of an institution. However risky that future looked, it offered more possibility than the certainty that trapped him now.

The worst part, he told me later, was telling his mother. 'Her whole edifice collapsed.' Her identity, her status in her village, her entire life were all absorbed in John's identity as a priest in the diocese. She became suicidal and refused ever to see Mary.

John and Mary spent days talking and walking the streets of London. They decided to move to Dublin, live apart and see what became of their relationship. Even with just a few pounds and nowhere to stay but a friend's couch, John felt liberated. When he and Mary finally decided to get married, he was unemployed and penniless. A church wedding was forbidden and, though invitations were sent, neither John's parents nor his sister replied; only his brother-in-law risked family opprobrium by attending. It would be twenty-five years before they were all reconciled.

People in authority who could have helped didn't. But others did. Working as a counsellor with women who had been victims of domestic violence, John's role was to ease them back into being able to talk to men. Knowing that he too had been excluded from society was what made the women trust him. His powerlessness made him effective. And for John and Mary, time was on their side. The church was losing its grip on Ireland. Celibacy came to be seen as a problem, not a virtue. Changing social mores, the scandal of paedophilia along with the growing number of priests leaving the institution meant that the church was losing respect and trust, its glory past.

Over time, John came to be seen less as a rebel and more as a trailblazer. Many now saw what John had felt: that the church had become mired in the past, unable to adapt to a future it didn't see or comprehend. 'I'm so thrilled you got out of that old dungeon you'd been in,' is how one parishioner put it. Many old friends were delighted for them – for the escape they'd made, the freedom they'd found. John found many ways to be useful, in social work and, after the banking collapse in 2008, deploying his financial skills to guide the poor and debt-laden through a gruelling crisis. After many years, even his mother forgave him. Today, he is working on a PhD about artificial intelligence and ethics.

There's a vibrant undertone of the zeitgeist in John and Mary's story. In refusing to accept a role that had been defined for him by others, John claimed that he alone – not his family or any institution – had the right to determine who he was. Such existential crises are intense experiences of free will, the possibility of choice. The way John puts it is simple: action is how you search. Giving up the need for certainty gave him the freedom to discover.

John and Mary's story bears an uncanny resemblance to the narratives of abused women, runaway slaves, refugees, of anyone forced to flee for their lives: the absolute certainty that the only possibility of safety lies in choosing danger. Only if you concede that the future is inevitable are you truly trapped.

2

Companies have existential crises too: defining moments when, if they aren't to die, they must forge a new future for themselves. The mythology of this moment follows a hyperbolic narrative: long-term wilful blindness to creeping failure puts the organisation in jeopardy. It teeters on the brink until a heroic guy (almost invariably a guy) rides into town and singlehandedly saves the day. Heads roll, weaklings are thrown overboard, ruthless cost-cutting and savage deal-making deliver victory. The hackneyed simplicity of the story implicitly casts the old guard as idiots and the hero as a genius technocrat, slaying bureaucratic dragons with inspirational bravura.

The reality is more complex and subtle. It is also more emotional. When great old companies fail, grown men weep: at their folly and weakness, at the loss of reputation and legacy, at the end of an institution's history. Their tears acknowledge that companies are more than buildings and balance sheets; they are living organisms containing personal dreams. When businesses die, personal hopes go with them.

One of the most radical corporate reinventions in recent times has been the reincarnation of Nokia, once the world's dominant designer and producer of mobile phones. In the 1990s and early 2000s, the company transformed what had been a luxury item for high-paid executives into a must-have for every consumer in the world. They were the first company to put cameras into phones and a pioneer of tablets and mobile games. For many, Nokia was all anyone knew about Finland, where the company's revenues represented 25 per cent of national exports and 4 per cent of the nation's GDP – more than all the rest of the Finnish companies combined.[1]

Contrary to Silicon Valley mythology, the launch of the iPhone in 2007 did not spell an inevitable end for Nokia. Comparing Apple's invention with the Nokia smartphone N95, reviewers dissed the newcomer, lauding the incumbent. In the first quarter of 2008, Nokia shipped 115 million phones, compared to a mere 1.7 million devices from Apple. It didn't even look like a contest. But when the Android operating system launched later that year, the market changed and accelerated.

Endemic demons started to surface: weaknesses in Nokia's Symbian operating system made it too difficult and slow to update, while the phones were so rugged that the touchscreen almost needed a hammer. These problems weren't secrets, but the company's culture was so polite and hierarchical that nobody talked about them. The huge global coverage of Nokia – in 140 countries – became a burden, as it made design permutations too complex. What had been assets became liabilities: the technology, the culture, the management structure. Each new product came to the market too late and it began to look as though the company was caught in a death spiral.

Towards the end of 2009, comparing it with thousands of other companies, McKinsey's Organizational Health Index placed Nokia in the bottom twenty-fifth percentile. McKinsey's data predicted that any company at this level would cease trading within two years. But at this stage, calculating probabilities was no help. In desperation, the board did what so many businesses do: prayed for a saviour CEO.

In 2010, the incumbent Olli-Pekka Kallasvuo was fired and replaced by Stephen Elop, an executive from Microsoft who became the first non-Finn to run the 150-year-old company. His famous memo made it clear where the company now stood: 'We've poured gasoline on our own burning platform. We have lacked accountability and leadership to align and direct the company through these disruptive times. We haven't been delivering innovation fast enough. We're not collaborating internally . . .'[2]

Knowing you are in a crisis is essential to surviving one. But it's rarely enough. Plenty of companies (Sharper Image, British Home Stores, Washington Mutual, Lehman Brothers, Polaroid, Toys "R" Us) have been incinerated on their platforms. Routine responses — layoffs, cost-cutting, exhortations to work harder — breed cynicism, division and contempt. To define a future no one can see yet requires radical imagination. When time is tight and money is running out, a company can't afford binary choices; it needs lots of options. But, under pressure, thinking often becomes even more constrained and hackneyed, rigid with fear. In its new chairman, Nokia got lucky. Risto Siilasmaa was, by background and mindset, an entrepreneur, accustomed to risk and to thinking freely for himself. As a board member, he had chafed for four years at the company's formality and complacency. Now he had a licence to challenge.

What distinguished his approach was that, at a time when focus typically narrows, Siilasmaa was prepared to go broad. Instead of trying to cut his way to prosperity, Siilasmaa cajoled, encouraged, nagged and berated board members and employees to question everything. No sacred cows. No hostages to fortune. No deference. He conducted what now looks like scenario planning on speed: multiple plans, diverse configurations of what a new Nokia could look like. When you know you can't afford to stop, he said, it's much easier to keep going.

The idea of constructing and testing out a variety of scenarios seems obvious, but in a crisis, most companies work frantically to construct a single, perfect plan. (Governments often do likewise.) They feel they don't have time for multiple plans. Overwhelmed by complexity, they shrink their options just when they need to expand them.

What surprised Siilasmaa was that thinking together helped everyone trust each other more. When you feel you are being listened to, he observed, you start to appreciate your listener. It was a great way for executives and the board to learn and to search, a fast and transformative way to get a deeper, richer contribution from everyone. Refusing to trust that any one plan would prove perfect, they kept recombining different pieces of the puzzle until, by 2013, the company found a first step: selling the handset business to Microsoft would buy the company time. Siilasmaa's quiet, consultative style even persuaded Microsoft's famously incandescent Steve Ballmer to negotiate in good faith.

At no point did Siilasmaa think about Nokia as just a financial entity. The company contained huge meaning for employees, business partners, customers and the Finnish nation as a whole, all proud of a business that had pioneered one of the coolest technologies of their lifetime. Nokia's crisis could not be solved by compromising standards, only by rising to them. The company's 'Bridge Programme' wasn't a typical corporate euphemism for laying people off – it offered training for new jobs, money for a new education, backing for entrepreneurial ventures or help finding work with a new company. Of those who went through the programme, 85 per cent said they were happy or very happy. The way in which they'd been treated built trust and energy among those who remained.

Nevertheless, when the Microsoft deal was done, many in the company wept; the glory days were over, but the crisis was not. What was to become of the company's remaining, strategically incoherent assets? Again, Siilasmaa and his team searched for multiple configurations for a new company until finally, in 2016, with the acquisition of French telecommunications equipment company Alcatel-Lucent, Nokia emerged as one of the top three telecom infrastructure businesses in the world. Today, whenever you send a bit into the internet, it goes through Nokia equipment or software somewhere along the way.[3]

The Nokia story isn't a melodrama of death and resurrection. As perhaps befits a nation famous for taciturn stoicism, it is a story of hard grind and nerdy negotiation delivered with patience and trepidation by thousands of individuals for whom the company is more than a job and their colleagues more than economic units of production. That the company had a tradition of reinvention may have helped: it had started as a lumber mill in 1865, became a power generator, then a manufacturer of electrical cables, rubber boots and power supplies. The company's legacy is all around change, adaptation and reinvention. Looking for an image to represent the company's future, it's no wonder Siilasmaa points to a blank whiteboard.

Wildly creative strategic thinking — being prepared to consider anything — was essential to Nokia's survival. But it wasn't sufficient. As important in generating that open exchange of ideas was the relationship between company leaders. Although Siilasmaa had been critical of Nokia's board in the beginning, over time he came to see how much they cared about the business. And as they laboured together to save it, what had been formal relationships deepened. On one level, what enabled

Nokia to survive was the emotional commitment its leaders made to each other. 'In business,' Siilasmaa said, 'we forget that we are human. Many strong leaders think they should not be friends with their colleagues. I disagree. Business is emotional. I like to be friends with my colleagues. You get through a crisis because you care so much.'

'The way I used to think was: he who cares wins,' Paul Matthews told me. Matthews was working at Standard Life when, overnight, the deputy CEO learned that what had appeared to be the insurance company's £9 billion surplus was, in fact, a £1 billion shortfall. Millions of insurance policies – on lives, houses and pensions – were underfunded.

Once the CEO had been fired, everything about the business had to change. The crisis was exacerbated by the Standard Life business model, which paid high commissions to financial advisors who acted as their agents, selling its policies to consumers. To save the business required ending those commissions and persuading the advisors to earn their income from fees paid by clients – something that, at the time, nobody in the industry did.

Matthews and his team needed to go to every financial advisor, explain what had happened and why the business model had to change. This could have a devastating impact on the advisors' own business: anyone who had sold SL products to a thousand clients could find all their income wiped out at a stroke. It was, Matthews said, a horrible experience.

Everyone in the industry insisted that selling products without commission was impossible, but Matthews and his team took years proving it could be done. The work was emotionally and physically taxing: absorbing the stress and anguish of his workforce who were themselves absorbing anxiety and rage from their customers. Matthews was clearly great at motivating his team – but through a marathon of abuse and apology, what kept him going?

'Longevity matters,' Matthews reflected. 'I was inspired by the people around me. When people have worked with you for a long time, they know you and trust you – and when you're in a crisis, you've got that!' It was, he added, 'pretty much the opposite of the gig economy . . .'

Forced to be creative, the company found a way to sell insurance without commission via financial advisors who charged for their work, just as any lawyer, dentist or accountant would. When, in 2008, the banking crisis revealed just how corrupt and perverse commission structures had become, financial regulators insisted that the entire industry move to this new way of working. Standard Life was already there, poised and ready.

Everyone I've spoken to about this period – from junior salespeople to the CEO – describes it with amazing energy. In such moments, leadership can get simpler, the sense of urgency shared and pervasive. But more than a few companies dissolve at this point too, when low levels of social capital surface all the lurking demons of rivalry, fear, blame, suspicion. Matthews is right; longevity does count, because teams grow stronger over time, more loyal to one another, more open, more trusting and more robust. Gig economies, by contrast, make complex systems more fragile; their very efficiency means there is nothing to fall back on. But going into a crisis with high levels of trust and solidarity provides an irreplaceable advantage.[4]

History can be an asset too, not because it repeats itself but because it can communicate values and standards and make people feel that they belong to something more meaningful than a temporary gig. Alan Mulally found this when heading up Ford during the financial crisis. Spending weekends in company archives, he sought out imagery and stories connecting the resilience of the company's past with the demands of the future. After the banking collapse, Joe Garner, as CEO of HSBC UK, drew inspiration from the bank's wartime history when the bank's general manager set up supply lines to get money and food to prison camps. So when a rogue trader brought down Barings Bank in 1995, its history of survival was the first note of the crisis: '1890. It's happened again.'

This might sound like code, but to the corporate lawyer Nicholas Gold, the meaning was clear. The Barings Bank Panic of 1890, a moment when Argentinian debt had nearly triggered a global financial meltdown, was legendary. That such a thing could have happened again seemed inconceivable, but by the time Gold joined the meeting of directors, he learned that the bank had lost all but £10,000. The chairman, Peter Barings, sat in disbelief, repeating: 'This cannot be happening. This cannot be happening.'

Gold says that crises are what he's good at. His entire career had been spent advising executives under pressure: pursuing a takeover or under threat from one. The previous year, his part of the business – Barings Corporate Finance – had been rated the best advisory business in the City of London, ahead of Goldman Sachs, ahead of Warburgs. Gold was proud of the team's reputation and determined to protect it. He was instantly pragmatic. At work on Glaxo's hostile bid for

Wellcome, he knew his client work, on completion, would bring the bank £10.5 million. Whatever else happened, that money could buy time. The trading division of the bank might be in disarray, but corporate finance would stay productive.

Over a weekend, ideas came in from everywhere. Barings was a venerable name in the industry and bankers hoped to save it. Would the Bank of England step in, as it had done before? What about the Bank of Japan? Could the other banks chip in to cover Baring's losses and keep it afloat? Could the charitable Barings Foundation take over the commercial bank? Tommy Suharto, the son of the president of Indonesia, owned $17 billion worth of platinum; perhaps that could be used as collateral to recapitalise the bank? The most promising scenario proposed a former customer, the Sultan of Brunei, might be able to help, but the Bank of England would still need to guarantee the deal.

By the end of a long weekend, all the ideas had failed. The Bank of England wouldn't step in; the other banks couldn't contribute enough. Suharto wasn't up for the challenge. To put a charity in charge of a bank would make it impossible to operate. At 8:36 p.m., news came that the Sultan of Brunei had decided not to proceed. At 9 p.m., the news echoed across the trading floor: Barings had collapsed. CEO Peter Norris wept.

Only two options remained: to go into administration or to sell the bank. But, laden with debt, what was there to buy? All the debt was on the trading side of the bank; all the value lay in corporate finance. But only if the team stayed. Gold says there wasn't a moment's hesitation. The way they had worked at Barings was so different. 'It was human and humane. And we wanted to keep it that way.'

In the end, Barings was sold to a small, unknown Dutch bank called ING for £1 and a billion pounds of debt. The trading side of Barings fell apart but corporate finance survived. The following year, they were named the top advisory business in the City again. Gold stayed at Barings until his retirement fourteen years later.

When asked how he had managed to weather such an immense crisis and stay so cool, Gold laughs, always uncomfortable with praise, demurring to the quality of his colleagues. Having lunch together every day, he thought, kept them united. And he identified another source of strength: he had always operated on the basis that anything could end tomorrow. So he lived on his salary, never spending his bonus. That kept him focused on what was at stake – the bank itself, not his own personal financial security. It's the only way, he says, not to muddle what might be best for the institution with what might be advantageous for you. But headhunters are notorious for circling the minute news of any crisis breaks – what had kept the team together? Gold laughs again, remembering how everyone had run rings around recruiters. 'We wanted to work together. We loved Barings. We just loved it . . .'

It's often said of business that, in a crisis, cash is king. There's a brutal truth there: money buys time to craft a survival strategy. What it won't buy is the motivation people need to keep going, to endure humiliation, recrimination, anger and grief. Only deep bonds, of trust and concern, built over time, will supply that. At Barings, Gold found that in the colleagues with whom he lunched every day. He also had one further resource. The day the news broke, after the strategising, after the management meeting, his head reeling with work, he phoned his best friend. 'I just had to talk to someone who would understand,' he said. 'Understand what it meant to me – this old place that had dignity, that had always been so careful . . . It was the most shattering and emotional experience of my life.'

Friendship is a topic rarely talked about in the upper echelons of business, but it should be. Nobody survives these crises alone. Survivors have friends: people not necessarily in the business but who know what it's like, what it means, people who have only each other's best interests at heart. Every successful business leader I've known or worked with has such friends, and everyone can describe the crises through which they've sustained each other. These relationships aren't transactional, they're not networking. Some leaders refer to their friends as their 'north star', others as the bridge between intellect and character. What gets people through crises and into the future is each other.

Yet recently, when I was working with a group of rising leaders of important organisations – high achievers from both public and private sectors – they all conceded that they had few, or no, friends. They had had them once. But now they were too busy, there was no time. Lunch together? It was inefficient. Friendships had faded and time to think was rare. It left me wondering: who will give us stamina and solidarity when the storms come?

3

In 1981, the Center for Disease Control and Prevention (CDC) reported the occurrence of a rare cancer in otherwise healthy gay men, and, even though just 180 cases were seen that year, the Center declared the disease an epidemic. On 4 July 1982, Terrence Higgins was one of the first British men to die of the mysterious disease. He was just thirty-seven at the time.

His friend Rupert Whitaker was also sick and had moved to London for treatment of what was assumed to be a weird form of cancer. He couldn't climb more than a flight of stairs and doctors didn't expect him to live more than a year. Higgins's death left him traumatised, puzzled, and angry. He didn't understand why Higgins had died in an isolation unit, or why the clinicians treating him wore full barrier clothing. Whitaker decided to become a doctor at least in part because, he says, 'I couldn't get my head around the bizarreness of this disease. We just had no idea what had happened . . . We just kept thinking: *This is going to kill us*. We are going to lose all the people we love . . .'

Together with friends, Whitaker set up the Terrence Higgins Trust to support people dying from the mysterious disease. But the complexity of the crisis did not allow for neat priorities; the battle had too many fronts. Homophobia and public ignorance. The disease itself, which was unknown, was undefined and might be untreatable. Government prejudice and apathy. A scientific research establishment that was arrogant, remote and slow and, in the US, a healthcare system that was expensive and exclusive. Hospitals turned away the dying and undertakers turned away the dead. Politicians saw no advantage to helping a marginalised community and drug companies did nothing to respond to a disease nobody understood.

Nor was the gay community homogenous. Some homosexuals believed in coming out; others stayed in the closet. Many aspired to conventional acceptance while others condemned assimilation as selling out. What constituted normative sexual behaviour became an incandescent, divisive question. Even in the face of death, such burning issues of identity defied solidarity. Add to this issues of race, class and gender and the complexity of the community became paralysing. The one thing everyone had in common was a sense of doom. 'In all the history of homosexuality we have never before been so close to death and extinction,' the playwright Larry Kramer declaimed.

The AIDS epidemic became a global existential crisis of a kind, on a scale that defied planning and prediction. No models showed how to attack such a vast, diffuse enemy, not even a way to map out a plan. Many activists were inspired by the anti-apartheid movement in South Africa. But that fight for the future had structure: a single mission (dismantling apartheid), leaders (Mandela, Mbeki, Tambo) and a big, clear enemy (the all-white government). When companies face existential crises, at least their choices are stark: find the cash to keep going or find a buyer. But in the AIDS crisis, the gay community had no such clarity, no precedents, no plan.

In the second year of the epidemic, Kramer and five colleagues founded Gay Men's Health Crisis to raise money for research, disseminate information about the disease and man a helpline. In the UK, the Terrence Higgins Trust did similar work, building a buddy network to support people suffering from a disease that still had no name. The most these organisations could do was share information and help people die well. But, in a crisis, you have no choice but to start where you are. Time is too precious to wait. 'We had no roadmap at the beginning, no plan,' Whitaker recalled. 'We just had fear and love. It was grief – and the losses that were starting to happen very fast.'

When Jonathan Blake, a young London actor, checked into the Middlesex Hospital, a biopsy revealed that he had HTLV-3, which is what the disease was called at the time. A terminal diagnosis. He was sent home, not yet ill enough for palliative care. By December 1982, he'd decided to commit suicide. All that stopped him was the thought of leaving others to clean up his mess. Isolated and afraid, any thought of the future was paralysed.

In the UK, the National Health Service made the disease a matter of government concern. Norman Fowler, the secretary of state for health, instigated a health information campaign, 'Don't Die of Ignorance', providing explicit information and advice about how to reduce the risk of infection. By the end of 1983, Luc Montagnier had isolated the HIV virus but still couldn't prove that it caused AIDS. No diagnostic test existed. And no treatment.

In New York, Kramer grew increasingly frustrated by Gay Men's Health Crisis. He thought it had become too bureaucratic, too friendly with power, playing safe in a dangerous world. The crisis was too urgent for conventional, managed planning. ACT UP was created in a deliberately different mould: no leadership, no bureaucracy, just ferocity. Its weekly meetings called for ideas to ratchet up demands for a cure. Anybody could join, there were no leaders, nothing was off limits. The structurelessness of ACT UP was a strength, because it welcomed everyone with ideas. But it was a weakness too, because those ideas represented no battle plan but outrage. 'I often describe it as democratic to a fault,' Larry

Kramer recalled. 'We were making it up as we went along. There were no rules.'[5]

ACT UP! FIGHT BACK! FIGHT AIDS! Much of the organisation's energy focused on massive, public provocations: an invasion of the New York Stock Exchange, obstruction of the post office on the day citizens filed their tax returns, a die-in at St Patrick's Cathedral where activists played dead in the aisles to protest the church's perverse stance on condoms. These were brilliant, crazy, unforgettable public events that forced the public to pay attention to the young and old dying around them.

As a young journalist, David France reported the rise of gay activism as he lived through the AIDS crisis and his partner died from the disease. 'If we did nothing, we knew we'd die. That much was certain,' he recalls. 'ACT UP used to brag about saving lives – but they were just casting about like the rest of us. We had no idea what would work so we had to try anything. Everything . . .'

Between the end of 1983 and 1984, the number of AIDS cases and deaths in the US more than doubled. In 1985, a test for the infection was finally available and the CDC estimated that over a million people worldwide were infected. By 1986, just five years after the first reported death, Anthony Fauci at the US National Institute for Allergy and Infectious Diseases estimated that a million Americans were infected and that, within five or ten years, the number would rise to three million. The Reagan administration, however, urged people not to worry since the disease was confined to gay men and intravenous drug users. Wilful blindness prevailed.

Gay Men's Health Crisis and ACT UP fought over hard cop/soft cop tactics: should they collaborate to get the establishment onside, or attack? Doctors couldn't agree about how or even whether to treat people with AIDS. Scientists debated the most promising avenues of research; politicians fought over funding. Drug companies wavered between hoping their existing drugs would find a new market and trying to decide whether to invest in new drug research. Every one of these communities needed to work together – but nobody had the power or authority to bring them together. This was complexity at its most lethal.

Developing new drugs could take decades – and still fail. At the time, drug approval alone, regulated by the Food and Drug Administration in the US, took an average of seven to ten years. That was too long, so ACT UP invaded and shut down the FDA. This shamed them but it didn't get any drugs. In desperation, members of the community started to experiment with their own treatments – some crazy, some dangerous, but none a cure. Chinese watermelon enemas, AL721 extracted from egg yolks, swallowing hydrogen peroxide. In London, thinking he'd be dead within a year, Rupert Whitaker tried injecting himself with proteins; with no treatment, why not experiment? The germ of an idea emerged: people with AIDS had to take an active role in finding a cure.

Into the tragic chaos walked Iris Long, a chemist and housewife. She wasn't gay; she was just interested in AIDS. That she would prove a linchpin in the fight against AIDS was completely unexpected. 'This woman just shows up one day,' Larry Kramer recalled, 'this straight woman – and after a few meetings, she gets up and she says, "You guys don't know shit." And that's in her nice way. And, "I'll teach you." And she did.'

Long recognised that accelerating drug development would require that the activists force the FDA and the whole, complex ecosystem of science and medicine to involve people with AIDS in every level of their decision-making. That meant a radical institutional fight with bureaucrats and scientists. For the battle to be won required expertise; people with AIDS had to learn what drugs were being developed, how clinical trials operated and how to get drugs into bodies fast. If people with AIDS didn't become as expert as the experts, they could always be patronised and marginalised and they would all die. An organisation, a strategy of sorts, began to emerge.

Attending one of his first ACT UP meetings, film archivist Mark Harrington listened as Long delivered a lengthy, complex presentation about current treatments. He understood almost none of it. He wrote down every word he didn't know, looked it up, created a glossary and distributed it to ACT UP. He became, in essence, a cultural translator for the group, enabling it to communicate with anyone about anything connected to AIDS.

By 1987, following nearly 20,000 deaths in the US, the new drug AZT became available for the first time. After five terrifying years, this was the first glimmer of wild, incredulous hope. ACT UP had made it a principle never to recommend any treatment, merely to disseminate information, but they now had the expertise to provide a considered assessment. 'One of our early successful actions was an effort to force the National Institutes of Health and the FDA to lower the dose of AZT,' Mark Harrington recalled.'[6] For the first time, the medical establishment had taken activists seriously.

But academic researchers were fascinated by molecules, not suffering. Pharmaceutical companies weren't used to meeting the dying. Government institutions were authoritarian, arrogant and unaccustomed to being held directly accountable to citizens. All were hostile: how dare these crazy, sick, gay people challenge their authority? A pattern started to emerge, too inchoate to call a plan: actions of civil disobedience kept in the public mind that over a hundred people a day were dying horribly of AIDS. Demonstrations in Washington, at the FDA, at scientific conferences, in pharma companies, hoped to shame medical institutions into change. And the citizen-scientists were learning where to intervene.

ACT UP collected data showing that there were more than forty new drugs ready for clinical trials. That seemed like good news. But, incredibly, thirty-nine of them had no people with AIDS enrolled in them. Only AZT, with its known problems, was being meaningfully tested, to refine dosages and identify when, in the course of the disease, it was most effective. For people with AIDS, like Silvia Petretti, the pace was surreal, as though there were no crisis at all.

'I thought I had one, maybe two years left to live,' Silvia Petretti recalled. A self-described 'party girl' she had contracted AIDS in London. Diagnosed days before her thirtieth birthday, she had been told she might not get any medication because only good girls got drugs. She felt lonely, tainted, dirty and scared. When she saw a doctor, all she could do was cry. In the absence of drugs, only the companionship of others provided comfort. 'My doctor told me about Positively Women: a room full of women and kids,' Petretti said. 'I thought they would all be dying – but they were knitting!

Knitting to make money. It was only here I felt safe and not judged. And we kept each other going, because we were the only ones who knew what it was like.'

'It was like the trenches in World War One, this decimation,' Jonathan Blake said. 'It was so lonely.' What brought Blake out of his isolation was helping others. In the coal miners, Blake saw another group being persecuted and marginalised. He joined Gays and Lesbians Support the Miners (GLSM) out of solidarity and because, he says, if he was going to die anyway, why not help someone? GLSM raised money to support striking miners' families, organised what became the legendary 'Pits and Perverts' benefit ball and visited mining towns to show solidarity. A distraction from hospital visits and funerals, the work was creative, collective and generous.

But, by 1989, the number of AIDS deaths in the US had passed the million mark. Government-funded AIDS research was described as corrupt, secretive, ethically barren. There was no plan. By 1990, one person died from AIDS every minute in America. In cities, it had become the leading cause of death for women aged 15–44. Promising drugs remained untested. Congress voted $800 million for treatment – but none of the money was ever released. Rumours of deportations, mass incarceration and suicides swirled around the community. Activists were dying; they were also burning out. But as they retired the field, others replaced them, fired by the certainty that if silence meant death, acting up at least meant possibility. 'Faith defies uncertainty' is how David France put it. Without optimism, there was nothing.

Glimmers of hope began to emerge. With AZT still the only available treatment, and too toxic for many, it had proved profitable. That encouraged other drug companies to tackle AIDS too. A few medical researchers spotted at conferences secretly carrying away 'Silence = Death' posters seemed to signal a shift in attitude. When Merck entered the field, the company created the first ever formal community advisory board with ACT UP. For Merck, this was a risk – drug companies are paranoid about leaked trade secrets – but the company recognised that involving self-educated people with AIDS could inspire research that was better, faster, cheaper and more likely to succeed.

But the 1990s seemed to reprise the '80s: a lethal roller-coaster of hope, activism and expertise, followed by crushing disappointment with millions more dead. Ten years after the first reported case, in 1991, 2.4 million people died of AIDS. In 1992, 3.3 million; 1993: 4.7 million.[7] Bereaved lovers, children and parents carried their loved ones' cremated ashes, hurling them onto the White House lawn with the words 'I love you'.

In 1994, 6.2 million died. The mood became apocalyptic. An ACT UP member was now on the approvals board of the FDA. But in 1995, in the year that 8.2 million people died of AIDS, the disease became the leading cause of death for Americans aged 25–44. When a promising drug at Merck failed, scientists despaired, questioning whether a solution could ever be found. They considered giving up, but it was the activists who kept them going. At Merck, Emilio Emini took the moral challenge personally: 'I have no right', he said, 'to say I can't do this.'

A new category of drug, protease inhibitors, triggered the same excitement and fear that had greeted AZT. Another false dawn? Arguments broke out again over how fast it should be tested and approved: too fast and it could prove lethal, too

slow and lives would be lost. The caution wasn't ill-placed –
the first protease inhibitor, Saquinavir, proved to be effective
for just sixteen weeks. But if no single drug worked for long
enough, would combinations of them do better?

In 1996, at an annual medical conference in Washington
D. C., Merck and Abbott presented their data on combination
therapies. The results made the audience gasp. A single trial
had kept very sick people with AIDS alive for two years. A
few days later, a New York press conference convened by all
three major drug companies announced their results. They
couldn't fully explain why or for how long the combination
of drugs worked, but they knew they'd made a breakthrough.
Not for the first time, technical jargon got in the way and
one scientist, sensing confusion, interrupted to translate:
'Maybe you are not understanding what I am saying . . .
This is the biggest news ever in this epidemic. This stuff is
actually clearing the virus out of people's bodies. People are
getting better! We don't know for sure yet, but we think
these drugs – this whole class of drugs – might allow people
to live a normal life . . .'[8]

The triple drug therapy received FDA approval in just
six months.

In London, Jonathan Blake counted himself lucky that he
had refused to enrol in trials of AZT. His doctors had helped
him manage opportunistic infections but, over time, he lost
weight, got shingles, neuralgia and reached a point where he
could scarcely move. Though still reluctant to trust the medical establishment, his doctor persuaded Blake that he had run
out of options: 'He works out this combo for me. A week goes
by: nothing. Second week: same thing. Third week: I still have

to take all these pills and – nothing. Fourth week: I wake up one morning and I have such energy I can't believe it. Like Lazarus rising from the dead! I go outside and lay a patio in my garden. Phenomenal. Extraordinary . . .'

Nothing about this triumph was inevitable or foreseeable. Many diseases exist today that remain incurable one hundred years after their discovery; the extinction so feared by the gay community could have been its history. So what made the difference? It wasn't just one thing – no one action, no one plan. Not one organisation. Not one leader. Not even one drug. It had taken everything and everyone: men, women, activists, scientists, bureaucrats and radicals; the healthy and sick, the living and the many, many dead and years of failure.

David France said the sheer scale of the tragedy ultimately made it impossible to ignore – a bitter advantage. Rupert Whitaker thought it came down to two things: shame and expertise. Shaming the medical establishment, he believes, was the only way to get their attention – and expertise secured it. Silvia Petretti says that nobody could have survived without peer support, the only protection against stigma. Everyone pays tribute to allies and friends, many now dead and not all gay, who stood shoulder to shoulder, bringing food or comfort, knowledge or ideas, all breaking through the isolation of fear, discrimination and despair. What kept the movement going was a passionate faith in a better future. The thing about courage, Whitaker told me, is that seeing courage instils courage.

There are so many lessons to be taken from a terrifying crisis that was met with unbridled conviction, daring, imagination and courage. Talking to AIDS activists and historians, I was wary of suggesting parallels; I didn't want to belittle such immense suffering and achievement. They, of course, were bolder in their thinking, having already identified similarities between the threat they had confronted and those we face today.

David France smiles, thinking about American school shootings and the high school students running the March for Our Lives against the National Rifle Association. 'Those Parkland kids, their die-in at a grocery store chain where the executive had a role in the NRA: their technique and strategy are lifted straight from this. There have been die-ins before, but ACT UP made it into an art form! It helps that these kids feel their personal peril, they were mowed down. These kids are fighting for their lives.'

The Parkland kids have also learned the lesson of finding allies. In the run-up to the 2018 US mid-term elections, working alongside OurLivesOurVote and Gabrielle Giffords, they raised money to support gun control candidates and to encourage young people to vote. Where, between 1994 and 2014, just 20 per cent of the vote came from the young, in 2018 it was 30 per cent. The kids, France says, don't just know what to fight for, but also who to fight against. For everyone, it's personal.

'I see real comparisons with climate change, especially in terms of not knowing what to do, having no plan,' Ian Green said. Diagnosed as HIV positive at the age of twenty, he is amazed to find himself alive, thirty years later, running the Terrence Higgins Trust. 'The story of HIV and AIDS is all about people taking action and not sitting back. It was hell but we had a real community, we all knew each other and we came together in adversity. It was personal, we felt each other's pain, going to funerals all the time. And it was a multi-factoral response: government, activists, families, scientists. The real lesson: sit back at your peril; what you can't be is patient or passive . . .'

In the fight to address climate change, all the hallmarks of the AIDS epidemic recur on a vast scale. Uncertainty about where to begin tackling the emergency. Ambiguity around where solutions will be found: in technology, in lifestyle, in corporations, in experiments. A plethora of organisations determined to drive change and to support the traumatised and displaced. Widespread disagreement about tactics and priorities. Decentralised activism launching huge public actions. The willingness to disrupt and the courage to sacrifice time, effort and personal reputations. Emergent, unexpected leadership, in Iris Long and Greta Thunberg. All amid a crisis so large and terrifying that many institutions and individuals feel paralysed, preferring to turn a blind eye or hope that a miracle (or miracle worker) will spontaneously save the day.

But there are further lessons to be taken from the AIDS crisis, lessons that apply to any existential crisis. While our love of narrative might predispose us to fantasise a magnificent denouement, progress in these fights is lumpy – advancing, stalling, accelerating and disappointing. They don't end neatly or conclusively, but solutions emerge – and continue to emerge. Despite generations of new treatments and prophylactics, AIDS remains a live issue as social stigma remains and new therapies are expensive and often inexplicably withheld.[9]

While loose structures might frustrate lovers of managerial neatness, it can allow leaders to arise from unpredictable places. Efficiency can be lethal; only the extravagant oversupply of creative thinking rises to meet the challenge. Allies are essential – especially alliances with presumed enemies. Cultural translators like Mark Harrington are critical too; being able to explain in easy, accessible language brings in more people and answers can come from anywhere. Shame and expertise, as Rupert Whitaker saw, are both needed because either alone is inadequate and too slow. As important as the fight is caring for the injured and traumatised.

Crises are always personal. John and Mary fought for a future they could share. Companies are saved by individuals who care about each other. Adults change their minds about the climate crisis when the arguments come from their children, especially teenaged daughters.[10] It can be tempting to sentimentalise crises, looking back with nostalgia to the sense of solidarity and meaning that they provoked. The deeper, harder truth is that going *into* a crisis with years of generosity, reciprocity and trust already deeply embedded provides resilience and stamina. The efficiency of the gig economy, the splintering of communities into competitive individuals, our dependence on technology all undermines this, eroding the lifesaving power of loyalty and friendship that these crises demand. Staying human, not just a user or a consumer, is the first way to prepare for an unpredictable future.

Expect surprises. When Jonathan Blake supported the coal miners, he did so because he wanted to help another group under threat. No longer feeling helpless was reward enough. He never imagined that it would result in the National Union of Miners pushing gay marriage onto the Labour Party platform. It's in the nature of complex systems that such weird, unforeseen events will emerge. As David France said, faith defies uncertainty.

CHAPTER NINE
WHO WANTS TO LIVE FOREVER?

It seems to me that one ought to rejoice in the fact of death — ought to decide, indeed, to earn one's death by confronting with passion the conundrum of life. One is responsible for life: it is the small beacon in that terrifying darkness from which we come and to which we shall return.

— JAMES BALDWIN, *The Fire Next Time*

Even people who didn't know her looked up. As Olivia crossed the club's dining room, heads turned. Aged ninety-two, she had shrunk to under five foot and no longer wore the high heels of her debutante days. But even as she approached the end of life, her glamour and presence commanded attention.

Any time my work takes me to Texas, I try to make extra time to visit my godmother. She's been a wise support all my life, funny, stylish and smart. Now she is in her nineties, it takes her longer to get dressed — she wouldn't be caught dead looking anything less than gorgeous — but this morning, we will still talk for hours, catching up on her life and mine. She laughs about the fact that her social life these days mostly revolves around funerals and bridge, adding that her biggest fear is that she might soon run out of friends to lose. Her late husband, a rigid and conservative man, might have felt her comment to be in poor taste, but one of the delights of her old age has been watching her grow bolder in what she thinks and dares to say. Who's going to stop her now?

At lunch, she still eats like a bird and relishes the fact that I don't. Tonight, she will give me the keys to her car and I will drive us to dinner. She will enjoy the fact that now I am looking after her, and I'm proud to do it. When we were both younger, we might visit museums or go shopping, but now it's enough to be together. In the past two decades, her life has steadily shrunk: not just her physical height, but the reach of her social life. Ten years ago, she gave up the trips to Europe she adored. Then she stopped going to New York. A few years later, eye problems meant she gave up driving. She still plays bridge twice a week and her children and grandchildren are good at staying in touch. But there are many days now when she just stays home, looked after by friends and helpers she's known most of her life. My visit is precious for both of us. Each time I come, we both know but neither of us says: this could be the last time.

Olivia may be ninety-two but she's more daring than when she was at the height of her beauty and social success. I wish, she told me, I hadn't been such a conformist when I was younger; I wish I'd known that I was more than just pretty. Her political views have changed (she swore me to secrecy); her wicked confidence is now more assertive. So it would be wrong to see her old age as nothing but loss. At an age where most people might expect to stop changing, Olivia is still becoming. And she is happy.

When I come to visit, we've always plenty to talk about. She's curious about my work, my family and such an acute social observer that it is still fun to hear her acerbic take on the local gossip. In all of this, Olivia reflects our current understanding of ageing: that as we grow older, we get happier. This takes many forms. Across a lifetime, negative feelings tend to decline but positive ones stay fairly stable; towards the end of life, that leaves most people pretty cheerful. Older people are drawn more to positive images and remember them longer than young people given the same choices.

Much of this research has been pioneered by Stanford's Laura Carstensen, and what it reveals is a picture of ageing around the world quite different from the standard gloomy narrative of decline and failure. She and her colleagues followed a group aged 18–94, asking each person to carry a pager over a ten-year study. Each member was regularly interrogated about their emotional state: were they happy, sad, frustrated, anxious? What they found was not that one generation was universally more contented than the rest, but that each individual became happier over time. So those who started adulthood grumpy became less so, those that were cheerful to begin with got even more so. Carstensen says, laughing, that when they hear of her research, many young people ask her how they can get old faster.[1]

In addition, the elderly retrieve happy memories more easily and frequently than sad ones – and these memories may be more positive than when they were first made. Diaries kept during the Blitz, for example, are replete with intense negative emotions – fear, anger, loneliness – that, decades later, were supplanted by memories of solidarity and purpose. We call this nostalgia but it isn't just a rewriting of history. Rather, our experiences teach us emotional coping skills and we get better at managing our own feelings.[2]

A second explanation for greater happiness in older people is simpler: time is short and what is scarce becomes valuable. Younger adults have longer futures to consider and may be more keenly aware of what they lack. That means they might waste time – going out with people they don't really like, taking jobs they don't enjoy. But the opposite is true for older adults: with shorter futures, they prioritise emotional goals, searching for meaning in what they have. They know better what they like and dislike and don't want to waste time. This makes them better – at times, quite ruthless – at moving towards the positive and negotiating their way out of the negative. So while Olivia may have fewer friends, those that she still sees are rich in the memories and support that they bring. The future is easier to navigate when there is less of it.

More meaningful than how long we have been around is how long we have left. So HIV positive patients who are symptomatic care about the same things as the very old, no matter how young in years they might be. HIV positive patients who are *not* symptomatic behave more like the middle-aged, while the young share priorities with the completely uninfected.[3] Age, it turns out, is a poor indicator of progress along the course of life. What's clear is that, regardless of chronological age, as life shortens, emotional ties deepen and strengthen, sometimes to a point of almost unbearable intensity. This could be seen tragically throughout the AIDS crisis and is a deep and recurring theme in much art. *La Traviata*'s Violetta, *La Boheme*'s Mimi, Munch's *Sick Child*, Strauss's *Last Four Songs* all attempt to capture the ineffable value of life as it runs out. I think now that it might also explain the crystalline gaiety of my first husband, who understood, far better than I, the true implications of a congenital heart defect.

'Here is something real' was how a friend commented on his cancer diagnosis. In sharp contrast to the ephemeral urgency of daily life – the missed train, the lost promotion – here was an experience undeniable, non-negotiable and surprisingly rich. 'Such clarity,' he recalled. 'Small moments of intense domestic delight. Such awareness of life all around me. Noticing all the time . . .'

He wasn't alone. Ulla-Carin Lindquist, a Swedish TV presenter, wrote towards the end of her life: 'It is now for the first time that I feel myself to be living in the present. Death brings me closer to life.'[4]

Every moment human beings are alive, they continue to change and to grow. This is what fuels the drama of *King Lear*: that this old, flawed man can gain wisdom. At the beginning of the play he is foolish and self-satisfied, thinking himself wise, but the fact that he won't meekly submit testifies to his ferocious appetite for life. That his wisdom comes so late is Lear's tragedy, but that he does learn, right to the bitter end, is his redemption and it is why we weep with him. *Lear* asks us: how much can we still learn? And it challenges its lead actor, typically towards the end of their career, to excavate their talent and capacity – physical, intellectual, emotional – to move us. Taking on the part of Lear requires every kind of stamina and courage, never more so than when, at the age of eighty, Glenda Jackson chose the role for her return to the stage after twenty years' service as a member of parliament. This was an actor not meekly retiring from politics but storming back into the theatre with a whole new level of performance.

When the idea was first suggested to Jackson, she'd dismissed it, thinking she'd been away from the stage too long – and that the British would never accept a woman in the role. But when she proposed it to the Old Vic Theatre and they agreed, her first thought was that she'd been mad to suggest it. 'My big fear', she said, 'was that I wouldn't have the physical or vocal strength to do it.' She went into training – swimming and walking – and condemned herself to solitary confinement with the script. Only after the first read-through of the whole play did it start to feel possible. 'I actually got through to the end and I didn't feel as though I was going to die,' she said with relief.

An exercise regime, hugely supportive cast, cutting down smoking (every day but Sundays) and the sheer energy inside what Jackson calls the greatest play Shakespeare ever wrote: these got her through the fear and challenge of the role. But what made her performance so ferocious was more than the professional risk she was taking. After twenty years in parliament, Jackson's King Lear scintillated with political shrewdness and acumen. There was nothing about politics this actor couldn't sense, know and show. Those who had seen Jackson on stage at the beginning of her career realised that they now saw an actor working at a level beyond anything she had done before. To demand so much of herself and so triumphantly succeed at the age of eighty revealed to the world just how much age has to say.

Far from winding down or petering out, it is not unusual for artists towards the end of their lives to unleash a final period of exuberant creativity and invention. That paradox – that the less of life that remains, the more we treasure it – fuels the energy and daring of what has become known as 'Late Style'.

The idea of the Late Style originated with the cultural critic Theodor Adorno, who recognised it as distinctive, even if he struggled to define what it was. Writing about Beethoven's late works, he describes them as 'relegated to the outer reaches of art . . . as if, confronted with the dignity of human death, the theory of art was to divest itself of its rights and abdicate in favour of reality'. How much artists ever concern themselves with theory remains debatable, but Adorno is not alone in sensing in these works an explosive quality of liberation: from convention, from expectation, from what *ought* to be. Beethoven's late quartets, written two years before his death, summon up all of his genius, providing to a mere four players a powerful distillation of everything his life's music has given him. 'Touched by death,' Adorno writes, 'the hand of the master sets free the masses of material that he used to form' and such is the energy and urgency of the work that it can feel unfinished as it breaks through to new territory.

The excruciating, raw honesty of Rembrandt's self-portraits, painted in the year he died, when all hope of success and love were gone, go straight to the question of what it means to be human. Ibsen's last plays, written ten years before his death, remain relentless, ambiguous, anxious and unsettled in their quest to understand failure and transfiguration. Goya's last paintings scream across the centuries, rejecting placatory platitudes. Schubert, dying at the age of thirty-one, created in *Winterreise* images and sounds of agonising beauty and exquisite despair. In the last ten years of his life, Matisse took up scissors, using only colour, shape and composition to change the way we think about art; many consider these the greatest of all his works. The radical simplicity of Peter Brook's late plays ache with the desire to strip theatre down to its essence. What Late Style artists have in common is that they distil their past to accelerate beyond it. With nothing to fear or hope for, these late works explode with questions, doubts and new ideas that remain to inspire and terrify future generations.

Though such achievement falls to few, Late Style and Carstensen's research point to a creative experience of old age. Anthropologists and psychologists have argued for over a century that death is so terrifying that we have had to invent religions, or devise complex systems of deep denial, in order to be able to go on living. But the analysis of blogs written by the terminally ill, or poetry by inmates on death row, suggest that the approach of death does not deprive life of its meaning. This late stage in life, with time so precious, can become a period of rich achievement, continued exploration and deep satisfaction.[5]

This is not to belittle the pain of illness, fear and suffering in dementia, or what can be the brutal consequences of mistakes, bad luck, poor decisions. It would be naïve and unjust to imagine that a different way of thinking about old age automatically alleviates pain and suffering. But it is equally incorrect to overlook how vivid life becomes when in short supply. What psychologists like Carstensen or any of the Late Style artists show us is that the certainty of life ending offers much that is powerful, inspiring, hopeful and vividly alive. They do not see death as a problem.

In that, they are unusual. Death is frequently portrayed as a technical challenge or a failure. The education of doctors focuses overwhelmingly on improving and saving lives; in all their medical training, doctors spend roughly just twenty hours with the dying. The physician Atul Gawande has written poignantly about his own well-intended but misguided and excessive attempts to prolong life. He had never spent much time looking at how old people actually live, but when he did, he came to a startlingly simple conclusion: that making their lives better often required *reducing* purely medical imperatives. Death isn't an error for doctors to correct, or a bug for software engineers to fix: it is a natural process that can be honoured and dignified.

But when my 91-year-old neighbour was diagnosed with breast cancer, she felt the full force of medical mechanics. A jolly and understated woman, Alison had led a quietly heroic life. Working in a London hospital during the Second World War, during bombing raids she would go and sit with patients whose wounds made it impossible for them to be moved to shelters. She made no big deal about the courage this required; it was just a happy memory of being useful. When, in her late eighties, she fell ill and received her diagnosis, she refused treatment. But so irate was her doctor that he stormed out of the room, leaving her on her own.

Casting death as failure denies the dying the opportunity to die well. So too does the rhetoric which casts disease as an enemy and the patient as a soldier. When Raj Thamotheram was diagnosed with cancer, he revolted against the cancer-as-war metaphor. A long-time peace campaigner and climate activist, he knew, and all his friends knew, he was a fighter.

But as a physician, he also knew that however his disease progressed and whatever happened next wasn't a moral judgement on him. The disease was bad enough; the idea that he had to prove himself by defeating it belittled him.

Viewing death as a moral challenge is one of the most ancient forms of egotism, imbuing survivors with a fantasy of invulnerability. This attitude was at its most self-righteous during the AIDS crisis, when millions, suffering a terrifying, unknown disease, also had to endure the vicious opprobrium of an ignorant public. Positioning death as punishment or failure, and those who escape it as superior, is just a self-serving form of denial. Worst of all, it hijacks the possibility of a good death.

***

To the transhumanist movement, death is a bug in the software, a problem to be solved. Where recent academic research has concluded that longevity plateaus at around 115 years, they insist that we will soon be able to eliminate death altogether. (Predictions vary from 20 to 100 years, a safe margin for error.) This vision is perpetuated by a strange cast of doctors, scientists, engineers, billionaires and crackpots, each with varying concepts of what eternal life will look like. Of these, one of the least crazed is Aubrey de Grey. He foresees what he calls the 'Methuselarity', according to which we can get ahead of ageing, by fixing failing parts of our body before they become seriously impaired. He concedes that this is tantamount to kicking the can down the road and could mean spending a large proportion of life undergoing medical procedures. But the rewards would be that 'We can stay as young adults, both physically and mentally, absolutely as long as we live. The only risks of death that we will have will be risks faced by young adults – being hit by a truck or the planet being hit by an asteroid.'

Acknowledging that pioneering technologies are notoriously difficult to predict, de Grey gives his vision a 50–50 chance of arriving in the next twenty years (as long as his fundraising is successful), but an 80 to 90 per cent chance in the next 100 years. Born in 1963, he might just make it himself if he doesn't meet a truck. His premise is breathtakingly simple: more life must mean a better life. Although he claims to be working to save the lives of millions – 'thirty September 11s every week!' – he seems strangely uninterested and ignorant about how those lives are lived. He takes it as a given that anyone not young should have a lot to complain about, that their lives must be worthless, detritus unworthy of attention, fatally flawed by age and mortality. So when asked how much time he spent with older people, he was flummoxed. Why would he want to do that? He wanted to *save* people from old age, not talk to them about it! Nor did he have any idea of how they might want to use the decades of life he laboured to achieve. What would they do with all this extra health and extra time? He hadn't asked them, but seemed certain he knew what they ought to want. Didn't everyone yearn to be a perpetually young adult? 'It is a reasonable supposition', he rallied, 'that people who still have the physical and mental vitality that young adults have would do whatever it takes to get the most out of life, to not get bored.'

That was the best vision he could offer: an infinite life of not getting bored. What de Grey couldn't imagine was that an endless life might be filled with infinite losses: habits, mores, rituals, language, fashions, old civilities that one might have embraced, invented, loved — and then lost as the world changed and life moved on. He couldn't grasp that individuals might feel burdened (even bored) by how much past they would be doomed to accumulate forever. We might no longer feel at home in a world where everything we were born with had vanished, to be replaced by new experiences and habits that would also vanish, to be endlessly rendered obsolete by a continuous and furious future that left us with more loss than we could handle.

The more obvious, practical question is where this immortal population might live. De Grey, acknowledging that he's neither an economist, sociologist, politician or environmental scientist, sneered at the question. Obviously, he insisted, as societies become more affluent, the birth rate falls, so the population will inevitably stabilise or decline. Would the planet cope? Well that was simple too: newer technologies such as renewable energy, desalination and artificial meat would mean that the average person would create 'less pollution'. The tone of boredom with which he stalwartly swatted away such petty considerations suggested that how the earth could supply the raw materials for immortality was clearly a question for lesser minds.

The logic of de Grey's vision is itself pretty simple. The increase in life expectancy over the last 150 years has derived primarily (but not exclusively) from disease prevention, so he is merely extrapolating that into the future. At a pinch, it's arguable that he might be doing us all a favour by forcing us to confront the dangers inherent to infinitely increasing life spans. But what was, for him, a thrilling prospect, seemed so dreary. He cherished no great project that he craved more time to complete: no symphonies, no inventions, no permanent solution for climate change . . . nothing but just more time. To what purpose would these long lives devote themselves? He had no ideas. What makes him think that anyone will endlessly strive to get more out of life when there's an unlimited supply of it? Why do today what can be put off to the next century?

Combating ageing is big business. Not just the face lifts and the gym memberships. If, instead of a natural process, ageing is defined as a disease, then every person in the world becomes a potential customer with an infinite lifetime value (and data). Calico is Alphabet's (Google's) subsidiary that aims to 'devise interventions that enable people to lead longer and healthier lives'.[6] The company is one in a crowded network of academic medicine, big pharma and high tech that is doing with messianic hype what such organisations have always done: searching for medical problems whose treatment will be profitable and, in some cases, beneficial. Disparaging age while idolising youth has always been the pitch. At one end of the spectrum, this is puffed up business as usual; at the further end – and it isn't clear where Calico sits – are more radical outfits, with flavours of transhumanism that make de Grey's ambitions look pedestrian.

Google's chief engineer, Ray Kurzweil, declares that his strategy for life is never to die.[7] He hopes to attain this goal with a healthy lifestyle, a strict low-fat, low-carb, low-calorie, no-sugar diet and the regular consumption of a very large number of vitamins and supplements. (These products, newly branded as 'Transcend', are for sale, of course.) But he has also committed to having his body preserved in liquid nitrogen until such time as he can be 'reanimated'. Several companies provide this service, catering to the band of biohackers determined to discover, and sell, ways to perpetuate their existence.

If whole-body cryogenics is too pricey, the cheaper option is to have your head cut off and frozen, awaiting the day when it might be possible to take a comprehensive scan of the brain (neurons, connections, processes) that becomes a blueprint for reconstruction in some kind of supercomputer or substrate. Even Kurzweil has acknowledged misgivings – the technology might not work, his legal status would be unclear, he might lose control over the process.

His goal here is not just defeating death. Over the past decade, he has written extensively about the point at which artificial intelligence and human intelligence merge. By the 2030s, he argues, computers will be so powerful that we won't be able to keep up unless we enhance ourselves with their capabilities. (You could argue we are already doing that with the deep integration of smart phones into all aspects of our lives.) But Kurzweil goes further, imagining our brains uploaded into computers (or computers becoming embedded inside our brains), at which point distinctions between machine and human become moot.

By 2045, when Kurzweil will be ninety-seven, he believes that technology will surpass human intelligence and be capable of solving every problem. His so-called Law of Accelerating Returns argues that because human evolution and technological advances are exponential, we will finally be able to transcend physical and mental limitations to become pure intelligence. What seems to thrill him most about this vision is not so much the prospect of immortality – though he is deeply invested in that – but the opportunity to cast physical biology aside in exchange for engineering perfection. Is that the same as life?

From one perspective, this is just a modern rewriting of ancient myths around death and transfiguration. Where once we believed in gods, some now believe in technology. Investing in cryogenic storage is not that different from the medieval kings and barons who endowed chantry chapels in which sung masses for their souls would resound throughout eternity. (Most are silent now.) Religion and technology both ring with the rhetoric of inevitability, in which the voice of individuals is drowned out by the overweening powers that only a few enlightened (and powerful) prophets understand. It's a curious thought, to imagine Silicon Valley replacing in power and arrogance the dominance of the medieval church. In both, the glory of tomorrow always absolves responsibility for pain and suffering today.[8]

Intellectually, Kurzweil's vision might be dazzling to technophiles, but it isn't without its risks. All computer systems develop bugs, at the rate of about one per thousand lines of code, and even the most sophisticated engineers acknowledge that they often don't know why. Kurzweil can have no idea where these digital mutations will lead, but entrusting all life to a single platform means it's also potentially a single point of failure. Hardly robust.

But what is striking about transhumanists isn't their enthusiasm for machines so much as their dismal dreariness when it comes to describing life. I can admire the intellectual dazzle of Kurzweil's analogies between biology, technology and the stock market; I'm just puzzled by a mind that can't see that the stock market is already an inadequate model of economics and an even poorer one for life. Why is he, like fellow transhumanists Peter Thiel and Sam Altman, so uninterested in real problems, like the *fall* in life expectancy, even in rich countries like the United States? Or the immediate climate crisis that could, after all, make eternal life pretty miserable? The vision feels literally disembodied and strangely *in*human. Was it these technologists that Tim Cook had in mind when he said: 'You cannot possibly be the greatest cause on the earth, because you aren't built to last'?[9]

These men seem incapable of imagining a world being any good without them. Is that the bug they're trying to fix? The transhumanist world is largely white, male, middle-aged and middle-class. It isn't apparently optimised for women who might anyway be redundant with the advent of compliant sex-bots. And the disabled could disappear completely in a future that 'fixes' people. The transhumanist visions of life perfected are all about power – computing power, super-intelligence – whose aim is domination: the colonisation of space. They are authoritarian and amoral, with seemingly little concern for anyone who can't afford such longevity. Kurzweil acknowledges that things could go badly wrong and thinks that somebody (not he) needs to spend a lot of effort inculcating liberal values of tolerance, diversity and liberty. But those tasks feel secondary, requiring moral maids or nannies to clean up the mess after the master has departed on a higher mission. We are back in the land of prophecy as propaganda, where technology promises to relieve us of the burden of thinking for ourselves.

Much transhumanism comes across as merely adolescent. Having grown up in an era that celebrates youth, these men feel entitled to hang on to it forever. Would they ever bother to have children, or would their future be permanently populated by the same un-old people? Sacrifice is certainly not their game. Nor do they appreciate the value of death. All humans produce mutations throughout our lives. These produce variation, and the natural selection of varieties is evolution. But the accumulation of mutations (which is evolutionarily worthless after reproductive age) is ultimately what kills us. But there is no evolution without mutations. So death is necessary, an essential part of life. On a more mundane basis, imagine the despair of a nation under the spell of a demagogue, dictator or sociopath who will never die: Franco forever, a permanent Pol Pot. Do we really want everyone to live forever?

It is a gross failure of understanding and imagination not to see that death, however fearful, confers real benefits. In de Grey's case this seems particularly obtuse and ungrateful, as the money that funded his research came to him after his own mother died, leaving him a small fortune. Where would he be without her death? Instead of trying to eliminate mortality, we do better to see it as a final gift.

***

'I remember feeling an immense sense of relief when my father died,' Lucy told me. 'I know I was loved and cherished, and when that's gone, it's a shock. But after a few months, I had a feeling of freedom. Wow! I have thirty, forty years of active life left, maybe more, and this is my FIRST chance to live my life as I want! It was an incredible realisation: you used to think you were free but now, you really are.'

Lucy spoke to me on condition of anonymity, that's how profoundly she felt that her emotions at her parents' deaths were taboo. Though it is almost never spoken about, many people feel just as she does: not that they did not love their parents but that their death inaugurated a new phase of adulthood. After their parents' deaths, many loving children discover a mother's or father's opinion has subtly limited their choices, decisions or self-image. Love imparts a degree of compliance, a desire to please, at least to avoid conflict. When those psychological constraints are lifted, the world looks different.

Looking back, Lucy could see how dutiful she'd been – going home at Christmas, getting married where her parents could attend. These weren't regrets, but the sense that such compromises were over came as a liberation. Lucy was glad she had been a good and loving daughter. But she was also exhilarated by this new phase in her life, when she feels free to make different choices that are fully her own. Life has become, she said, much simpler: there are fewer constituents to placate.

As a parent myself, this is, of course, a bracing thought. I am reminded of the CERN scientists working on experiments the results of which they won't live to see. When I asked them how they felt about this, the reply stuck in my mind. It was important, they told me, to make way for the next generation who will have their own ideas. It would be wrong to stand in their way. Thinking of my own children, I can appreciate that leaving them can be my final contribution to their future.

Nobody understands this better than hospice workers, who spend their working lives helping the dying to find a good death. 'In so many cases, a good death is the last great gift that parents can give their children,' Penny Moorcraft says. 'When you are dealing with the dying, it isn't helpful to think only about them – you have to think about the ones left behind.'

Moorcraft works as a family support therapist at St Margaret's hospice in Taunton, Somerset. Where better to explore how people think about their final future than in a setting where it is the daily focus of everyone's attention? The hospice movement began in the 1960s when Cicely Saunders opened the first purpose-built centre to provide for the physical, social, psychological and spiritual needs of the dying, their friends and families. Original to Saunders was the idea that the whole life of the patient, not the disease, should be the focus of attention. This was a radical thought at a time when the industrialisation of medicine was gaining momentum. It remains a challenging proposition in many circles today: that death is part of life and should be treated as an equal part of human experience. Saunders also believed that the dying couldn't and shouldn't be considered in isolation, that their mental and physical states depended profoundly on a broader community of loved ones. Every death that occurs resonates for a very long time.[10]

For hospice workers, dying well is not a matter of biology but of biography, connecting the past with the future. So Moorcraft and her colleagues work with the whole family, and much of their work involves children. They strive to create positive memories of parents and grandparents that the children can take into the future. But they also have to consider the needs of the dying, their desire to cuddle children, but not frighten them. This has led them to think about transitional objects.

'The idea is to help with separation anxiety,' Moorcraft explained. 'We had an admin assistant who does fantastic crochet, so we asked her to make two animals: a big one and a small one. The parent/patient gets the smaller one and the child gets the big one. It's a bond. It helps them walk through what each is feeling. We had one patient with brain metastases and we could see her, cradling and hugging the little animal. As she got worse, the children moved away from her, but she still had her animal and they had theirs – and the kids saw that. It allowed them both to withdraw very gently. And that family has been very resilient.' At St Margaret's, every child and dying parent now gets their own set of animals.

Those who work in the hospice movement see themselves as endlessly researching what is required for a good death. Most people who think about their own death concentrate on paperwork, drawing up wills and detailed funeral plans, but such administration too often becomes a displacement activity, avoiding deeper conversations about impending death. But the failure to think this through explains why people often don't get the death they want. At St Margaret's, the staff suggests that we talk early to loved ones about where we want to die, who we want to be with us (and who not), how much pain relief we want, what activities or objects should be part of our life to the very end.

To achieve a good death requires being willing to think about and discuss such things in the period between becoming aware of disease and the time we die. Fear of what will happen is common to everyone. Not many people drop down dead; very few deaths are sudden. Most of us will die slowly but not painfully. Cancer is more manageable than heart disease. Most, but not all, death is quiet, a gentle winding down – and hospices have become renowned for their skill in providing this. St Margaret's is surrounded by gardens, fresh flowers are everywhere. It is full of friendly faces and fresh air. Staff, visitors and volunteers work together as a community to support each other. In fact, most of St Margaret's' work isn't done in their building at all but in private houses and nursing homes, where most people prefer to die.

Complex cases come into the hospice itself, but those too are managed so that the dying remain in control. Sally Reader, the palliative care consultant, described one long, difficult death of a man with an eleven-year-old son. Suffering from a head and neck tumour, he chose every form of treatment to stay alive as long as he could. He came into the hospice one day bleeding. He wouldn't go to bed, he wouldn't take any pain relief and he continued to bleed. It looked, Reader recalled, like a blood bath, but it was a good death because the patient called the shots. Doctors and nurses might have wanted him in bed, but he wanted to sit and hold his wife. That's what they wanted and that's what they got.

Everyone at St Margaret's can describe in detail the many good deaths that they have witnessed. Even as we lay dying, they say, we remain ourselves. Penny Moorcraft told me of two children who carried to university the hospice blankets they'd held as their mother died: not because it was a terrible memory but because it was a treasured one. Patients and their families aren't easily forgotten. Many family members return to the hospice, to stay in touch, volunteer or just to sit quietly in the place where their loved one died and to talk to people who aren't afraid of the subject.

Why are such conversations rare? In part it is because we don't see death in our daily lives. In the past century, world wars made death a shared experience: public, visible and honoured through ritual. Tony Whitehead, a survivor of the AIDS crisis, says now that one of the strengths that the epidemic experience gave him was an appreciation of the privilege of helping loved ones through the end. 'Sitting with my mother as she died, I thought: *I have been here before*. Maybe I'm better able to deal with these things. Because I've seen it so many times, I can be useful. That's very empowering, not being afraid.'

Such respect for death is unusual today. When my first husband died, I remember driving down Irish roads behind his casket, strangely moved as strangers on the street stood silently and removed their hats. They didn't know Michael or me; honouring the dead was an old ritual that paid respect to a common humanity. Returning to London, I sometimes noticed the exact opposite: acquaintances avoiding me because they didn't know how to be.

It's so hurtful when, told of a colleague's fatal illness, many at work say nothing, unable to do the right thing because they're so fearful of saying the wrong thing. All the staff at St Margaret's had stories like this to share, feeling that in our avoidance of death we injure the living and the dead alike.

Yet, increasingly, all over the world, a good death is coming to be seen as a human right. There is even a 'quality of death' index: one area in which Britain leads the world. While definitions are heavily influenced by cultural and personal values, globally they share two fundamental elements that cleave closely to Cecily Saunders's original work: a good death requires respect for patient judgement and the alleviation of all forms of pain. Death need not be associated with suffering – that's why hospice workers have become so expert in palliative care and why many regard the need for euthanasia as a failure.

I don't think I have ever visited a workplace that was more joyful than St Margaret's hospice. This is not because the people who work there – doctors, nurses, psychologists, social workers and, yes, accountants and HR executives too – feel themselves immortal. It is because they know that they are not. They appreciate that these last, precious moments of life influence the future – how those that remain feel about themselves and their loved ones. The work done in hospices is driven by the desire to make this experience not merely untraumatic but one saturated with beauty, meaning and love that will live on for years to come.

'People think hospices are all about death and dying,' St Margaret's CEO, Ann Lee, laughed. 'But ironically we are all about living, making the end of life a comfortable experience. Most people think you'll die a painful death. They always ask: "What's going to happen?" And we tell them that at some point over the last few hours, breathing will stop. They ask: "Is that it?" And the answer is yes, most deaths are that simple. We try to get dying understood – it is going to happen but it needn't be scary.'

Unsurprisingly, everyone working at St Margaret's uses their experience to inform their own plans for their death, talking to their families, considering what matters most and sharing those intentions. Sitting around the table, discussing what they do and don't want at the end of life proves a surprisingly jolly conversation. The plans are, they tell me, somewhat akin to those that mothers make during pregnancy: a list of hopes and principles made in order to feel involved and in control of the process. Death plans are designed to give the dying power over what happens to them, in part because this leaves survivors better able to carry positive memories into the future. Hospice workers often become involved in these plans well in advance, ensuring that the dying and their family can preserve their relationships and not get sucked into the overzealous medicalisation of death. St Margaret's has even developed its own funeral service, so that the families they have worked with needn't, so abruptly, have to confide in strangers at a moment of such intimacy. Even at the very end of life, when contingencies and choices contract, we still touch the future.

'When they're dying, people don't cease to be themselves; they often are more themselves than ever,' Ann Lee says. 'And people like to say goodbye.' She recalls one patient who threw a huge garden party, like a funeral that he got to attend. Raj Thamotheram did something similar: an evening of talk, discussion, food and drink full of all the people and ideas that sustained him throughout his life. The community that came to support him poured huge amounts of time into planning it: how could they say they didn't have the time? When else might they get the opportunity to be so explicit about their love and respect?

At the end of life, it's easy to feel that such events are a waste of time. But they aren't. Ann Lee explains to patients that it is important to show your family how to die. 'How you do that and how you demonstrate how to cope is one of the best lessons you can give. It will make such a difference to them, to the rest of their lives. They find it quite empowering. It's a final gift.'

When it comes, the moment of death is both obvious and indescribable. In an instant, a person becomes a body. For survivors, this feels impossible: that it is real, that it is now and that it is forever. Many hope that all the grief they've already experienced will soften the blow, though that's rarely true. However fully we allow ourselves to know, with absolute certainty, that someone we love will die, the difference between the idea and the reality is everything.

Death is transition. For the religious, this is codified and ritualised. For the rest of us, it is internalised. The people I have loved and lost remain with me forever. They continue to shape who I am and how I think. I don't remember when Michael told me that he thought second marriages, after bereavement, were proof of a good first marriage – but the memory of that conversation was permission to have a full life after he'd gone. Memories of my father's dirt-poor hometown have forever informed the way I think about poverty. My complex feelings about my mother become wonderfully simple when I go to the opera that she taught me to love. I frequently recall a conversation with Alan that stopped me in my tracks and changed the way I thought. I will never forget driving with John on Riverside Drive. And any mention of Texas will always remind me of Olivia: her glamour, her laughter, her refusal to be simplified, and I will remember her not at one age but for all the time I knew her. These people are immortal in me, trace elements of a future that my children will inherit, often not knowing where they come from. I will never be certain where they go. The best I can do is set them free.

CHAPTER TEN

BE PREPARED

Can I get there?
Where the deer pounces on the lion,
Where the one I'm after's
After me?

— RUMI, *The Blocked Road*

On 11 September 2001, Richard Hatchett was on a bus heading to work at the Sloane Kettering Cancer Center in New York City. He was reading about self-organising systems and thinking about the role that narrative plays in decision-making. Like most New Yorkers that day, what he chiefly remembers is how ordinary it was at the beginning and how extraordinary by the end. In a matter of hours, Hatchett found himself engulfed in a self-organising system that emerged as he and his colleagues scrambled to establish a triage area. Out of the measured pace of a cancer treatment centre, a four-storey field hospital suddenly appeared, and it left Hatchett thinking about the contours of order required by unpredictable events.

Hatchett, an English major, had wanted to be a writer. But that day's experience left him with an abiding curiosity about medical policy. What could have prepared New York's hospitals better? Was there any kind of infrastructure that might have made the city able to respond faster? He began to move from the traditional management focus on efficient planning to a more expansive, imaginative concept of preparation. In a world punctuated by events that are generally certain but specifically ambiguous, preparedness might offer a more robust approach.

Today, Hatchett is the chief executive of the Coalition for Epidemic Preparedness Innovation (CEPI) that describes itself as 'a global insurance policy to defend against future epidemics'. It grew out of four key insights: first, that epidemics come without warning; they are inherently unpredictable. In a world of global travel, they move fast: an outbreak could spread to all major capital cities within sixty days. Since the 1970s, new pathogens have been emerging at the unprecedented rate of one or more a year. Finally, no two epidemics are the same; they don't repeat themselves. There is no profile of an epidemic, because new strains of a wide array of diseases constantly evolve, because separate geographies with distinct medical, education and transportation systems require a variety of logistics and supplies, because wildly diverse cultures respond to different messages and authorities in specific ways and because successful approaches are both medical and non-medical, albeit in different proportions.

Much of this thinking grew out of the Ebola crisis of 2015/16, which had presented a paradox: the response had been successful – for the first time in history, an effective vaccine was developed in the midst of an epidemic – but it had also failed: doing so had taken too long, costing over 12,000 lives.[1]

The question for CEPI, and for Hatchett, was: what could be put in place ahead of an epidemic to accelerate an effective response whenever and wherever it was needed? At the very heart of CEPI was an acknowledgement that prediction would not be the answer – but preparedness could be.

Vaccines, says Hatchett, are the be-all and end-all of epidemic responsiveness. But developing candidates is expensive and slow. The first Ebola vaccine was in development in 2003, tested in monkeys in 2005 but then stalled because, with outbreaks so sporadic, it was impossible to test it. But the fact that the process hadn't had to be started from scratch accounted for the signal success of ending the 2015–16 epidemic. It would be prohibitively expensive to develop vaccines for every possible disease, so CEPI chose to focus on three kinds of diseases that pose the biggest risk and where a successful vaccine is most likely: MERS, Lassa and Nipah. 'We are playing roulette,' Hatchett acknowledged. 'But we have to put our money down somewhere. Lassa is endemic in Africa and has 300,000 cases a year. Nipah is just a very scary disease, with a very wide geographic dispersion spread by bats. And we feel like the world has put us on notice that we have to deal with beta corona viruses, like MERS and SARS, because they have pandemic potential.'

Each disease requires three to six vaccine candidates because some will fail. Researchers don't know which part of the immune response is critical to controlling the disease, or what the antibody needs to be or how fast the disease will change in response to the vaccine. So these are 'just in case' candidates: in case the disease breaks out, in case one of them works. The failure of some will look inefficient but having several options makes it more likely that CEPI will have vaccines already at an advanced stage of development when the next outbreaks occur. The organisation isn't banking on a single theory of vaccines but making bets on categories of disease – those with high likelihood and big impact – because these provide more robust options.

But when the time comes for the mass production of a successful vaccine candidate, then efficiency must be a priority. The second prong of CEPI preparedness adopts a just-in-time approach. (Just-in-time management systems, developed in Japan during the 1970s, aim at maximum efficiency by buying and shipping everything at the last minute, when uncertainty is minimal.) That means that Hatchett is developing systems now that will be able to mass-produce vaccines fast: 'Mainstream pharmaceutical markets don't care about manufacturing speed, but we do: the time it takes to produce the vaccine, the time it takes from injection to immunity and the time it takes to manufacture at scale. These aren't market imperatives so we have to work with all kinds of companies and technologies that offer us the greatest utility and speed against a future we can't predict.' In practice, that means that CEPI invests in and facilitates manufacturing processes that are specifically designed for emergencies.

The third prong of CEPI's preparedness requires an appreciation of what it is that vaccines *don't* do best. Before coming to CEPI, Hatchett spent a decade exploring different models of responsiveness. After 9/11, he worked in Washington D.C. setting up a medical reserve corps and writing a national food plan for the US in the face of chemical, biological and nuclear threats. Fifteen years of thinking about how to prepare for unquantifiable risks has made him alert to how flexible any response to complexity must be.

He had been tempted to look at models as a way of simulating experiments. Science has often turned to mathematical simulations where data is scarce and, in epidemics, it is always scarce because each one is different – or, as data scientists put it, $n = 1$. But the more that Hatchett dug into simulations, the more he came to see their shortfalls. As an English major, he sensed that they were poor at capturing subtle, contextual and cultural information that was too hard to quantify: 'The danger arises when you turn to models to make decisions,' he says. 'It's too easy to mistake the simulation for the real thing, to believe they're more precise than they can be.'

For policymakers with little first-hand knowledge, the danger of computer simulations is that the model looks so much like reality that it is tempting to think that the right answer for the model will produce success in the real world. Models, says Hatchett, 'are not designed to give answers; they're at their best when they help you to think and to ask questions. So we think about everything we can relating to vaccines – but we can't leave out our understanding of all the other components, the social aspects of a successful response to an epidemic.'

In the 1918 flu pandemic, for example, some urban populations proved more resilient because they implemented social interventions earlier: closing schools or banning massed gatherings. The earlier the social interventions, the stronger the reduction of the peak of the epidemic. The same was found during the bird flu epidemic in Mexico in 2009.[2] However crucial vaccines are, they have to be part of a wider system that takes into account all of the social, political, economic and geographic complexities of context. These are resistant to mathematical modelling – quantifying them is difficult, if not impossible, because it's hard to gain consensus around what matters, why and how. What CEPI can't do is conceive of epidemics as purely medical problems. So the third prong of its preparedness is its participation in a global ecosystem of epidemic responsiveness. 'All of this is less about prediction and more about understanding the terrain,' Hatchett says. 'There is no entity in the world, not even in the US, that could do this alone. We have to own it collectively and find a collective solution.'

Epidemics are always crises, so everything depends on speed. Just-in-case vaccines, manufactured just in time, work only if accepted by the culture and people that need them. That means relationships have to be carefully nurtured and negotiated *before* an outbreak – or, as Hatchett puts it: 'Don't exchange business cards in a crisis.' But, to reiterate, an epidemic is always a crisis. So as important to CEPI as the vaccines and manufacturing platforms are human relationships: between researchers, physicians, local doctors, health professionals and governments in countries where outbreaks are most likely. During the 2015 Ebola outbreak, for example, a big chunk of the five months that it took to set up clinical trials was spent building relationships that hadn't been done in advance. That cost lives. Many Ebola victims died because of a suspicion of vaccines – were they poison? – and the invasion of foreigners in SUVs who might, or might not, have come to help.[3] Changing such attitudes takes time – fostering public engagement, behavioural understanding and cultural awareness can be harder than the pure science. So, in Nigeria, CEPI works with the head of Nigeria's Centre for Disease Control and other Nigerian scientists to make decisions together about advancing vaccines at an early stage. Hatchett hopes to do that with every vaccine, in each country at risk, so that when the time comes, everyone will have spent years creating a shared approach. Building the necessary trust, generosity and reciprocal relationships – some of which (like the vaccines) may never be used – takes time. Investment today is the only way to guarantee speed tomorrow.

How much can you do before you need it? That was the question Hatchett had asked on 9/11 and that continues to drive him to understand the whole system involved in epidemics. Negotiating partnership agreements that may need to last for years requires careful judgement about what details to nail down now and what to leave for later when there's less uncertainty but also less time. CEPI is trying to streamline the due diligence needed for contractual relationships in order to accelerate them. Hatchett and his colleagues are educating and enlisting the global financial system to be informed, ready to provide capital the minute an epidemic breaks out. The whole organization has to consider the ecosystem of intellectual, political, financial, medical and social capital so that, when they're needed, they're available.

Preparing for events, some of which may never happen, might sound like a leisurely activity. It is exactly the opposite – Hatchett feels he is in a race to get ahead of events. That need for speed is real: in 2018, there were outbreaks of six out of the eight diseases designated 'priority' by the World Health Organisation: Ebola, MERS, Zika, Nipah, Lassa, and Rift Valley fever. He's discovered that you can't prepare for speed; the whole organisation has to get used to working fast all the time.

I first met with Hatchett when he was six months into his job. Just one year later, it was obvious that operating at speed is how CEPI itself functions. The standing start was the hardest and slowest; with each year, CEPI gains momentum. In the time since we'd met, nine partnerships had been established, nine vaccines were in development, two rapid response partnerships were each working on three vaccines and total funding had increased to $750 million for the first five years. With so much progress, CEPI has added two more vaccines to its portfolio: Rift Valley fever and chikungunya. But most important of all, they have demonstrated the value of preparedness: the 2018 Ebola outbreak in Équateur did not develop into an epidemic. Within eleven days of the first case, everyone who had been in contact with the disease had been vaccinated. That was faster than the disease's incubation period – so the disease had no time to spread.

Much of Hatchett's work resembles that of Chris Llewellyn-Smith's at CERN: immense amounts of diplomacy and negotiation to create a coalition of disciplines, institutions, individuals and industries rich enough in their understanding and perspectives to address extreme complexity. Beyond expertise, the job also demands a significant capacity for cultural translation. Hatchett's earlier desire to be a writer has not gone to waste. 'I get more mileage out of stories than out of arguments,' he laughs. 'Being able to tell real stories, like what happened to Ebola in Équateur province, completely changes the dynamics. And the stories illustrate how you can't think that this is just one thing – it's not just the vaccine. It requires the whole system.'

Strictly linear, command-and-control stories won't work. Hatchett has to be able to tell a story in which everyone has a role and a contribution to make: 'We need Citibank to help with currency exchanges, we need companies like Envio, Profectus, Emergent to develop vaccines. We need to work with my Nigerian colleagues to receive and test vaccines. We don't have control over *any* of these people – yet they're all eager to play their parts. Here is something that has tortured humanity for as long as humanity has existed and being able to talk about what this means, and to whom . . . well, I'm better served by my understanding of narrative than by all my scientific expertise.'

Preparedness has come to comprise four components. Just-in-case thinking means making significant, informed bets within a context of uncertainty. This produces vaccines. Just-in-time thinking maximises the efficiency of any aspect of the work that can be standardised, measured and predicted, such as manufacturing. Becoming trusted participants and investing in a dynamic ecosystem accelerates the effectiveness of vaccines within stricken communities. Cultural translation articulates, reinforces and adapts insight and experience. These four mark the contours of control that Hatchett so dimly glimpsed on 9/11. This approach is both efficient, where processes are predictable, and robust, where outcomes are uncertain. Collective human intelligence and the sense-making of stories underpins the resilience of the whole system.

Preparedness here is specifically non-ideological. Trusting to the market during epidemics has already been shown to be inadequate. An efficient mindset would try to force-fit a predictable model of disease onto unpredictable environments.

That would fail because the diseases can't be commanded. But a completely robust mindset would fail too because it would prove exorbitantly expensive. Expertise alone won't work without the glue of social capital. Like a human body, where specific organs play defined roles but all are connected and inter-dependent, preparedness generates the levels of adaptation and responsiveness that the problem demands.

This approach accepts complexity and change from the outset. There is no overheated rhetoric about eliminating epidemics, no war against viruses, no slogans of heroism and triumph. As you might expect from biologists, there's a humble, human response to the complex environment in which our species has always learned to adapt and thrive. Confidence doesn't derive from force-fitting a determined model but from a quiet belief in the human ability to keep asking better questions, to find and build better answers. Models speak to this as a means of exploration, but not as an engine of solutionism.

It may be easier to prepare for events whose horror has been visceral for centuries. But that doesn't mean it's impossible to prepare for events that have never happened; it just takes an act of imagination to extrapolate from early warning signs. After both 9/11 and Hurricane Katrina, the American agriculturist Cary Fowler started to wonder about what he called 'sooner or later thinking'. Experts had said a Category 5 hurricane would hit New Orleans sooner or later; intelligence agents had expected another terrorist attack on the World Trade Center. Why, Fowler wondered, instead of talking about it, hadn't people done anything? But then he turned that question on himself: what was he doing about threats to the world's agricultural diversity?

On his computer, Fowler kept a file of gene bank horror stories. In 2002, looting had wrecked Afghanistan's seedbank. In 2005, the Iraqi seed collection at Abu Ghraib was destroyed, and in 2006, the national seedbank in the Philippines had been wiped out by a typhoon. Seedbanks encompass millions of unique regional varieties, dating back to the beginning of agriculture. As such, they represent a compendium of successful evolutionary responses to every known environment. Some may be very useful, sooner or later, but we can't predict which. Because nature and climate keep changing, it's impossible to know what varieties could suddenly become life-saving. So the robust solution is to protect our entire genetic inheritance. Otherwise, Fowler reasoned, the world risked what he called 'a gigantic permanent extinction event' in which unique samples of crop diversity are lost forever. That's why he started to search for what he called 'a failsafe way to protect the world's stockpile of diversity'. What it required, he thought, was the safest place on earth. Just in case.

Svalbard is now home to the world's largest seedbank. It's an archipelago a thousand miles north of Norway, as far north as it's possible to fly in a commercial plane, and it is naturally very, very cold – so to the seedbank doesn't depend on refrigeration. Those natural advantages, however, aren't enough. Fowler needed to gain the trust of countries around the world in order to persuade them to donate seeds and find someone to manage the facility properly. So he went to talk to the Norwegian deputy foreign minister.

'If I get you correctly, this seed diversity that you want to conserve, this is the most important natural resource on earth?' the minister had asked. Fowler said yes. 'And you are also saying that this territory, that Norway has sovereignty over, is the best place in the world to conserve it?' the minister continued. Fowler said yes again, at which point the minister just threw his hands up in the air, saying, 'How can we say no?' The scale of the project might seem huge – but trivial when compared to the risk.

Today, the Svalbard seed vault is a long tunnel, running 130 metres into a mountain. Its construction, in a windy environment regularly visited by polar bears and where the temperature runs at -40°C, stretched engineering limits. Designed to function for thousands of years, Fowler's team had to contemplate climate change scenarios in which all the earth's ice melts, sea levels rise and the vault is hit by the largest tsunami in history. When it was ready, Fowler had to persuade countries to entrust him with every seed known to man, passed down through the generations for the past 13,000 years. A few people asked him what he'd been drinking, but Fowler is well known within his professional ecosystem; fellow agriculturists liked the idea and trusted him. Visiting the site is, for some of them, almost a religious experience. Svalbard has become a new cathedral project.

'I've seen people go out of that room with tears in their eyes,' Fowler says. 'This is not just a living history of human beings on earth, but it is also everything that our agricultural crops, and thus we, can be in the future.'[4]

Svalbard is a huge just-in-case project, which, like CEPI, is humble in the face of global complexity – wars, disease, ecological disaster – that can't be controlled or predicted. Both organisations act on the belief that imperfect strategies today beat perfect planning sometime in the future. They are designed to be adaptable and robust enough for events that *will* occur – even where there's wild uncertainty about when, or where or how. Both operate on the principle that just because there is no single source of control over events needn't exclude the possibility of positive action early.

***

Today, the rise of autonomous vehicles and drones makes the advent of killer robots a similar but manmade threat that can't wait to be addressed. The non-profit organisation Article 36 was established to develop treaties and frameworks to prevent unintended, unnecessary or unacceptable harm caused by weapons developed in the future. (The name refers to Article 36 in the 1977 Additional Protocol of the Geneva Convention, which calls for scrutiny of new kinds of warfare.)

After a career that involved working on nuclear weapons and cluster munitions, Richard Moyes is part of a team working towards a treaty that defines and enforces 'meaningful human control'. That three-word phrase is what Moyes calls a 'terminological meme': a simple, memorable phrase that both explains and defines the agenda, in much the same way that 'drugs into bodies' did for the AIDS crisis. The meme maintains everyone's focus even in the fog of future technologies. 'You can't directly produce the outcome you want,' Moyes explains. 'The issues are too complex, there are too many stakeholders. But, having done this kind of work before, we know there are certain things we will need. A lot depends not on rules but on modes of thinking: agreeing what's important, what the law says, ensuring that all the key players, including

victims (or potential victims), are seen and heard as partici-
pating stakeholders in any treaty.'

So being prepared also means considering the needs and
rights of those who aren't present and cannot represent themselves. For Article 36 negotiators, this means children. For
national governments, it can mean children too. Most legis-
lators think hard about the immediate consequence of their
work, but the election cycle rarely provides much impetus to
think beyond that, which means that a longer future is rarely
considered. The endemic short-termism of government was
precisely what the National Assembly of Wales attempted
to address in 2015 when it passed the Wellbeing of Future
Generations Act.

The idea for the Act was initiated by Jane Davidson, when,
as a minister in the Welsh government, she became fed up with
all the lofty talk about sustainability – and the absolute dearth
of action. The United Nations' Sustainable Development Goals
gave status, structure and urgency to her rage; the country
had committed to the SDGs but made little progress towards
attaining them. She was supported by a new generation of
bright young civil servants eager to turn her idea into action.

After the legislation passed, the first Future Generations
Commissioner for Wales, Sophie Howe, set to work in 2016.
The guiding principle of the work is sustainable development
applied to seven areas: making the country more prosperous,
resilient, equal, healthy, cohesive, globally responsible and cul-
turally vibrant. Each of these aims has its own convenor, who
is expected to integrate long-term thinking into public bodies,
collaborate with a broad cross-section of the population and
stop existing problems from getting worse. The convenors are

non-partisan and expected to focus on 'the art of the possible'.[5]

The first test came when Howe challenged a 25-year-old plan to expand the M4 motorway past Newport, a notorious congestion point. The plan, she argued, did not take into account the rise in rail passengers and changes in working patterns, with fewer people commuting to work. It overlooked the fact that fewer young people had cars, and those that did drove less. No one had considered poor air quality or that an extended motorway would make it harder for Wales to meet its carbon-reduction targets. But the huge borrowing require-ment for the project meant that future generations would be stuck with the bill for years to come.

'I asked the people backing this project to explain to me how it met our goals for a healthier Wales, how it addressed the goal of a more equal Wales, when 25 per cent of people don't have a car – and they couldn't!' she laughs. 'I definitely put my neck on the block coming out against it, but if I'd gone along with it, the Act would have meant nothing.' At the end of the public inquiry, the inspector recommended that the exten-sion go ahead, but when the final decision went to the first minister, the scheme was cancelled. 'That's when people really started talking about the Future Generations Act,' Howe says. 'They thought the first minister had made the right decision. And the BBC said that in the next five or ten years, my job would be the most powerful in Wales!'

Howe has only soft power: to commission research, review the way that public bodies make decisions, make recom-mendations about how those bodies can better take the long term into consideration and to assess, every year, how well they are doing so. But that means she can shape the debate and encourage different modes of decision-making. Previous efforts along similar lines in other countries have been killed off by politics, so Howe thinks it's an advantage that the role is not held by a party politician. But she's canny. Howe served as a local councillor for nine years but left government in frustration. She then worked at reforming public services in policing, local government, housing and equalities policy. 'I know', she said, 'how the system works, and how to have influence. I know where the bodies are buried, so I'm not afraid of calling things out. So this is my dream job.'

Looking at policies through the lens of future generations upends ancient assumptions. In public health, Howe noted that just 10 per cent of life expectancy depends on healthcare services. By contrast, 29 per cent depends on housing conditions (clean air, houses, green space), 18 to 19 per cent on social capital and 30 per cent on jobs and welfare. But, traditionally, medical healthcare has always dominated the national budget and, prior to the Future Generations Act, there was no mechanism to address health holistically. But Howe is now challenging health, housing, environment and welfare bodies to work together to craft a preventative strategy.

Similarly, she's shaken up industrial policy, asking why the government should subsidise old, dirty industries like car manufacturing, when a country so rich in wind and waves could invest in and lead the modern, renewable energy industry instead?

It was fine for the Education Department to restructure the school curriculum, but the Commission is now enquiring what is being done to retrain the staff who have to teach it. 'People may need to do less work in the future and we'll have more old people,' Howe adds. 'We might go on a pathway of saying we want to have a four-day working week, because on the fifth day, we want you to look after your neighbour. I know it's utopian, but how else are we going to think about these trends? We have to set out a vision for the Wales we want.'

Howe has a team of only twenty people. But she's resourceful, grabbing civil servants in other departments to come and work with her on secondment. That way, when they go back to their permanent positions, they've absorbed a way of thinking about the future that she hopes will inform their home department. A practical, political understanding that 'everything has a consequence for everything else' can, she believes, lead to better integrated policymaking. She is also fond of what she calls 'back-casting': working from a future that the citizens endorse to figure out what needs to be done now. 'The legal definition of "a prosperous Wales" nowhere mentions GDP,' she says. 'So we have to escape the trap of thinking that prosperity is only about economic growth. It has to encompass far more than that. We have a legal and a moral obligation to leave the world better than we found it.'

The dream job is intense, not least because Howe is also on a mission to take the Welsh blueprint to the rest of the world. Canada has just amended legislation to reflect responsibility for future generations. In the UAE, much of the wellbeing strategy is being taken from the Welsh experience. Gibraltar is trying to pass legislation that is, she says, virtually identical, and she is in discussion with the New Zealand government too. 'I could', she says, 'be in a different country every week because their governments are getting to know about what we're doing here and want to know more.' When we spoke, she was just back from the United Nations, whose director general had seen in the Future Generations Act a mechanism to smash some of the siloes forming around the sustainable development goals. 'They're treated as single issues,' she says, 'but they are all interconnected. Sustainable needs have to be taken laterally.'[6]

Wales is serious about preparing for its future. This is typical of small countries. Unlike rich, powerful nations, the Welsh don't have the luxury of natural resources or economic clout to imagine they can call the shots, so they have to be nimble, creative and collaborative. Being small may also make it easier to get things done, but being clear-eyed about their vulnerability is a real prompt to action. The speed with which the idea has spread is testament to the power of small things – ideas, individuals, countries – to make a big impact on complex environments. One of the key requirements in mapping the future is to notice these, and to share and copy them prodigiously.

A mixture of the pragmatic and the utopian, the Act implicitly recognises that any five- or ten-year plan for the future would be an absurdly simplistic response to the complexity of the real world. But it also rejects the view that passivity or predictions provide the only alternatives. Instead, it galvanises all parts of the population to participate in their future, to feel powerful and responsible, regardless of age or status. The seven guiding principles help to shape experiments and design scenarios for possibilities that they can start exploring today. Howe would be the first person to say the Act isn't perfect. But it's a start. The only way the Welsh can prepare a better future for their children and grandchildren is by defining it for themselves. In accepting both their power and their vulnerability, we can see ourselves.

***

Being prepared in an age of uncertainty can intensify the craving for models. If the old model doesn't work, what is the new one? The perhaps unsatisfactory response has to be that there isn't one. Not only because of the flaws intrinsic to models, but because complexity won't fit them. Nor can a better future be made by zealots or ideologues. It is too diverse to yield for long to a single big idea or a binary view of the world, however tempting such simplification might be.

Being prepared means developing a very practical form of resilience. It also helps us kick our addiction to planning, making more time to pay attention to the details, contradictions and paradoxes all around us. Accumulating memories with which to plot a journey forward, as full of options and deviations as those envisaged by Eleanor Maguire's cab drivers. We aren't all artists, but we can all allow our minds to wander off the predictable path to explore what lies beyond it. The richer our knowledge and experience, the more easily we can identify where the opportunity for experiments lies. Makers of the future won't be downhearted when their results differ from expectations but will persevere, uncover and understand more meaning in uncertainty. Not knowing the future doesn't leave us passive, but puts the onus on us to be proactive in mapping it.

We all inhabit multiple interconnected ecosystems: the small ones we control; larger ones that we might influence;

and many that influence us, but over which we have no control and little or no influence. Preparedness requires knowing these ecologies in fine-grained detail, being alert to their changes, to the possibilities and problems they reveal and seeing where need and resources intersect with personal passions. Ignoring these connections, being ignorant of what they are and how they behave, is dangerous. Scenarios use all the material that our experiments and wandering minds have gathered. The stories we make about where we are and where we could be are a form of preparedness, be they positive (what we might hope to achieve) or negative (what we fear for ourselves and from others). The need to do this work is particularly acute in organisations, each of which can expect 'plastic straw' moments of their own: occasions on which supposedly solid ground disappears from beneath our feet.

Making the future is a collective activity because no one person can see enough. No one can have an adequate argument alone or in an echo chamber. So the capacity to see multiple futures depends critically on the widest possible range of contributors and collaborators. Leave perspectives out and the future is incomplete or invisible. This isn't only a democratic imperative but a frank acknowledgement that those not involved in making the future will have knowledge and motive to upend it. The emergence of open strategy, in which individuals at all levels can contribute to mapping their organisation's future, is much more than a tacit acknowledgement that insight and intelligence exists everywhere. For decisions to be credible, seen as being for the good of the whole, they must be developed by more than a few authorities or experts. That this process can be intelligent, meaningful and productive is demonstrated repeatedly in deliberative polling, citizen juries and assemblies. Engaging diverse minds is a more robust way of capturing the complexity of the environment in which decisions, policies and laws succeed or fail. In many ways, CEPI, the Svalbard seedbank, Article 36 and similar organisations are doing what Mary Warnock did with her fertilisation and embryology commission: preparing for uncertain future events and technologies by consolidating understanding and consensus to support positive, early action. She understood that decisions, however good, fail if not regarded as legitimate.

Our institutions, corporations and organisations need reform to be prepared, to maintain trust and to stay relevant. This requires the development of a mindset prepared constantly to review their relationship with the society they serve, and with the ecosystems in which they operate and influence. Imagining that whole swathes of the population and environment can be overlooked in preference to a focus on financial performance might once have been considered operational discipline. Now it just looks like institutional wilful blindness. For the public to believe that its institutions and economy are legitimate requires that they visibly support everyone touched by them. That is the only pragmatic protection against surprise. To be prepared requires that, in some shape or form, every organisation has its commissioner for future generations.

This calls for a new kind of leadership. Those who will rise to that challenge will be outstanding convenors, better chosen for their scepticism than their confidence. Collecting voices, structuring exploration, keen listening and synthesising success and failure will be the focus of their work. They will need to be excellent interrogators of the ecosystems in which they reside, aware of where they fit and the impact of their decisions on others. Being able to reconcile opposites – efficiency and robustness, just-in-time and just-in-case – will prove a hallmark of their adaptive minds. The unborn children who will make great leaders will be able to hold the tension between urgency and integrity, to stiffen the resolve for what is confusing, frustrating and frightening and to resist simplifying what is innately complex.

Like the director general at CERN, or the leaders of backbone organisations, like Richard Hatchett or Sophie Howe, Oliver Burrows or Fiona Wilson, an effective leader's principal asset isn't power but the ability to make a better future feel possible, practical and meaningful. They will need the moral authority to be honest about sacrifices and they will have to resist the rhetorical allure of over-simplified fantasies. Where will they come from? From everywhere, identified by courage and energy or, like Iris Long in the AIDS fight or Greta Thunberg in the climate crisis, they may emerge unpredictably, living evidence of the huge impact of small surprises. Such leaders are characterised by rational optimism, a grounded belief in human capacity. They don't accept that, as a leading psychologist put it, 'We've seen the enemy and it's us.' They scoff at the goal proposed by a science technologist 'to defeat mother nature'. Instead, they find in humanity and nature all the strength we need to seize the day. Progress will be indirect, lumpy and hard to measure, accelerating at times and stalling at others. Those who can work together will fare best.

The need for legitimacy doesn't render expertise useless or trivial. As the astronomer Martin Rees argues, there is no ivory tower or penthouse high or remote enough for scientists and engineers to disown accountability for the uses to which their work is put. This means that the choices we face, of any kind, have to be informed and led by values beyond those that science, engineering or any single discipline can provide. None of the challenges we face will be solved by expertise alone, but it places on experts the responsibility to explore humbly all the consequences and ramifications of their work on everyone. It is only together that legitimate boundaries for technology can be defined.

The future is also personal. Teen daughters are changing attitudes to the climate crisis, just as attitudes to AIDS shifted when parents watched their sons and daughters die or when scientists met patients and activists. Such epiphanies can't happen without love and friendship. That means making time for each other in order to develop bonds of trust and respect strong enough to weather crises. So the future is personal but not individual, because so many of our private decisions have consequences beyond ourselves.

Perfection is a problem. The great cathedrals weren't built following immaculate plans; they evolved through conviction, collaboration and a stubborn belief that the work mattered. In confronting the existential challenge of climate change, we could have, should have, started earlier. Waiting for the perfect plan wasted precious time. But the emergency is here now and we need all the qualities and insights discovered, at high cost, by the survivors of all crises: the determination to act on every front, before the last detail is known, to make common cause with those we might consider enemies, to experiment everywhere, to keep visible the deadly damage being done today, to be honest about unavoidable sacrifice, to support the broken and downhearted and to remember that courage drives courage.

Threats to our future come from anyone or anything that disparages or diminishes those gifts. Of these, the biggest insult to our power to craft a fitting legacy for successive generations comes from technology. The automation paradox is a physical reality. The more we surrender to the authority of devices, the less independent and imaginative our minds become, just when we need them most. Extravagant claims for artificial intelligence don't just denigrate real intelligence but mask a determination to force the world into predictable patterns. In a complex world, replete with contingency and uncertainty, nothing could be more dangerous than to constrain imagination, freedom and creativity. When industry leaders acknowledge that 'the goal of everything we do is to change people's behaviour at scale', they tacitly acknowledge that we aren't merely data, that we are complex and unpredictable and that the only way they can make predictable profits is to shackle us to their digital devices with rewards and punishments. But we become digital slaves only if we think of ourselves as no more than data. Nothing is inevitable, unless or until we surrender the right to use the freedom that we have.[7]

Every time we use technology – to nudge us through decisions or to interpret how other people feel – we outsource to machines what we could and can do ourselves. It's an expensive trade-off. When we surrender our emotional intelligence to parenting apps, we give up on the chance to learn about ourselves and our children. The more we meet people we are programmed to like, the less we can cope with those who are different. And the less compassion we need, the less compassion we have. So the more we let technology think for us and act for us, the less we will be capable of thinking and acting for ourselves.

The companies enforcing this sterile, monoglot view of the world are so few, so homogenous and so powerful that they represent a big and obvious threat to the economic and cultural diversity of the world we inhabit. At a time when both humanity and the planet are struggling to preserve the variety that evolution demands, a single, impoverished definition of life's meaning undermines the will and skill needed to build a better future for us all.

Imagination, creativity, compassion, generosity, variety, meaning, faith and courage: what makes the world unpredictable are also the strengths that make each of us unique and human. Accepting uncertainty means embracing these as robust talents to be used, not flaws to be eliminated. This book began with two questions: what do we need to do, and what do we need to be, to map the future? What we need to *do* is to hold fast to the gifts we have, and to develop them together. What we need to *be* is human. The future will always be uncharted, but it is made by those active enough to explore it, with the stamina and imagination not to give up on themselves or each other. We have no need to be slaves and we have no right to enslave future generations. All we owe to ourselves and to generations yet to be born is to hone the gifts we have to create the best that we can imagine, exercising daily the self-determination that built cathedrals. It doesn't matter where we start, only that we do.

POSTSCRIPT

I did not predict the Covid-19 pandemic. That epidemics appear throughout the book merely testifies to what we know about them: that they are always with us but, lacking any defining profile, they are unpredictable. As such, they are the perfect emblem of uncertainty. That combination of knowing and not knowing is what makes it so intensely painful.

Nothing since publication in February 2020 has changed my views of how unpredictable the world is or about the means we have to deal with it. But I underestimated how deeply intransigent our craving for certainty about the future is and therefore how profound the shift that we now need to make. Once the implications of Covid-19 began to emerge, some individuals and institutions moved quickly and intuitively to a whole new mindset – but most have not. They are still mired in linear thinking and convinced, in the midst of complexity, that somewhere certainty is to be found in models and prescriptions. That anachronistic frame of mind has turned out to be both damaging and inadequate.

At the outset of the pandemic, many pinned their hopes on forecasting and super-forecasting. Such quasi-religious faith renewed fascination with Philip Tetlock's original research with the result that many (most notably Dominic Cummings and his acolytes) hinted at their own super-forecasting powers. But they overlooked one vital requirement: the best forecasters are open-minded, comfortable changing their minds. In other words, they are specifically non-ideological. That, Tetlock had explained decades earlier, is why famous forecasters fail, because they're held hostage by their big ideas, blind to anything that undermines their personal fame and power. To be able to develop informed insights about the future always requires open, sceptical and undetermined minds. But these are not, for the most part, the people we saw making decisions in government. Instead of seeking to understand the emergent nature of science, many sought to co-opt its authority.

Boris Johnson seemed to confuse strong leadership with certainty. Not a big deal, under control, over by Christmas: you can call such forecasts wishful thinking or wilful blindness but what you can't call them is helpful. The mathematician David Spiegelhalter appropriately castigated what he calls 'numbers theatre': using maths to create an illusion of control. But a pandemic caused by a novel pathogen, about which almost nothing was known, was actually a moment for doubt. Simulating confidence that was fake or foolish, ministers missed their chance to provide a way of thinking about the pandemic, to explain what was predictable and how much was not. Nobody wanted to admit how long vaccine development can take, that the record to date had been four years and the average ten, or that there are many diseases (like HIV) for which as yet no vaccines exist. This failure to communicate the ambiguity and complexity of our predicament presented grave difficulties later when other promised resolutions didn't deliver.

Instead, reliance on what politicians insisted on calling 'The Science' slowed down the pace at which the public came to understand that there is no such thing as The Science. There is only science, a process by which the best insights of the moment are constantly over-written by new knowledge as it emerges. Every day of the pandemic has been replete with minute discoveries, which often reveal how much more there is to discover. Nine months after the first known case, scientists were still learning about the difference in viral spread between aerosols (which remain airborne for some time) and droplets (which fall onto surfaces). The full story of this pandemic, its worst mistakes and luckiest judgements, will be understood only years after it is over when all the data is in. And even then, interpretations will be contentious.

Instead, still aiming at an outmoded image of strong leadership, the government perpetrated the myth that perfect decisions were possible and that outcomes could be predicted. What we all needed to understand (and have learned through failure) is that complexity requires decisions made with imperfect data. Just as Eliza Manningham-Buller knew, move too fast and leaders lay themselves open to charges of panic or wasting money; move too slowly and people die unnecessarily. What that means is that all decisions will be uncertain. Where a choice costs little but could bestow a real benefit, it is worth making. That was the case with masks; here data still remains ambiguous but wearing them isn't a huge burden. But when even that level of certainty can't be found, a good decision should be defined as one that can be both explained (the principles that inform it) and understood.[1] Absolute confidence is impossible and implausible and invites provoking distrust – and once trust in decision-makers is lost, influencing events becomes infinitely more difficult. Far more urgent is to build a shared perception of what is really going on.

We might not have been in such a mess had we prepared better. And we almost did. Certainly, the British government had spent a lot of time thinking about the threat. The 2015 National Security Risk Assessment identified a flu pandemic as a major risk, making it clear that not all risks could be prevented and that, therefore, adequate resources had to be made available to deal with them. In October 2016, Exercise Cygnus, a major planning exercise involving all government departments and the NHS, showed that the NHS would be stretched beyond breaking point with a shortage of beds and PPE.[2] Apparently, the subsequent report was so frightening that it was not released to the public.[3]

In July 2018, Minister of State for Security and Economic Crime Ben Wallace introduced the UK's biological security strategy, saying, 'We cannot predict all the ways in which this risk landscape will evolve in the future, but it is by breaking down barriers, working in a co-ordinated way across and beyond Government, and thinking globally that we will be best prepared to meet the threat of significant disease outbreaks (however they occur).'[4] Not much was said about how barriers were to be broken down and the report is stuffed with abstract nouns and vague intentions.

The report went on to say that, 'The UK has in place world-leading human, animal and plant health systems that are able to respond to a wide range of potential crises – from frontline responders to expert treatment.' Sadly, the report's contents were primarily a bureaucratic overview of existing systems with no substantial data about how they worked or even how they had been tested. Worse still, the reassuring tone that imbues the report suggests that little or no thought was devoted to what might go wrong, even though doing so typically leads to better design. Sometimes called a pre-mortem, thinking ahead about how failure might occur also makes it easier to learn when it does.

More detailed was the 2019 National Security Risk Assessment, which recommended that PPE be stockpiled, that procedures be established for tracking and tracing whatever pathogen caused the pandemic and that plans be put in place to manage a surge in deaths. 'A novel pandemic virus could be both highly transmissible and highly virulent,' it said. 'Therefore, pandemics significantly more serious than the reasonable worst case . . . are possible.'[5] These years of paperwork might explain why, in 2019, the World Economic Forum placed the UK second in a list of countries 'best prepared to deal with a pandemic'. (The United States came first.)[6]

But the Threats, Hazards, Resilience and Contingency Committee, which was responsible for overseeing pandemic planning, was suspended by Prime Minister Theresa May in order to release government capacity to focus on Brexit. And when Boris Johnson came to power in July 2019, the committee was scrapped altogether. There was, apparently, no spare capacity to consider remote possibilities like a pandemic when the immediate reality of Brexit consumed full attention. It wasn't just the NHS that lacked robustness; government did.

Hovering over this failure is the ghost of efficiency.

Preparedness is always at odds with efficiency because it calls for work and spending on things that might never be needed. Since the Industrial Revolution and the division of labour, efficiency has always been accepted as an unqualified good. But it delivers benefits only in circumstances with high degrees of certainty and predictability. In times of uncertainty, which is unquantifiable, efficiency becomes dangerous because it erodes the capacity to respond to surprises.

In the UK, a decade of austerity that followed the economic crisis had led to a loss of approximately 32,000 overnight hospital beds in England.[7] In the year before Covid appeared in the UK, between 80 and 85 per cent of critical care beds within the NHS in England were occupied. This was very efficient – so little waste – but it left very little margin for major incidents of any kind.[8] It also meant that, for English adults, there were just 9.1 beds per 100,000 people, compared to 34 beds per 100,000 in Germany. The difference proved important as it meant that, when Covid-19 struck, the German healthcare system had capacity to admit patients before their condition worsened but the NHS did not.[9] And in the period between January and the end of March 2020, there were 84,393 advertised full-time vacancies within the National Health Service in England.[10] This too might have been construed as efficient cost-saving, but it proved catastrophic.

That neither the government nor the National Health Service had the capacity to respond effectively to unpredictable events revealed a twentieth-century mindset, one that continued to believe in efficient planning, as though the world still operates along complicated, predictable lines. Super-forecasters would be able to see everything coming and to manage with technocratic efficiency the planned needs of the nation. This was leadership as anachronistic as 1938, when the British Army allocated the bulk of its transport budget to horses.

In part, it was dawning alarm at how ill-prepared for epidemics most governments were that had led to the creation of the Coalition for Epidemic Innovation (CEPI) in 2017. (The UK joined in 2020.) In retrospect, we might all wish it been launched earlier, but the foresight of establishing the organisation has been vindicated as countries and companies around the world have now piled in to support its work. This meant that the work didn't begin from a standing start. CEPI had already provided early stage funding in the Moderna vaccine and has gone on to assemble the biggest and most diverse vaccine portfolio in the world. Developing different technologies and platforms has been critical as it is impossible to predict which will work best, or to know which parts of the world's population will discover different needs. That there are so many isn't efficient, but because each takes a different approach, CEPI's approach is almost the definition of true robustness in science.

As the vaccine projects progressed, CEPI was quick to sense rising concerns around trust and integrity in the testing and distribution of vaccines. The organisation responded fast by creating a centralised network to assess and compare the immunological responses to all vaccine candidates. In the fetid atmosphere in which this highly competitive work is pursued, this might be seen as duplicative (inefficient) but it adds robustness to the health system: more verification is safer than less. In addition, a new initiative, COVAX is designed to ensure rapid, fair and equitable access to Covid-19 vaccines as soon as they become available. More than 170 countries (70 per cent of the global population) rushed to join, recognising that until everyone is protected, everyone remains at risk of the disease, its adverse economic effects, or both. A pandemic is no time to insist on pinpoint efficiency. That both initiatives were launched so quickly in the midst of the pandemic validated Richard Hatchett's early recognition that the way to prepare for crisis is to get used to working fast.

It's a lesson everyone had to learn. Almost overnight, it seemed, companies that had long resisted flexible working (a charter for slackers, some thought) moved large parts of their workforce to working from home. This was an enforced experiment and, to the surprise of many, productivity often went up, not down. Giving trust was rewarded with trust. During lockdown, many deeply rules-bound bosses seemed to intuit that caring was more important than carping. Frequent, two-way communication exploded as many companies sought to ensure that their workforce was keeping healthy and resilient. And, as real-time research by Veronica Hope-Hailey showed, many executives found that there was more to their workforce than perhaps they had realised. 'It was clear people can be trusted to do the right things,' one Human Resources director found. 'They don't need to fill in time sheets. People do the right things if you do the right thing by them.'[11]

Hierarchies started to crumble when Zoom and Teams screens were tiled with faces each occupying equal space. In refusing bonuses or taking pay cuts, many senior teams acknowledged that it was more important to look after the people who were keeping the company alive than to worry about their own income or status. Microsoft's director of human resources summed up what many organisations saw and did, saying, 'What makes the difference is knowing that I trust my colleagues, I trust my peers, I know they've got my back, I know I've got their back. We've pulled each other through.' In some organisations' value system, even share-holder value ceded its pole position.[12]

An exceptional experiment was taking place; did that mean that others would follow? For one euphoric moment, many spoke of a 'Big Reset', when the shared experience of Covid-19 would smash silos of ideology and class, galvanising the solidarity and determination that the crisis had demanded. Could this even be the moment when, at long last, the capacity for collective action that the climate crisis so urgently needed would finally be forced into being?

Not yet. With the speed that has come to characterise the pandemic, responses to it quickly split. On the one hand, having settled their workers at home with laptops and comfortable chairs, many executives went back to thinking, talking, dreaming about a return to normal. They continued to see the pandemic as an interruption, not a sea change. Having managed the working from home experiment and found in themselves an empathetic style of leadership, it soon looked as though that was enough change for them and many senior teams started to question how far they had really led anything. 'So who drove your digital transformation,' one Huawei executive quipped, 'the CEO, the CTO – or Covid-19?'[13]

Overwrought debate around office space, property prices and office work patterns fell into the trap of trying to predict what the future of work would look like. This was the moment for more experimentation, not less, but instead the search was on for a template, a road map, any confident prediction of the perfect home/office blend. Even though this experiment in remote working offered a chance to refresh organisational culture, few seized the strategic opportunity to do so. Instead, pundits made out like bandits with forecasts, models and thinktanks. And after all that outpouring of empathy, business leaders quickly began to talk of layoffs. Some managers suggested that it would be better if these were done by senior leaders because *not* knowing the people would make the decisions easier. Many firms had the financial capacity to make different choices but the rhetoric of inevitability quickly infested these discussions. Insidiously, old bad habits crept back.

To my surprise however, in the early months of the pandemic, a serious consideration of uncertainty seemed to grip economists and financial regulators. Alert to the dangers of an economic crisis, an unemployment crisis and the concurrent climate crisis, commentators and CEOs alike started to ask whether or not balance sheets and annual reports should contain some measure of robustness: how well prepared is this organisation for unpredictable threats? After all, in an age of complexity, investors couldn't be confident if all their information was retrospective and so little of it prospective. Uncertainty, they now saw, moves fast and it is impossible to get the full measure of an organisation if you can't see how well prepared it is. As the past now stood revealed as a poor predictor of the future, it seemed crucial that any business should be made to measure its own robustness; a requirement to do so would drive each to be better stewards of their assets.

A new idea started to emerge: that the quality of leadership of any organisation (business, charity, healthcare, education, government) could be seen in terms of preparedness.

These new observations seemed suddenly obvious and pragmatic in the first, febrile days of lockdown. How far they will withstand the gravitational pull of efficiency remains to be seen. Around the world, enforced change has demonstrated how creative, imaginative and risk-taking people could be. But technically, working from home could have been introduced over a decade ago. That so-called leaders had managed for decades to persuade so many to work in ways they hated was the perfect illustration of the status quo trap: the preference for lousy certainty over innovation.

That trap took on a grimmer mien when, in the midst of the first lockdown, the tragic killing of George Floyd sparked off renewed Black Lives Matter protests. BLM had been active for seven years, a burning issue fuelled each year by black deaths at the hands of the police. But what serious experiments had institutions and organisations done to create more just environments? If organisations insist on waiting for the perfect prescription for the elimination of systemic racism (and many do) then they are doomed to years of anger as deaths and protest recur. If only dire necessity is powerful enough to drive change then our chances of dealing with the crises heading our way are slender. We could, we should, get ahead of them. But will we?

In some organisations, a new plasticity emerged. At St Margaret's Hospice, thinking that a novel flu in China might cause problems in the UK, the in-house funeral service took the precaution of ordering extra coffins. When the crisis came, they shared these with less prepared local funeral homes. In this, they made partners of their competitors. They also made 198 taxis Covid-safe, to get their patients in and out of hospital safely. Not one caught the virus. Having already decided that a residential care centre was financially unviable and geographically discriminatory, CEO Ann Lee's team had already decided to care for all patients in their homes, because that's where they wanted to die. That left the residential centre empty, until Lee proposed that the local cancer treatment centre take it over to continue chemotherapy. In the first six months, it came rent free. But as demand for St Margaret's services soared, the cost of PPE tripled, no cost-of-living increase came from the NHS and fundraising dried up (charity shops were shut and events prohibited), a long-term rental agreement provided the hospice with much needed income. In the face of crisis, St Margaret's became more relevant than ever.

Within the NHS, early attempts at old-style command and control leadership mostly failed fast. Those who thought their moment of glory had come were quickly overwhelmed by the sheer scale and complexity of events and dismissed as power grabbers. But their defeat in turn collapsed a vast and intricate hierarchy into a single organism, which generated levels of collaboration and cooperation across all levels and between other services (ambulance, fire and rescue, social care) with an ease and speed managers had previously only ever dreamt of. No longer 'doomed to hit targets but miss the point', one doctor said, 'It was incredible, the ease with which we could do the right thing . . .' Free from all the tools of bureaucratic control, many went to exceptional lengths to improvise what the rules had previously made difficult. Many decisions were pushed down to a local level and to individuals.

At one NHS hospital, recognising that local care home workers had no PPE, doctors and nurses made the decision, at the end of a shift, to load their cars with it and drive it to their colleagues. Others went to extraordinary lengths to keep families together. Dentists became nurses and many doctors discovered (just as David Ring had done at Dell Medical Centre) that video consultations did not have to be the cold transactions everyone had feared. After years of centralised control, this freedom was a huge experiment for everyone – one that has shown them much about themselves and their colleagues. And one that they now labour to preserve.

At Ford, a collaboration with ventilator designer Penlon and manufacturer STI produced 17,000 ventilators in a few months, an achievement that would previously have been regarded as impossible in under a year. And while many famous names publicly or secretly failed the government's ventilator challenge, individuals discovered in themselves more capacity than they'd imagined. Martin Stanton, a former tech entrepreneur who ran a diving centre in Somerset, had earlier designed a rebreather, a small device for maximising the oxygen available to divers. Conventional hospital ventilators were expensive and Stanton noticed that hospitals were forced to close when they ran out of the pure oxygen on which the costly machines rely. Surely a rebreather could do a better job.

He contacted the Cabinet Office and secured their support – but also the overhead of process consultants assigned to help (or monitor) his tiny team. After the budget ran out (most of it going to the consultants), Stanton persevered. He believed in his device because he saw that, in countries where pure oxygen was unaffordable or inaccessible, it could be a life saver: his device needed just 10 per cent of the oxygen that ventilators require. And while conventional machines cost tens of thousands of pounds, his price ran in the hundreds. A few months after his support and helpers had vanished, Stanton's device passed all of its safety and standards tests and he secured a distribution deal for it to reach rich and poor countries needing a cheaper, faster way to keep their Covid patients alive.

As remarkable as the device, however, was the change in him. I've known Martin for sixteen years; he'd always been a very clever man with immense drive. But seeing his invention through to practical success gave him a different kind of energy. This was about helping people, about saving lives, about using his ingenuity to do something meaningful in the world. When it was done, he was exhausted – and he was different. He had discovered a sense of himself as a good man. Perfecting his product was not business as usual.

That the search for meaning intensifies in crises is as true for companies as for individuals. It isn't just that past usefulness can become redundant overnight (travel agents, theatres or restaurants), but that seeing communities in turmoil provokes a need to help strong enough to overcome the fear of experimentation: cider companies making hand sanitiser, chefs cooking for key workers and high-end restaurants turning to takeaway. Such sudden experiments were more than just a desperate need for cash; they articulated the desire to stay relevant and valued by their communities. The mentoring firm Merryck & Co. provided free coaching and mentoring to forty NHS leaders for no other reason than that they wanted to be helpful. In doing so, they also learned how to make many of their own practices faster at helping organisations in crisis.[14] And they discovered that a project which enlisted almost everyone in the company, imparted a sense of solidarity and camaraderie.

The John Lewis Partnership was already grappling with the crisis in retail when the pandemic struck. It might have confined its future thinking to cutting cost-cutting and redundancies. But when customers started coming into Waitrose stores offering to work for free just to keep the company afloat, that prompted a deeper line of enquiry. If the organisation meant so much to people, what more could it do to be socially useful? With a housing crisis, could redundant stores be turned into homes? With a social care crisis, was this an area the Partnership should explore? If customers felt so deeply about the company, what should the company do for them? How imaginatively the business dares to embrace the richness of that challenge remains to be seen.

The management thinker Peter Drucker once said that no healthy business could survive in a sick society. For artists, this took on a visceral reality. With exhibitions cancelled, galleries closed and many part-time positions on which artists depended axed, the extreme vulnerability of artists turned into crisis fast. DACS, the Design and Artists Copyright Society, collects royalties due from the reproduction or resale of artworks. Although it already distributes more money to visual artists than the Arts Council, much more would be needed if the visual arts communities weren't to die. How far could DACS reconfigure its services, expertise and knowhow to support all artists better?[15]

The Society convened multiple discussions with artists

about the effect of the pandemic on their work. The news was worse than they thought: very few artists could afford studios or materials and government schemes offered no protection. None wanted charity, they just wanted to be paid something for their work. From a conventional collecting society, DACS began to reimagine itself as an organisation that deployed intellectual property law, new technology, knowhow and global connections to build a more robust ecosystem supporting the livelihoods of visual artists. Its ambition now greater, all kinds of new possibilities suddenly sprang into view.

All around, small cathedrals were being built. Or reconceived. It's impossible to categorise where such deep exploration has been most prevalent because it has not been confined to any specific sector or size or industry. Underlying all of these new strategies is a shared awareness that the status quo is the most implausible of all scenarios. But these difficult reconfigurations have emboldened companies because they have accepted uncertainty as a persistent reality. What all of them are doing is asking the questions that Richard Hatchett asked himself at the birth of CEPI: in the future, what will we wish we had been doing *now*? Where are the contours of control? On the brink of an economic crisis, an employment crisis and already mired in an inequality and climate crisis, where can we make an impact?

Asking such a question mid-pandemic might seem incredible, even impossible. But consider the gathering of world leaders for three weeks at the Bretton Woods Hotel in July 1944. With the Second World War not yet won, victory not yet guaranteed, 730 delegates recognised an urgent need to design a new economic order for the moment when the war was over. They dared not wait – and not just because the hotel owner was eager to re-open as soon as they were gone. Instead, they negotiated, argued, designed, redesigned and reconfigured over dinner and through the night. Because the elegant but vast New Hampshire hotel had just one lift that had to accommodate everyone, John Maynard Keynes could be seen running down hallways and charging up and down stairs, so urgent did he feel it was to reach an implementable agreement. When he failed to attend the last night's dinner, delegates wondered if he had died. But he was still working. The future, he knew, would come faster than anyone could control and he could not wait.[16]

This is, in essence, what Paul Polman did when, as CEO of Unilever, he re-oriented the company towards decoupling growth from environmental degradation. Instead of waiting for a mandated prescription for dealing with climate change, he sought to get Unilever ahead of the climate crisis and fit for a demanding future. The crowd didn't race to copy him (traditional business models seemed more predictable) but a growing number have been inspired by his lead. Instead of fretting over unanswerable questions about the short term, or waiting for the perfect masterplan, they are asking themselves forward-facing questions: in this new world, what people, talent, products, intellectual property, constituents, reputation and knowhow do we have? How do we reconfigure those to make them more relevant to a world in crisis? They are moving quickly, convening those they serve and depend on to help explore what could be possible and useful. Their sense of urgency, like Keynes's, is extreme. They've had a taste of the acceleration that crises bring and they are not going to wait until the fog clears. These individuals and their organisations are invigorated, more than up to the task of building cathedrals and eager to get started. Doing scenario planning on speed, like Nokia's Risto Siilasmaa, comes easily to them because it is a form of action. And action is how they search.

How far will that mindset characterise the age of crises in which we now find ourselves? It's impossible to know. The political scientist Robert Putnam noted that, following 9/11, America changed dramatically. Community feeling and connectedness increased measurably and the country felt different. How long did that last? It took just six months, Putnam said, before levels of social capital were back at their original low levels. The fact that the pandemic has already lasted longer than six months, with no immediate end in sight, might embed change better. And in his more recent work, reviewing how America moved from the gross inequalities of the Gilded Age to a period of rising equality and growth between the 1930s through to the 1960s, Putnam posited that formal leadership may be a lagging indicator. Real change starts at the grassroots, where it's often hard to see. In which case, the necessary mind-shift we need may already have begun. The pandemic has changed us all, even if we can't yet see how. We have not been here before and nobody knows what happens next.

When I originally wrote this book, it was from my sense that we deeply misunderstood the world we inhabited, that we were trying to force-fit determinist thinking onto a world that was inherently unpredictable. Mostly I thought that was because doing so was comfortable and profitable. I still believe that is part of the explanation. But I've come to see that many have simply failed to recognise, or adapt to, the profound consequences of the world's increasing complexity. When the World Economic Forum talked about the Fourth Industrial Revolution, it didn't just mangle a metaphor. It implied that the major change was a technological one. They underestimated. A smooth transition to a digital world is not the only or the most pressing challenge; a new way of thinking, deciding and acting is.

The inability to predict and to plan requires a whole new way of thinking, working and living together. The pandemic is a test: do we have the courage to experiment and the imagination to see how and where? We can't acquire these skills until we accept uncertainty and start to do the extra work needed to produce communities, companies and countries that are robust. Not merely efficient. Not simply rich. But able to withstand shocks we cannot see coming. That means we all need to get good at change. At convening. At listening. At seeing each other as a source of strength. Nobody imagines this will be easy and many will experience a deep sense of loss as they relinquish old, comforting illusions.

If we can't find the change in ourselves, younger generations might. They have never known a predictable world. The seminal experiences of those born in the 1990s are these: 9/11. Banking crisis. Economic crisis. Migrant crisis. Brexit. Trump. Climate crisis. Pandemic. That's their world. They are routinely underestimated and belittled with praise for being 'digital natives', as though their only value comes from being able to tweet and code. They have far more to offer. A burning demand for justice. No expectations of guarantees, permanence or formulaic solutions. A sense of solidarity with others not like themselves, but who are similarly impotent, overlooked and underrated. A deep experience of injustice, as the group most profoundly disadvantaged by the crises their elders have so mismanaged. Everything these young people do in the world today is an experiment because no certainties are available to them. That they have never grown up with certainties may be their greatest strength and our greatest hope. It is high time that we gave them our power, our resources and our support to create a better future for themselves.

ACKNOWLEDGEMENTS

If I needed a lesson in unpredictability, writing this book was it. Like every other book I've ever written, this one had a schedule. Unlike every other book I've written, this schedule kept being blown up. So I apologise to all the people I didn't see, meetings I didn't make, parties I missed and the many kindnesses I'm sure I overlooked. Writing this book has been a daily reminder that uncertainty may be full of possibility, but it can also be full of shocks and horrors.

In the face of dire predictions that print was doomed, Natasha Fairweather, Suzanne Baboneau and Sue Stephens have been steadfast in their championing of books and writers. I am indebted to them for their steadfast support, their insight, understanding and faith.

All of the people in this book contributed far more than appears on the page. In particular, I am indebted to Jonathan Blake, Silvia Petretti, Tony Whitehead and Ian Green; I shouldn't be surprised that AIDS activists are brave and generous, but I am grateful. Likewise, I'm indebted to all the staff at St Margaret's Hospice, who have plenty to do without giving their precious time to me. Alberto Fernández was a remarkable host and guide to Mexico and I'm indebted to him and his colleagues for their hospitality, insights and generosity. Similarly, Adam Kahane and his team at Reos Partners could not have been more open in demonstrating the skill and nuance of scenario planning.

Off the page, my colleagues at the Forward Institute, the University of Bath, and at Merryck & Co., have been inspirational, provocative and remarkably patient with the demands this book made on my time. I'd also like to thank Ben Story, Clare Gilmartin, Dominik Kaiser, Lisa Myers, Marco Amitrano, Sandy Crosby and Matthew Brockman for sharing with me their daily experience of leading organisations in periods of deep uncertainty. And along the way of this winding book, David Fishkin, Anab Jain, Danica Remy and Elsa van der Zee proved very useful guides.

The team at TED has been stalwart in their support of my work and I am indebted to Juliet Blake, Bruno Giussani, Lisa Choi Owens and Chris Anderson for their encouragement and enthusiasm. I'm also grateful to Hugh Levinson, Adele Armstrong, Sheila Cook and Jasper Corbett, who've allowed me to explore some of the ideas in this book through the miracle that is BBC Radio. Robert Phillips, Ben Page and Laurence Evans were excellent guides to the wonderful world of polling and its history. I've also been fortunate in many friends and colleagues who a have gift for asking brilliant and surprising questions: Jennifer Board, Charlotte Calkin, Lorna Davis, Sarah Gillard, Jonathan Gosling, Thelma Holt, Pico Iyer, Juliane Jung, Mike Jones, David Kedmey, Brooke Masters, Eve Poole, Massimo Portincaso, Stefan Stern, Christian Wolmar and many more. It is impossible to think alone and I'm indebted to my many and diverse thinking pals.

Nicki Defago, Jenni Waugh and Clemency Calkin provided excellent research despite often daunting briefs. Stephanie Cooper-Lande somehow kept her cool as my schedules fell apart. But it is always families who bear the burden of books and never more than this one. My children tolerated with grace my endless interrogations into how they saw their future. But it was my husband Lindsay above all whose steady, stalwart belief in this project kept me going.

This book is dedicated to four friends who faced existential crises of their own during the course of its writing. Their creativity and fortitude sharpened my resolve, reminding me that, for all of us, the future is not an abstract idea but a real, often daunting, reality. I will always be grateful for their inspiration and friendship.

Farrington Gurney
2019

ENDNOTES

INTRODUCTION

1 Tetlock, Philip and Gardner, Dan, *Superforecasting: The Art and Science of Prediction*, Random House, New York, 2016
2 O'Connor, M. R., *Wayfinding: The Science and Mystery of How Humans Navigate the World*, St Martin's Press, New York, 2019

1 FALSE PROFITS

1 Ott, Katherine, *Fevered Lives: Tuberculosis in American Culture Since 1870*, Harvard University Press, London, 1996
2 Friedman, Walter A., *Fortune Tellers: The Story of America's First Economic Forecasters*, Princeton University Press, Princeton, N. J., 2014
3 Babson, Roger W., *Actions and Reactions: An Autobiography of Roger W. Babson*, Harper & Brothers, New York, 1950
4 Ibid.
5 Ibid.
6 Fisher, Irving N., *My Father Irving Fisher*, Comet Press Books, New York, 1956
7 MacFarquhar, Larissa, 'The Deflationist: How Paul Krugman Found Politics', *New Yorker,* 1 March 2010
8 Testimony before Congress, 'The Financial Crisis and the Role of Federal Regulators', Thursday 23 October 2008
9 Friedman, *Fortune Tellers* (Keynes to Bullock, 11 February 1925), op. cit.
10 An elegant description of why this is the case goes as follows:

   a) No scientific hypothesis is ever confirmed with absolute certainty; there is always a possibility of it being wrong.

b) The decision of whether to accept or reject a hypothesis depends on whether the evidence is sufficiently strong.

c) Determining sufficient strength is always a value judgement.

d) Therefore scientists make value judgements.

For more on this, see Eric Winsberg's *Science in the Age of Computer Simulation*, University of Chicago Press, Chicago, I. L., 2010

11 Author interview with Robert Skidelsky, 2 August 2018

12 Engelberg, Joseph, Sasseville, Caroline and Williams, Jared, 'Market Madness? The Case of *Mad Money*', *Management Science*, Vol. 58, Iss. 2, 2012

13 This is one reason why Warren Buffett has advised his wife to invest in tracker funds after this death. The pollster Nate Silver makes the challenging observation that the rare group that does outperform the market is US senators, raising all kinds of questions about inside information. See Silver, Nate, *The Signal and the Noise: The Art and Science of Prediction*, Penguin Books, London, 2013

14 See *The Economist*, 17 March 2018, p.39

15 I'm indebted to David Kedmey for pointing this out

16 'The Risk of Automation for Jobs in OECD Countries', www.oecd-ilibrary.org/social-issues-migration-health/the-risk-of-automation-for-jobs-in-oecd-countries_5jlz9h56dvq7-en, accessed 14 October 2018 and 27 October 2019

17 '5 Things to Know about the Future of Jobs', www.weforum.org/agenda/2018/09/future-of-jobs-2018-things-to-know/

18 Google's Chris Urmson suggested that the autonomous vehicle 'has the potential to reduce current Federal spending pressures for roadways, parking and public transit'. Wolmar, Christian, *Driverless Cars: On a Road to Nowhere*, London Publishing Partnership, 2018

19 For examples here, see Eubanks, Virginia, *Automating Inequality: How High-Tech Tools Profile, Police and Punish the Poor*, St Martin's Press, New York, 2017, as well as O'Neill, Cathy, *Weapons of Math Destruction: How Big Data Increases Inequality and Threatens Democracy*, Allen Lane, London, 2016, and reports from the AI Now Institute: ainowinstitute.org

20 'Overcoming Speed Bumps on the Road to Telematics', www2.deloitte.com/content/dam/insights/us/articles/telematics-in-auto-insurance/DUP-695_Telematics-in-the-Insurance-Industry_vFINAL.pdf, accessed 20 August 2019. Also quoted in Zuboff, Shoshana, *The Age of Surveillance Capitalism: The Fight for a Human Future at the New Frontier of Power*, Public Affairs, New York, 2019

21 'Good Judgment Project research found that super-forecasters can anticipate events 400 days ahead that other forecasters can only see 150 days ahead', www.goodjudgment.com, accessed 29 January 2019

22   www.youtube.com/watch?v=mtrOquc4CJc

23   'Why Do People Find Probability Unintuitive and Difficult?', nrich. maths.org/7326

2 DOES HISTORY REPEAT ITSELF?

1   Woollett, Katherine and Maguire, Eleanor A., 'Acquiring "the Knowledge" of London's Layout Drives Structural Brain Changes', *Current Biology*, Vol. 21, Iss. 24, 2011

2   Mullally, Sinéad L. and Maguire, Eleanor A., 'Memory, Imagination, and Predicting the Future: A Common Brain Mechanism?', *The Neuroscientist*, Vol. 20, Iss. 3, 2014

3   'Ditch the GPS. It's Ruining Your Brain', www.washingtonpost.com/opinions/ditch-the-gps-its-ruining-your-brain/2019/06/05/29a3170e-87af-11e9-98c1-e945ae5db8fb_story.html?noredirect=on&utm_term=.70c11f4d7c07, and O'Connor, M. R., *Wayfinding: The Science and Mystery of How Humans Navigate the World*, St Martin's Press, New York, 2018

4   Gilbert, Dan T. and Wilson, Timothy D., 'Prospection: Experiencing the Future', *Science*, Vol. 317, Iss. 5843, 2007

5   Santayana, George, *The Life of Reason*, Ch. XII, Vol. 1, 1905. Can be accessed at ia801407.us.archive.org/11/items/lifeofreasonphas01sant/lifeofreasonphas01sant.pdf

6   Gibson, Irving M., 'The Maginot Line', *The Journal of Modern History*, Vol. 17, Iss. 2, 1945

7   Kahneman, Daniel and Tversky, Amos, 'On the Psychology of Prediction', *Psychological Review*, Vol. 80, Iss. 4, 1973

8   Nevertheless, it is strikingly difficult to persuade people that the aesthetic similarity between stories isn't meaningful. The most frequent argument for history repeating itself is always the invasion of Russia. Surely Hitler repeated Napoleon's folly. But military historian Michael Clarke dismisses the analogy swiftly. Charles XII of Sweden had taken on Russia and won. The military campaigns of Hitler and Napoleon were different in almost every detail. Hitler might have been victorious had he not made many unforced errors: getting distracted by Greece, failing to gain Ukrainian support, failing to find an effective way to work with Japan. The aims of the wars were different, as were the tactics, talents and circumstances.

9   Neustadt, Richard E. and May, Ernest R., *Thinking in Time: The Uses of History for Decision-Makers*, The Free Press, New York, 1988

10   Macmillan, Margaret, *The Uses and Abuses of History*, Profile, London,

2010. More recently, Boris Johnson tried to puff his own government by drawing an analogy between himself as Churchill (as he is wont to do). The historian Simon Schama blasted back: 'You are not Churchill and the EU is not the Third Reich. You do not have a war cabinet and THERE IS NO WAR. How DARE you invoke the sacrifices of those [who] fought one.'

11 More recently, Mervyn King, a former governor of the Bank of England, compared Theresa May's Brexit deal to Chamberlain's appeasement of Hitler in the 1930s too: 'In the 1930s, with appeasement; in the 1970s, when the British economy was the "sick man" of Europe and the government saw its role as managing decline; and now, in the turmoil that has followed the Brexit referendum. In all three cases, the conventional wisdom of the day was wrong', www.bbc.co.uk/news/business-46446105, accessed 5 December 2018

12 'From the Berlin Wall to the Arab Spring', www.counterpart.org/stories/from-the-berlin-wall-to-the-arab-spring

13 'Medvedev compares "Arab Spring" to fall of Berlin Wall', www.expatica.com/ru/news/country-news/Medvedev-compares-Arab-Spring-to-fall-of-Berlin-Wall_274177.html, accessed 30 November 2018

14 Remarks by the President on the Middle East and North Africa, obamawhitehouse.archives.gov/the-press-office/2011/05/19/remarks-president-middle-east-and-north-africa, accessed 2 May 2018

15 In Egypt, even as Tahrir Square filled, analysts started to question the revolutionary thesis. President Mubarak might be in peril but the real threat wasn't posed by students but by the army. Throughout modern Egyptian history, the military has always claimed the right to name the president's successor. When Mubarak started to seize that privilege, asserting that his son Gamal would succeed him, the army decided to curb presidential power and reinstate military influence. Three days after Mubarak resigned and many commentators continued to enthuse about a democratic revolution, the geopolitical strategist George Friedman saw something different – and far from inevitable: 'What we see is that while Mubarak is gone, the military regime in which he served has dramatically increased its power. This isn't incompatible with democratic reform. Organizing elections, political parties and candidates is not something that can be done quickly. If the military is sincere in its intentions, it will have to do these things. The problem is that if the military is insincere, it will do exactly the same things. Six months is a long time, passions can subside and promises can be forgotten. At this point, we simply don't know what will happen.'

Tahrir Square wasn't the Berlin Wall or the Boston Tea Party. In 2014, Field Marshal Abdel Fattah el-Sisi retired from his military career to run for president, winning with 96 per cent of the votes. In 2018, he was re-elected with 92 per cent. Today, most commentators see the uprisings in Tunisia, Egypt, Libya, Bahrain and Syria as more different than they were similar to each other and these countries as more complex than the simple narratives that were so easily attached to them.

16   Cederman, Lars-Erik and Weidmann, Nils B.,'Predicting Armed Conflict: Time to Adjust Our Expectations?', *Science*, Vol. 344, 2017

3 WELL-ORDERED SHEEP

1   storage.googleapis.com/kindersight/muse.mp4 on the Muse website: muse.socoslearning.com, accessed 9 April 2018

2   Foroohar, Rana, 'Vivienne Ming: "The Professional Class Is About to Be Blindsided by AI"', *Financial Times*, 27 July 2018

3   You might even question what it is that makes Ming so certain she will *not* win a Nobel Prize; there's still time

4   '"We Will Literally Predict Their Life Outcomes"', www.wired. com/2016/05/we-will-literally-predict-their-life-outcomes/, accessed 24 August 2017

5   See *The Digital Human*, Series 13, Oracle, a BBC Radio 4 programme by Alex Krotoski, www.bbc.co.uk/programmes/b09wrxtw, accessed 27 October 2019

6   The *Financial Times* reports that McKinsey employees list their MBTI type in the company's internal profile pages. See Murad, Ahmed, 'Is Myers–Briggs Up to the Job?', *Financial Times*, 11 February 2016

7   Emre, Merve, *What's Your Type?: The Strange History of Myers–Briggs and the Birth of Personality Testing*, Fourth Estate, London, 2018 (the book was published in the US under the title *The Personality Brokers*)

8   Srivastava, S., John, O. P., Gosling, S. D. and Potter, J., 'Development of Personality in Early and Middle Adulthood: Set Like Plaster or Persistent Change?', *Journal of Personality and Social Psychology*, Vol. 84, Iss. 5, 2003

9   Emre, Merve, *What's Your Type?*, op. cit.

10   The Pygmalion effect in the classroom was first written up here: www.uni-muenster.de/imperia/md/content/psyifp/aeechterhoff/ sommersemester2012/schluesselstudiendersozialpsychologiea/ rosenthal_jacobson_pygmalionclassroom_urbrev1968.pdf. See also Rosenthal, Robert and Jacobson, Lenore, *Pygmalion in the Classroom:*

Teacher Expectation and Pupils' Intellectual Development, Holt, Rinehart & Winston, New York, 1968. The subsequent study of the Israeli army platoons can be found here: psycnet.apa.org/?&fa=main. doiLanding&doi=10.1037/0021-9010.75.4.394

11 Estimates in the UK suggest 90 per cent of hiring uses algorithms: 'Beating the Recruitment Machines', www.bbc.co.uk/news/business-20255387

12 Perez, Caroline Criado, *Invisible Women: Exposing Data Bias in a World Designed by Men*, Chatto & Windus, London, 2019

13 Laszlo Bock, formerly head of HR at Google, rejected them for this reason

14 Of course, old-style recruiting doesn't offer us such a dream of perfection either. It is slow, expensive and riddled with bias. But it carries no promise of perfection. How it works is visible; we can call each other on demonstrable bias. And although it's been fashionable to point out how fallible it is, it's hard to find an organisation whose leadership believes all of its hiring has been mistaken.

15 The minimal group paradigm in social psychology was explored and defined by the social psychologist Henri Tajfel and later developed by Thomas Gilovich at Yale. See Tajfel, H., 'Experiments in Intergroup Discrimination', *Scientific American*, Vol. 223, 1970, and Tajfel, H., Billig, M. G., Bundy, R. P. and Flament, C., 'Social Categorization and Intergroup Behaviour', *European Journal of Social Psychology*, Vol. 1, 1971, and Frank, M. G. and Gilovich, T., 'The Dark Side of Self- and Social Perception: Black Uniforms and Aggression in Professional Sports', *Journal of Personality and Social Psychology*, Vol. 54, Iss. 1, 1988

16 Adorno, Theodor, *The Authoritian Personality*, available online: www.ajcarchives.org/AJC_DATA/Files/AP22.pdf

17 Clauset, Aaron, Larremore, D. B. and Sinatra, R., 'Data-driven Predictions in the Science of Science', *Science*, Vol. 355, Iss. 6324, 2017

18 Sinatra, R., Wang, D., Deville, P., Song, C. and Barabási, A. L., 'Quantifying the Evolution of Individual Scientific Impact', *Science*, Vol. 354, Iss. 6312, 2016

19 Davis, Nicola, 'Scientists Quash Idea of Single "Gay Gene"', *The Guardian*, 29 August 2019

20 Branicki, Wojciech, et al., 'Model-based Prediction of Human Hair Color Using DNA Variants', *Nature Genetics*, Vol. 129, Iss. 443, 2011

21 Zimmer, Carl, *She Has Her Mother's Laugh: The Powers, Perversions, and Potential of Heredity*, Picador, London, 2018

22 'Determine Your Risk – and Practice Prevention', www.ccalliance.org/colorectal-cancer-information/statistics-risk-factors, accessed 4 November 2018

23 Varghese, Sanjana, 'Ruha Benjamin: We Definitely Can't Wait for Silicon Valley to Become More Diverse', *The Guardian*, 29 June 2019. See also Benjamin's book, *Race After Technology*, Polity Press, Medford, Massachusetts, 2019

24 Davies, Paul, *The Demon in the Machine*, Penguin Books, London, 2019

25 Plomin, Robert, *Blueprint: How DNA Makes Us Who We Are*, Allen Lane, London, 2018

26 Warren, Matthew, 'The Power of Many', *Nature*, Vol. 562, 2018

27 Plomin, *Blueprint*, op. cit.

28 'DNA Tests for IQ Are Coming, But It Might Not Be Smart to Take One', www.technologyreview.com/s/610339/dna-tests-for-iq-are-coming-but-it-might-not-be-smart-to-take-one, accessed 4 November 2018

29 Not a hypothesis. In the BBC's outstanding documentary series *The Mighty Redcar*, this is exactly what happens. Or consider the only child persuaded not to attend university because the mother fears living alone.

30 Young rats brought up with stimuli – ladders, tunnels and toys – developed cerebral cortex volume that was 25 per cent larger than the rats left in cages with nothing to do: Renner, M.J. and Rosenzweig, M.R., 'Social Interactions among Rats Housed in Groups and Enriched Conditions', *Developmental Psychobiology,* Vol. 19, Iss. 4, 1986

31 Plomin, *Blueprint*, op. cit.

32 Ibid.

33 He wrote a novel, *Kantsaywhere,* describing a society driven by determined, designed self-improvement. The novel was never published and just one copy remains, now in the special collections of University College, London, where Robert Plomin works.

34 Chitty, Clyde, *Eugenics, Race and Intelligence in Education*, Continuum International Publishing Group Ltd., London, 2007

35 Brignell, Victoria, 'The Eugenics Movement Britain Wants to Forget', *New Statesman*, 9 December 2010

36 Emre, Merve, *What's Your Type?*, op. cit.

37 Brignell, Victoria, 'When America Believed in Eugenics', *New Statesman*, 10 December 2010

38 US Supreme Court Justice Oliver Wendell Holmes, *Buck v. Bell*, 1927, www.ushmm.org/information/press/press-kits/traveling-exhibitions/deadly-medicine/quotes-from-the-2004-exhibition, accessed 17 April 2018

39 'Thousands Sterilized: A State Weighs Restitution', www.nytimes.com/2011/12/10/us/redress-weighed-for-forced-sterilizations-in-north-carolina.html, accessed 27 October 2019

40 'Toby Young, Eugenics, IQ, and the Poor (part 1)', blogs.bmj.com/medical-ethics/2018/01/08/toby-young-eugenics-iq-and-the-poor-part-1

41 Mukherjee, Siddhartha, *The Gene: An Intimate History,* Scribner, New York, 2017

42 Ibid.

43 'Amazon Patents "Anticipatory" Shipping – To Start Sending Stuff Before You've Bought It', techcrunch.com/2014/01/18/amazon-pre-ships/?gucco unter=1&guce_referrer_us=aHR0cHM6Ly93d3cuZWNvc2lhLm9yZy9zZ WFyY2g_cT1hbWF6b24rYW50aWNpcGF0b3J5K3Nob3BwaW5nJmFkZG 9uPXNhZmFyaQ&guce_referrer_cs=tQBTN1R67wK4N8Ucod2ewA, accessed 21 August 2019

44 Of course, the company might make the wrong choices (it forever sends me emails recommending that I buy books I've written), but that's okay, because the first few I'll be allowed to keep as a gesture of goodwill

45 Zuboff, Shoshana, *The Age of Surveillance Capitalism*, op. cit.

46 Strangely this comment appears to have been made without irony or any awareness that our financial systems are imperfect. Pentland, Alex, 'Society's Nervous System: Building Effective Government, Energy, and Public Health Systems', hd.media.mit.edu/tech-reports/TR-664.pdf, accessed 20 August 2019

4 NO AVAILABLE DATASETS

1 For more detail, see Kania, John and Kramer, Mark, 'Embracing Emergence: How Collective Impact Addresses Complexity', *Stanford Social Innovation Review*, 21 January 2013. See also Kania, John and Kramer, Mark, 'Collective Impact', *Stanford Social Innovation Review*, Winter 2011 and Hanleybrown, Fay, Kania, John and Kramer, Mark, 'Channeling Change: Making Collective Impact Work', *Stanford Social Innovation Review*, January 2012

2 One example of this was an outstanding Somerset initiative to tackle post-natal depression. It proved highly successful and sustainable but the isolation of the organisation that designed it meant that it never proliferated. I encountered this when working with the charity, CreativityWorks, that initiated the project.

3 Szabtowski, Witold, *Dancing Bears: True Stories of People Nostalgic for Life under Tyranny*, Penguin Books, New York, 2014. A completely brilliant and original book.

4 Source is a conference of doctors held in Chicago in 2018, hosted by Advisory.

5 Stacey Chang, M.S., and Lee, Thomas H., 'Beyond Evidence-Based Medicine', *New England Journal for Medicine*, 22 November 2018

6   This is in striking contrast to medical record systems that are designed without doctors or patients in mind, as described by Atul Gawande: www.newyorker.com/magazine/2018/11/12/why-doctors-hate-their-computers

7   'The Citizens' Assembly Publishes Final Report', www.citizensassembly. ie/en/News/The-Citizens-Assembly-Publishes-Final-Report.html

5 GO FAST, GO FAR

1   Crime data from Poligono Edison, OXXO (email)

2   'Fighting Corruption in Mexico: Taking It to the People', www.foreignaffairs.com/articles/mexico/2016-06-22/fighting-corruption-mexico, accessed August 2019

     Shell scenario-planning videos can be found at: www.youtube. com/watch?v=nwub4Bhr-aM&frags=wn; www.youtube.com/ watch?v=GoBvGOmO8KQ&frags=pl per cent2Cwn; www.youtube. com/watch?v=srY-hJuqYTM; www.shell.com/energy-and-innovation/ the-energy-future/scenarios/new-lenses-on-the-future.html

3   See two articles by Pierre Wack on this period: 'Scenarios: Uncharted Waters Ahead', *Harvard Business Review*, September 1985, and 'Scenarios: Shooting the Rapids', *Harvard Business Review*, November 1985

4   Wack, Pierre, 'Scenarios: Shooting the Rapids', op. cit.

5   The scenarios and datasets are published here: www.shell.com/content/ dam/royaldutchshell/documents/corporate/scenarios-newdoc.pdf

6   Wilkinson, Angela, *The Essence of Scenarios*, Amsterdam University Press, 2014

7   Ibid.

8   Smerkolj, Alenka and Soos, Timotej, *Prototyping the Future: A New Approach to Whole-of-Society Visioning*. Both of the authors worked on the scenario exercise. To my knowledge it has not been published.

9   I asked Flowers how much of this transformation depended on language, how critical that one sentence – 'In 2050, Slovenians are a happy people' – had been: 'Language really matters. I have evolved a style – almost the opposite of a literary style. It has to be so clear and simple and transparent and self-effacing. The language has to get out of the way, so people can imagine themselves on the stage, not a passive audience waiting to be entertained. They need to be able to inhabit it. That means you have to exclude technical language because the stories aren't intended for experts. The more individualistic you make it, the more jargon you let in, the more people you exclude. In the headings and titles though, then you need little things, like poetry, to make them vivid and condensed enough so that

if someone just memorizes the headings, they can tell the whole story themselves. The headings become a kind of meme and then they really stick. I remember one set of scenarios for Shell because someone quoted the headings to me just yesterday – and that was twenty years later! Sticking inside you is how they become real outside you.'

10 Kahane, Adam, *Transformative Scenario Planning: Working Together to Change the Future*, Berrett-Koehler, 2012

6 LIVING THE QUESTIONS

1 Hellend, Frode and Holledge, Julie, *Ibsen on Theatre*, Nick Hern Books, London, 2018

2 'Clip-clippety-clip, out of the newspaper I clipped things', is how Atwood described the process of writing her novel, *The Handmaid's Tale*. Over several years, Atwood noted and collected stories, news items, the weak signals of shifts in thought, attitude, behaviour and rules. Nothing Atwood included in *The Handmaid's Tale* lacked a historical antecedent or modern reference. The details didn't need to be made up; by collecting and arranging them, she showed what they might mean.

3 The technology writer Jaron Lanier recommends that consumers be more like cats than Pavlov's dogs as a defence against the behaviourism imposed by social media. Lanier, Jaron, *Ten Arguments for Deleting Your Social Media Accounts Right Now*, Bodley Head, London, 2019

4 Interview in *The Paris Review*, Iss. 226, Fall 2018

5 Meyer, Michael, *Henrik Ibsen*, Vol. 3, Rupert Hart-Davis, London, 1967

6 Rilke, Rainer Maria, *Letters to a Young Poet*, Penguin Classics, London, 2016

7 www.youtube.com/playlist?list=PLM4S2hGZDSE4645tTLQ-q0CGiR4eSFlBW

8 Interview with Tracey Emin for the *Financial Times*: www.youtube.com/watch?v=nQQTI-X1OOw

9 See www.futurelibrary.no

10 Eliot, T. S., 'The Frontiers of Criticism' in *On Poetry and Poets*, Faber & Faber Ltd, London, 1986

11 'Toni Morrison, Towering Novelist of the Black Experience, Dies at 88', www.nytimes.com/2019/08/06/books/toni-morrison-dead.html?campaign_id=60&instance_id=0&segment_id=15916&user_id=533be8ef03dbf051b0bb06e1f1f74ec7&regi_id=3305561

12 'Greatness thrust upon him,' *The Economist*, 26 October 2019

13 The Auden reference is from his poem 'In Memory of W. B. Yeats', written in 1939

14 Firth, Joseph et al., 'The "Online Brain": How the Internet May Be Changing Our Cognition', *World Psychiatry*, Vol. 18, Iss. 2, June 2019

7 BUILDING CATHEDRALS

1 'Our Attitude Towards Wealth Played a Crucial Role in Brexit. We Need a Rethink', www.theguardian.com/commentisfree/2016/jul/29/stephen-hawking-brexit-wealth-resources

2 van Heijsbergen, Gijs, *The Sagrada Família: Gaudí's Heaven on Earth*, Bloomsbury Publishing, London, 2018

3 'Business Roundtable Redefines the Purpose of a Corporation to Promote "An Economy That Serves All Americans"', www.businessroundtable.org/business-roundtable-redefines-the-purpose-of-a-corporation-to-promote-an-economy-that-serves-all-americans, accessed 1 September 2019

4 'Helping Britain Prosper Plan', www.lloydsbankinggroup.com/Our-Group/responsible-business/prosper-plan, accessed 1 September 2019

8 SIMPLE, NOT EASY

1 Siilasmaa, Risto, *Transforming Nokia: The Power of Paranoid Optimism to Lead Through Colossal Change*, McGraw-Hill, 2019

2 Ibid.

3 'Nokia's Risto Siilasmaa: Transformation Lessons from the Chairman', www.cxotalk.com/episode/nokias-risto-siilasmaa-transformation-lessons-chairman, accessed 22 November 2018

4 The academic Veronica Hope-Hailey has demonstrated that companies going into a crisis with high levels of trust emerge stronger. Her three reports on the subject can be found on CIPD.com. 'Cultivating Trustworthy Leaders', www.cipd.co.uk/Images/cultivating-trustworthy-leaders_2014_tcm18-8971.pdf; 'Where Has All the Trust Gone', www.cipd.co.uk/Images/where-has-all-the-trust-gone_2012-sop_tcm18-9644.pdf; 'Experiencing Trustworthy Leadership', www.cipd.co.uk/Images/where-has-all-the-trust-gone_2012-sop_tcm18-9644.pdf, all accessed 24 October 2019

5 ACT UP oral history project, see www.actuporalhistory.org/index1.html

6 Ibid.

7 Number of deaths is worldwide. Source is France, David, *How to Survive a Plague*, Picador Publishing, London, 2016

8 Ibid.

9   The English government's reluctance to make the highly effective PrEP widely available is one example of inexplicable, incoherent policy.

10 Lawson, Danielle F. et al., 'Children Can Foster Climate Change Concern among Their Parents', *Nature Climate Change*, Vol. 9, June 2019

9 WHO WANTS TO LIVE FOREVER?

1   See especially Kennedy, Q., Mather, M. and Carstensen, L. L., 'The Role of Motivation in the Age-Related Positivity Effect in Autobiographical Memory', *Psychological Science*, Vol. 15, Iss. 3, 2004; Fung, Helene H., Carstensen, L. L. and Lutz, Amy M., 'Influence of Time on Social Preferences: Implications for Life-Span Development', *Psychology and Aging*, Vol. 14, Iss. 4, 1999; Carstensen, Laura L., 'The Influence of a Sense of Time on Human Development', *Science*, Vol. 312, Iss. 5782, 2006

2   Carstensen, Laura L., Pasupathi, M., Mayr, U. and Nesselroade, J., 'Emotional Experience in Everyday Life across the Adult Life Span', *Journal of Personality and Social Psychology*, Vol. 79, Iss. 4, 2000

3   Carstensen, L. and Fredrickson, B. L., 'Influence of HIV Status and Age on Cognitive Representation of Others', *Health Psychology*, Vol. 17, Iss. 6, 1998

4   Lindquist, Ulla-Carin, *Rowing Without Oars*, John Murray, London, 2005

5   Goranson, A., Ritter, R. S. and Waytz, A., 'Dying is Unexpectedly Positive', *Psychological Science,* Vol. 28, Iss. 7, 2017

6   www.calicolabs.com

7   'Ray Kurzweil's Plan: Never Die', www.wired.com/2002/11/ray-kurzweils-plan-never-die

8   It's important to note that Kurzweil is not alone in this nonsense. The founder of Bulletproof Coffee is equally obsessed by the importance of his own life: 'The Bulletproof Coffee Founder Has Spent $1 Million in His Quest to Live to 180', www.menshealth.com/health/a25902826/bulletproof-dave-asprey-biohacking/

9   2019 commencement address by Apple CEO Tim Cook at Stanford University, news.stanford.edu/2019/06/16/remarks-tim-cook-2019-stanford-commencement, accessed 8 August 2019

10 The hospice movement proved a tremendous ally to the gay community during the AIDS crisis

10 BE PREPARED

1   The World Health Organization considers the death toll of 11,310 to be
    a significant under-estimate. See 'W.H.O.: New Ebola Cases Could Hit
    10,000 Per Week', time.com/3505982/ebola-new-cases-world-health-
    organisation/, and Meltzer, Martin I., Atkins, Charisma Y., Santibanez,
    Scott, et al., 'Estimating the Future Number of Cases in the Ebola
    Epidemic – Liberia and Sierra Leone, 2014–2015', *Morbidity and Mortality
    Weekly Report*, 26 September 2014

2   'Characterizing the Epidemiology of the 2009 Influenza A/H1N1
    Pandemic in Mexico', journals.plos.org/plosmedicine/article?id=10.1371/
    journal.pmed.1000436

3   'Why Couldn't My Treatment Center Save This Baby?', www.nytimes.
    com/2019/01/30/opinion/ebola-treatment-democratic-republic-of-
    congo.html

4   BBC World Service, *Witness: The Doomsday Seed Vault*, https://www.bbc.
    co.uk/programmes/w3cswsjv, accessed 29 October 2019

5   See 'A Resilient Wales', futuregenerations.wales/a-resilient-wales/

6   It's important to acknowledge that there have been such initiatives
    before. In the 1990s, the French government set up a council on the
    rights of future generations but it proved insufficiently robust to survive
    controversy around testing nuclear weapons in the Pacific. The Israeli
    Knesset also had a Commission for Future Generations, but that lasted
    only six years. The Finnish parliament has a committee of seventeen
    members who are supposed to represent generations to come.

7   'The goal of everything we do is to change people's actual behaviour
    at scale. We want to figure out the construction of changing a person's
    behaviour, and then we want to change how lots of people are making
    their day-to-day decisions. When people use our app, we can capture their
    behaviors and identify good and bad [ones]. Then we develop "treatments"
    and "data pellets" that select good behaviors. We can test how actionable
    our cues are for them and how profitable certain behaviors are for us.'
    Zuboff, Shoshana, *The Age of Surveillance Capitalism*, op. cit. The book is
    replete with jaw-dropping interviews with Silicon Valley leaders proudly
    discussing the efficiency of inevitability when it can be forced.

POSTSCRIPT

1   I owe this insight to Professor Lenny Smith, director of the Centre for the Analysis of Time Series at the London School of Economics.

2   www.telegraph.co.uk/news/2020/03/28/exercise-cygnus-uncovered -pandemic-warnings-buried-government/

3   www.telegraph.co.uk/news/2020/03/28/exercise-cygnus-uncovered -pandemic-warnings-buried-government/

4   assets.publishing.service.gov.uk/government/uploads/system/uploads/ attachment_data/file/730213/2018_UK_Biological_Security_ Strategy.pdf

5   www.theguardian.com/world/2020/apr/24/revealed-uk-ministers-were -warned-last-year-of-risks-of-coronavirus-pandemic. See also www. oxfordresearchgroup.org.uk/writing-on-the-wall-the-uk-and-the-early- warning-signs-of-covid-19

6   www.weforum.org/agenda/2019/11/countries-preparedness-pandemics/ Another explanation might be that the WEF is frequently ideological in its rankings.

7   Lawrence, Felicity et al., 'From Austerity to Covid-19: How a decade of NHS cuts and privatisation left the UK exposed to a pandemic', *Guardian*, 1 June 2020.

8   www.england.nhs.uk/statistics/statistical-work-areas/critical-care- capacity/critical-care-bed-capacity-and-urgent-operations-cancelled- 2019-20-data/

9   Chazan, Guy, 'How Germany Got Coronavirus Right', *Financial Times*, 6/7 June 2020.

10 digital.nhs.uk/data-and-information/publications/statistical/ nhs-vacancies-survey/february-2015---march-2020-experimental- statistics#key-facts

11 Hope-Hailey, Veronica, 'Responsible Business Through Crisis', CIPD, November 2020. This is an outstanding review of management practices – good and bad – during the first six months of the pandemic.

12 Ibid.

13 Global Drucker Forum, 28 October 2020.

14 Full disclosure: I sometimes work as a mentor via Merryck & Co.

15 Full disclosure: I am now the chair of DACS.

16 The full story of the conference is well told in Conway, Ed, *The Summit: Bretton Woods, 1944: J. M. Keynes and the Reshaping of the Global Economy*, Pegasus, Cambridge, 2017. Keynes died some fifteen months after the conference at the age of sixty-two.

INDEX